From Jesus to the Church

From Jesus to the Church

The First Christian Generation

Craig A. Evans

WESTMINSTER
JOHN KNOX PRESS
LOUISVILLE · KENTUCKY

First edition
Published by Westminster John Knox Press
Louisville, Kentucky

14 15 16 17 18 19 20 21 22 23—10 9 8 7 6 5 4 3 2 1

Book design by Sharon Adams
Cover design by LeVan Fisher Design
Cover illustration: Ruins of the great synagogue of Capernaum, Israel,
by Zvonimir Atletic©shutterstock.com

Library of Congress Cataloging-in-Publication Data

Evans, Craig A.
  From Jesus to the church : the first Christian generation / Craig A. Evans.
    pages cm
  Includes bibliographical references and indexes.
  ISBN 978-0-664-23905-3 (alk. paper)
  1. Church history—Primitive and early church, ca. 30–600.   I. Title.
  BR165.E93   2014
  270.1—dc23

                                                            2013041175

Most Westminster John Knox Press books are available at special quantity discounts when purchased in bulk by corporations, organizations, and special-interest groups. For more information, please e-mail SpecialSales@wjkbooks.com.

Contents

Figures with Credits

Preface

This small book grew out of the Deichmann Lectures given at the Ben-Gurion University of the Negev in Beersheba, Israel, in May of 2010. I thank Dr. Roland Deines of Nottingham University and the Deichmann Committee for the invitation. I also thank Herr Dr. Heinz-Horst Deichmann, whose generous financial support makes the lecture series possible. I also thank Dr. Cana Werman, who translated the lectures into Hebrew for the Hebrew-speaking students. The purpose of the Deichmann Lectures is to support scholarship that is concerned with the intersection of Judaism and Christianity. It was an honor to take part in this worthy enterprise.

It is hard to imagine how a visit of this nature could have been more enjoyable and how hosts could have been more hospitable. My wife—Ginny—and I were treated to wonderful dinners, musical events, receptions, desert walks, and visits to important archaeological sites, with Dr. Deichmann and his musically gifted daughter; with Roland Deines, Pau Figueras, and Anders Runesson; and with Professor Zipora ("Zipi") Talshir and her husband (readers should know that Zipi is a chef of no mean accomplishment—though I doubt she will ever admit it!).

I am grateful to Greg Monette, who assisted with the preparation of the indexes; and to Anders Runesson, Alexander Schick, and Ginny, who generously gave me permission to use several of their beautiful photographs. Many thanks, colleagues!

Craig A. Evans
Acadia Divinity College

Abbreviations

AB	Anchor Bible (Commentary Series)
'Abot	Mishnah, *'Abot*
'Abot R. Nat.	*'Abot of Rabbi Nathan*
ABRL	Anchor Bible Reference Library
AGJU	Arbeiten zur Geschichte des antiken Judentums und des Urchristentums
Ant.	Josephus, *Jewish Antiquities*
ArBib	Aramaic Bible
AT	author's translation
b. 'Abod. Zar.	Babylonian Talmud, *Abodah Zarah*
b. Ber.	Babylonian Talmud, *Berakhot*
b. Git.	Babylonian Talmud, *Gittin*
b. Pesah.	Babylonian Talmud, *Pesahim*
b. Sanh.	Babylonian Talmud, *Sanhedrin*
b. Shabb.	Babylonian Talmud, *Shabbat*
b. Yoma	Babylonian Talmud, *Yoma*
BAR	*Biblical Archaeology Review*
BBR	*Bulletin for Biblical Research*
BETL	Bibliotheca ephemeridum theologicarum lovaniensium
Bib. Ant.	*Biblical Antiquities* (Pseudo-Philo)
BJRL	*Bulletin of the John Rylands University Library of Manchester*
BJS	Brown Judaic Studies
BNTC	Black's New Testament Commentaries
BZ	*Biblische Zeitschrift*
CBET	Contributions to Biblical Exegesis and Theology

CBQ	*Catholic Biblical Quarterly*
CD	Cairo Genizah copy of the *Damascus Document*
CEJL	Commentaries on Early Jewish Literature
CII	Jean-Baptiste Frey, *Corpus inscriptionum iudaicarum* I–II
CIS	Copenhagen International Seminar
CQ	*Classical Quarterly*
CSHJ	Chicago Studies in the History of Judaism
DJD	Discoveries in the Judaean Desert
DSD	*Dead Sea Discoveries*
FBBS	Facet Books, Biblical Series
FRLANT	Forschungen zur Religion und Literatur des Alten und Neuen Testaments
Gen. Rab.	*Genesis Rabbah*
GNS	Good News Studies
Hel. Syn. Pr.	*Hellenistic Synagogal Prayers*
Hist. eccl.	Eusebius, *Ecclesiastical History*
ICC	International Critical Commentary
IEJ	*Israel Exploration Journal*
JAL	Jewish Apocryphal Literature
JBL	*Journal of Biblical Literature*
JGRChJ	*Journal of Greco-Roman Christianity and Judaism*
JJS	*Journal of Jewish Studies*
JSJ	*Journal for the Study of Judaism in the Persian, Hellenistic and Roman Period*
JSJSup	Journal for the Study of Judaism in the Persian, Hellenistic and Roman Period: Supplements
JSNT	*Journal for the Study of the New Testament*
JSNTSup	Journal for the Study of the New Testament: Supplement Series
JSOTSup	Journal for the Study of the Old Testament: Supplement Series
JSP	*Journal for the Study of the Pseudepigrapha*
JSPSup	Journal for the Study of the Pseudepigrapha: Supplement Series
JTS	*Journal of Theological Studies*
J.W.	Josephus, *Jewish Wars*
KJV	King James Version
Lam. Rab.	*Lamentations Rabbah*
LCL	Loeb Classical Library
LXX	Septuagint (Greek translation of the Old Testament)

m. Sotah	Mishnah, *Sotah*
m. Yoma	Mishnah, *Yoma*
m. Zevah.	Mishnah, *Zevahim*
Midr. Pss.	*Midrash on the Psalms*
Midr. Tanh.	*Midrash Tanhuma*
MT	Masoretic Text
NETS	New English Translation of the Septuagint
NICNT	New International Commentary on the New Testament
NICOT	New International Commentary on the Old Testament
NIV	New International Version (2011)
NKJV	New King James Version
NovT	*Novum Testamentum*
NovTSup	Novum Testamentum Supplements
NRSV	New Revised Standard Version
NTL	New Testament Library
NTM	New Testament Monographs
NTS	*New Testament Studies*
NTTS	New Testament Tools and Studies
OGIS	W. Dittenberger, *Orientis graeci inscriptiones selectae* I–II
OTL	Old Testament Library
PAST	Pauline Studies
PG	J.-P. Migne, ed., Patrologia graeca
PNTC	Pillar New Testament Commentary
P.Yadin	Papyri Yadin
4Q266	sample ref. to numbered scroll from Qumran Cave 4
1QM	*War Scroll*, from Qumran Cave 1
1QpHab	*Pesher Habakkuk*, a commentary from Qumran Cave 1
1QS	*Rule of the Community*, from Qumran Cave 1
RevQ	*Revue de Qumran*
RILP	Roehampton London Institute Papers
RSV	Revised Standard Version
SBL	Society of Biblical Literature (and Exegesis [before 1963])
SBLDS	Society of Biblical Literature Dissertation Series
SBLMS	Society of Biblical Literature Monograph Series
SBLSP	Society of Biblical Literature Seminar Papers
SDSSRL	Studies in the Dead Sea Scrolls and Related Literature
Sifre Num.	*Sifre Numbers*
SJLA	Studies in Judaism in Late Antiquity

SNTSMS	Society for New Testament Studies Monograph Series
Spec. Laws	Philo, *On the Special Laws*
T. Benj.	*Testament of Benjamin* (sample ref. for a testament)
t. Hul.	Tosefta, *Hullin*
t. Meʿil.	Tosefta, *Meʿilah*
t. Sukkah	Tosefta, *Sukkah*
TBN	Themes in Biblical Narrative
Tg.	*Targum*
Tg. Onq.	*Targum Onqelos* (sample ref. to a Targum)
THKNT	Theologischer Handkommentar zum Neuen Testament
TSAJ	Texte und Studien zum antiken Judentum
TynBul	*Tyndale Bulletin*
VCSup	Vigiliae christianae: Supplement Series
Vir. ill.	Jerome, *De viris illustribus* = *On Illustrious Men*
WBC	Word Biblical Commentary
WUNT	Wissenschaftliche Untersuchungen zum Neuen Testament
y. Ber.	Jerusalem Talmud, *Berakhot*
y. Sotah	Jerusalem Talmud, *Sotah*
y. Taʿan.	Jerusalem Talmud, *Taʿanit*
YJS	Yale Judaica Series
ZNW	*Zeitschrift für die neutestamentliche Wissenschaft*

Introduction

When Jesus of Nazareth entered Jerusalem, shortly before Passover, and quarreled with the ruling priests, he set in motion a chain of events that would change the world. The purpose of this book is to examine the first link in this chain. This link is made up of the first generation of the Jesus movement, a movement centered in Jerusalem. It was almost entirely Jewish and was very much focused on the redemption and restoration of Israel.

Even during the first forty years, with the Jesus movement and the temple establishment fiercely competing for the hearts of the Jewish people, there was never any thought that the Jesus movement was somehow not Jewish or outside the boundaries of the nation of Israel and its great heritage. The Messianists, who up north in Antioch became known as *Christianoi*, or "Christians," were viewed as a Jewish sect (or *hairesis*), as were the Pharisees, Sadducees, and Essenes.

The death of James, the capture of Jerusalem, and the destruction of the temple changed the dynamics of Jewish society and, along with it, the relationship of the Messianists with their non-Messianist Jewish brothers and sisters. The Gentile branch of the church, energetically planted and deeply watered by Paul and other Jewish missionaries, rapidly expanding across the Roman Empire, soon dominated. Although the Jewish branch of the church did not cease, it did recede and in time exerted little influence. By the second century, especially in the aftermath of the Bar Kokhba revolt, the movement that Jesus had launched and that his apostles had spread had become largely a Gentile affair.

The present study is not a history of the early church; it is not even a history of its first generation. It is, rather, a study narrowly focused on

1

the clash between the family of high priest Annas and the family of Jesus of Nazareth, a clash inaugurated by a Jeremiah-related prophecy of the temple's doom, uttered by Jesus, and ended by another Jeremiah-related prophecy of the temple's doom, uttered by another man named Jesus. My goal is to draw attention to the importance of this prophecy, what motivated it, and the effects it had on both the followers of Jesus and on the followers of Annas, his family, and allies.

Even as narrowly as I have defined this study, several avenues have not been explored, at least not fully. This is rich, suggestive material. The more I probed, the more questions were raised. My hope is to alert scholars to the importance of a facet in early Christian history that has not been investigated. I begin with an "ambiguous" prophecy, which will provide the context for the prophecies of Jesus and others regarding the fate of Herod's glorious temple. Discussion of this prophecy will create the proper context for the remainder of my study.

An Ambiguous Prophecy

Writing primarily for an elite Roman readership a few years after the destruction of the Jewish temple (in 70 CE), Joseph bar Matthias—better known as Flavius Josephus—discusses a number of incidents that presaged the coming war and catastrophe (66–73 CE). Among these were the appearance of numerous false prophets and charlatans, all of whom promised deliverance (*J.W.* 6.285–88); the appearance of a star over the city of Jerusalem, which many wrongly assumed was a good omen (6.289–91); a cow that gave birth to a lamb, in the very precincts of the temple (6.292); the strange nocturnal self-opening of the massive brass eastern gate of the inner temple court (6.293–96); the appearance of chariots and armed battalions "hurtling through the clouds" (6.297–99); and the loud cry of a host heard one evening during Pentecost, saying, "We are departing from here" (6.300a). Many of these strange omens, leading up to the capture of Jerusalem and the defeat of the Jewish uprising, were also known to Roman writers.

Perhaps related to the star that appeared over the city was a prophecy—or in the words of the politically astute Josephus, "an ambiguous oracle"—which "more than all else incited them to the war." This oracle, found in the Jewish sacred Scriptures, foretold "that at that time one from their country would become ruler of the world" (*J.W.* 6.312). Although it is debated, the prophecy most likely in view is that of Numbers 24:17: "I see him, but not now; I behold him, but not nigh: a star shall come forth out of Jacob, and a scepter shall rise out of Israel; it shall crush the forehead of Moab, and break down all the sons of Sheth." Not only does this prophecy of a "star" cohere with the previously mentioned star that appeared above Jerusalem; the prophecy was also interpreted in royal and messianic terms in Jewish literature of late antiquity. Indeed, when the magi in Matthew's Gospel inquire after him who has been born "king of the Jews," because they have seen his star (Matt. 2:1–2), they are probably alluding to Numbers 24:17 (or at least Matthew's Jewish readers would assume so).[1]

Naturally, the Jewish people assumed that the prophecy of Numbers 24:17 spoke of the coming of a Jewish ruler. The prophecy is quoted in a collection of messianic texts in one of the Qumran Scrolls (see 4Q175 1.9–13). In 1QSb 5.20–29 the prophecy is cited along with Isaiah 11 and is applied to the anticipated "leader of the nation" who will conquer Israel's enemies. In the great war against the "sons of darkness," Numbers 24:17 will be fulfilled (1QM 11.5–7). In the *Damascus Document* the text is applied to the coming king and the "interpreter of the Law" (CD 7.18–8:1 [= 4Q266 frag. 3, 3.20–23; 4Q269 frag. 5, lines 3–4]). The Aramaic paraphrases of Jewish Scripture (i.e., the Targumim) regularly paraphrase and interpret Numbers 24:17 as referring to the anticipated royal Messiah: "When the strong king from those of the house of Jacob shall rule, and the Messiah and the strong rod from Israel shall be anointed." It is rather clear how the prophecy of Numbers 24:17 was understood in Jewish circles in late antiquity.[2]

Josephus, however, interpreted the prophecy not in reference to a Jewish redeemer, whether a messiah or something else. Contrary to the Jewish "wise men" of his day, he interpreted it in reference to the victorious Vespasian, the Roman general: "The oracle, however, in reality signified the sovereignty of Vespasian, who was proclaimed emperor on Jewish soil" (*J.W.* 6.313). Vespasian had defeated the Jewish rebels in Galilee, then occupied Jericho and awaited developments in Rome in the aftermath of the suicide of Nero. His patience paid off. After the rapid succession and failures of Galba, Otho, and Vitellius, Vespasian was proclaimed emperor. Josephus, who had foretold the accession of Vespasian (*J.W.* 3.401; 4.628–29), was vindicated, at least in the eyes of the Roman elite.[3]

Both Tacitus and Suetonius know of this prophecy and agree with Josephus that it came to fulfillment in Vespasian's victory and accession to the throne. Tacitus speaks of the prophecy, as well as some of the very omens described by Josephus:

Messianic Prophecies Known in the Time of Jesus

. . . The scepter shall not depart from Judah, nor the ruler's staff from between his feet, until he comes to whom it belongs; and to him shall be the obedience of the peoples. . . . (Gen. 49:8–12)

I see him, but not now; I behold him, but not nigh: a star shall come forth out of Jacob, and a scepter shall rise out of Israel; it shall crush the forehead of Moab, and break down all the sons of Sheth. (Num. 24:17)

There shall come forth a shoot from the stump of Jesse, and a branch shall grow out of his roots. [2]And the Spirit of the LORD shall rest upon him, the spirit of wisdom and understanding, the spirit of counsel and might, the spirit of knowledge and the fear of the LORD. . . . [3]He shall not judge by what his eyes see, or decide by what his ears hear; but with righteousness he shall judge the poor, and decide with equity for the meek of the earth; and he shall smite the earth with the rod of his mouth, and with the breath of his lips he shall slay the wicked. . . . (Isa. 11:1–4)

Prodigies had indeed occurred. . . . Contending hosts were seen meeting in the skies, arms flashed, and suddenly the temple was illuminated with fire from the clouds. Of a sudden the doors of the shrine opened and a superhuman voice cried: "The gods are departing": at the same moment the mighty stir of their going was heard. Few interpreted these omens as fearful; the majority firmly believed that their ancient priestly writings contained the prophecy that this was the very time when the East should grow strong and that men starting from Judaea should possess the world. This mysterious prophecy had in reality pointed to Vespasian and Titus, but the common people, as is the way of human ambition, interpreted these great destinies in their own favour, and could not be turned to the truth even by adversity. (Tacitus, *Histories* 5.13.1–2)[4]

The variations of language (e.g., the plural "gods" and the reference to Jewish Scripture as "priestly writings") are consistent with that of a polytheistic Gentile who has little familiarity with the religious beliefs of the Jewish people.

Suetonius speaks of a number of different omens that hinted at the rise of Vespasian, but he also mentions the Jewish prophecy and even the prophecy of Josephus himself:

> There had spread all over the Orient an old and established belief, that it was fated at that time for men coming from Judaea to rule the world. This prediction, referring to the emperor of Rome, as afterwards appeared from the event, the people of Judaea took to themselves; accordingly they revolted. . . . When he [Vespasian] consulted the god of Carmel in Judaea, the lots were highly encouraging, promising that what he planned or wished, however great it might be, would come to pass; and one of his high-born prisoners, Josephus by name, as he was being put in chains, declared most confidently that he would soon be released by the same man, who would then, however, be emperor. (Suetonius, *Vespasian* 4.5; 5.6)[5]

In view of these statements, especially regarding the Jewish prophecy "spread all over the Orient," Menahem Stern is justified in saying, "Presumably these Jewish expectations had become a matter of common knowledge by the initial stages of the rebellion, and did not sound strange to a world already familiar with eschatological terminology."[6]

The prophecies of the destruction of Jerusalem's temple reach back anywhere from one generation to a century or more before their fulfillment.[7] A very old prediction of the destruction of the Second Temple is found in the *Ethiopic Book of Enoch*. In a section that could date as early as 160 BCE, we are told that God will pull down the "ancient house" and a build a new one, "loftier than the first" (*1 Enoch* 90:28–29). It is possible that "house" here refers to the city of Jerusalem, but a later elaboration in *1 Enoch* suggests that the temple itself is in view: "A temple shall be built for the Great King for ever more" (91:13; 4Q212 4.18).[8]

The book of Tobit, dating to the second century BCE, also seems to anticipate a new temple. On his deathbed Tobit says to his son and grandsons:

> But God will again have mercy on them, and bring them back into their land; and they will rebuild the house of God, though it will not be like the former one until the times of the age are completed. After this they will return from the places of their captivity, and will rebuild Jerusalem in splendor. And the house of God will be rebuilt

there with a glorious building for all generations for ever, just as the
prophets said of it. (Tob. 14:5)

The first part of the verse anticipates the postexilic return to the land of
Israel and the rebuilding of the temple, what we call the Second Temple. It
is acknowledged that the rebuilt temple "will not be like the former one,"
the one built by Solomon. The author of the book of Tobit knows this,
of course, for this inferior temple was standing in his own lifetime (see
Hag. 2:3). But he writes from the perspective of righteous Tobit, an exile
in eighth-century-BCE Assyria. He foresees the inferior Second Temple
standing "until the times of the age are completed." Then all of the Jewish
people will return to Israel, and "the house of God will be rebuilt there with
a glorious building for all generations for ever." Clearly this house of God
is an eschatological temple that will replace the Second Temple, built soon
after the end of the exile.[9] It is not clear that the Second Temple would be
destroyed, but the anticipation that it will be replaced is quite clear.

A prophecy of the temple's destruction is found in the *Testament of
Levi*. In this pseudepigraphal work (ca. 100 BCE) the aged patriarch Levi
is portrayed on his deathbed, giving his final testament to his sons. He
tells them, "At the end of the ages you will transgress against the Lord"
(14:1). The description of priestly wickedness that follows matches the
complaints that we find in the literature leading up to the time of Jesus,
as seen in some of the Dead Sea Scrolls (mostly dating to the first century BCE) and in the *Testament of Moses* (dating ca. 25–30 CE). Priestly
wickedness will result in the destruction of the temple: "Therefore the
temple, which the Lord shall choose, shall be laid waste through your
uncleanness, and you shall be captives through throughout all nations.
. . . All who hate you will rejoice at your destruction" (*T. Levi* 15:1, 3).

Although Christian editing is present elsewhere in the *Testament of Levi*
(e.g., at 10:3; 14:2; and 16:3, 5), the prophecy of the temple's destruction
in chapter 15 is probably genuine.[10] There is nothing in the prophecy
that reflects knowledge of the temple's destruction in 70 CE (e.g., no
mention of siege or fire), whereas the anticipation that the priesthood
will be hated by the Gentiles stands somewhat in tension with what actually happened. After all, the ruling priesthood was for the most part col-
laborating with Rome; the Jewish rebels attacked and killed some of the
ruling priests, including the high priest himself; and Josephus, also of
aristocratic lineage, became a close friend and confidant of the Flavian
family. If anything, the dispersion foretold in 16:5 is based on the earlier
Babylonian sack of Jerusalem, not on the Roman capture of the city.

The fictional patriarch Judah also predicts the destruction of Jerusalem's temple, again due to the wickedness of Israel's leadership. Many evils will befall Israel, including "consumption of God's sanctuary by fire" (*T. Judah* 23:3). In this case the prediction could be a Christian gloss and not a genuine predestruction prediction.[11]

Some of the Qumran scrolls show evidence of anticipating the temple's destruction. In reference to the corrupt high priesthood, the *Commentary on Habakkuk* (*Pesher Habakkuk*) asserts that "in the last days their riches and plunder alike will be handed over to the army of the Kittim" (1QpHab 9.6–7). Most scholars understand the "Kittim" as a reference either to the Greeks or to the Romans. Later the commentary adds that "God will condemn" the high priest of the last days to "utter destruction" (12.5). The destruction of the high priest does not, of course, necessarily imply the destruction of the temple itself.

The commentary on Nahum reviews some of Israel's intertestamental history, explaining that Nahum 2:11b ("Wherever the lion goes to enter, there also goes the whelp without fear") refers to "Demetrius, king of Greece, who sought to enter Jerusalem through the counsel of the Flattery-Seekers; [but it never fell into the] power of the kings of Greece from Antiochus until the appearance of the rulers of the Kittim; but afterward it will be trampled [by the Gentiles . . .] (4QpNah frags. 3–4, 1.1–4, with restorations).[12] The expected trampling of Jerusalem may well have included an assault on the temple itself, perhaps even its destruction. Destruction or defilement of the temple would be consistent with an expectation that the temple of the last days will be created anew by God, as we find expressed in the *Temple Scroll*: "I shall sanctify my temple with my glory, for I will cause my glory to dwell upon it until the day of creation, when I myself will create my temple; I will establish it for myself for ever in fulfillment of the covenant that I made with Jacob at Bethel. . . ." (11Q19 29.8–10).

An eschatological temple seems to be in view in another scroll from Qumran:

This "place" is the house that [they shall build for him] in the last days, as it is written in the book of ³[Moses: "A temple of] the Lord are you to prepare with your hands; the Lord will reign forever and ever" [Exod. 15:17]. This passage describes the temple that no [man with a] permanent [fleshly defect] shall enter, ⁴nor Ammonite, Moabite, bastard, foreigner, or alien, forevermore. Surely his holiness ⁵shall be rev[eal]ed there; eternal glory shall ever be apparent

there. Strangers shall not again defile it, as they formerly defiled
[6]the temp[le of I]srael through their sins. (4Q174 1.2–6, with
restorations)

Several Qumran scrolls speak of a "new Jerusalem" (e.g., 1Q32, 2Q24,
4Q554, 4Q555, 5Q15, 11Q18), though whether a new temple is also
envisioned is not clear. In these fragmentary texts the temple is mentioned only a few times (e.g., 4Q554 frag. 1, 1.4; 2.18). The New Testament's book of Revelation also speaks of a "new Jerusalem," which comes
down from heaven, along with a "tabernacle of God" (Rev. 21:2–3). Is
this "tabernacle" or "dwelling" (Greek: *skēnē*), which probably alludes
to Ezekiel 37:27 ("My dwelling place [Greek: *kataskēnōsis*] shall be with
them"), the equivalent of a new temple? In a sense, it probably is. However, it is probably better to say that the very presence of God in the new
Jerusalem renders a temple building unnecessary. Of course, when the
book of Revelation was composed (near the end of the first century CE),
Jerusalem's famous temple had been long destroyed. All that is prophetic
in Revelation is the anticipation of a new Jerusalem and the very presence
of God.

First-century texts and individuals foretold the coming doom of the
temple. The *Lives of Prophets*, probably pre-70 CE,[13] contains two prophecies of the destruction of the first-century Temple:

And he [Jonah] gave a portent concerning Jerusalem and the whole
land, that whenever they should see a stone crying out piteously,
the end was at hand. And whenever they should see all the Gentiles
in Jerusalem, the entire city would be razed to the ground. (*[Life of
Jonah]* 10:10–11)

And concerning the end of the temple, he [Habakkuk] predicted,
"By a western nation it will happen." "At that time," he said, "the
curtain of the Dabeir [i.e., the Holy of Holies] will be torn into small
pieces, and the capitals of the two pillars will be taken away, and
no one will know where they are; and they will be carried away by
angels into the wilderness, where the Tent of Witness was set up in
the beginning." (*[Life of Habakkuk]* 12:11)[14]

These prophecies are probably not based upon the events of 70 CE.
In reference to the prophecy credited to Jonah, Douglas Hare thinks that
rather than pointing to the Romans specifically, the prophecy seems "to

reflect uneasiness regarding the increasing number of Gentile visitors and/or residents, which threatened to change the character of Israel's holy city." Hare adds that the "prophecy of 10:11 is best taken as reflecting an earlier situation, not the bitter experience" of 70 CE. In reference to Habakkuk's prophecy of the temple's destruction at the hands of a "western nation," Hare similarly concludes that the "prediction of [*Lives*] 12:11 that the temple will be destroyed by a Western nation was probably understood as referring to the Romans, but nothing requires that it be taken as a prophecy after the fact; the accompanying statements have the ring of unfulfilled predictions."[15]

Jesus of Nazareth is well known for his predictions of the siege of Jerusalem and the destruction of its famous temple:

> O Jerusalem, Jerusalem, killing the prophets and stoning those who are sent to you! How often would I have gathered your children together as a hen gathers her brood under her wings, and you would not! [35]Behold, your house is forsaken. (Luke 13:34–35)

> And when he drew near and saw the city he wept over it, [42]saying, "Would that even today you knew the things that make for peace! But now they are hid from your eyes. [43]For the days shall come upon you, when your enemies will cast up a bank about you and surround you, and hem you in on every side, [44]and dash you to the ground, you and your children within you, and they will not leave one stone upon another in you; because you did not know the time of your visitation." (Luke 19:41–44)

> And as he came out of the temple, one of his disciples said to him, "Look, Teacher, what wonderful stones and what wonderful buildings!" And Jesus said to him, "Do you see these great buildings? There will not be left here one stone upon another, that will not be thrown down." (Mark 13:1–2)

Other texts could be cited (e.g., Mark 14:58; Luke 21:20–24; 23:27–31). Of special importance was Jesus' appeal to Jeremiah 7:11 ("den of robbers") on the occasion of his demonstration in the temple precincts (Mark 11:15–18). Jeremiah 7 constitutes sharp criticism of the ruling priests of the First Temple and a warning that destruction is at hand. (More will be said about this later.) Today scholars are inclined to think that Jesus did actually warn of coming judgment upon Jerusalem and the temple. Jesus' demonstration in the temple's precincts, along with a prophecy or two that the temple would be destroyed, easily explains the actions taken against him by the ruling priests. It also explains the charge that Jesus had been heard threatening the temple (Mark 14:58), a tradition that resists dating to a post-Easter setting.

Probably the weightiest factor in favor of the authenticity of the prophecies is the observation that they do not reflect specific details of the destruction of the temple. There is no mention of the devastating fire that swept the precincts and was much emphasized in the graphic description narrated by Josephus (*J.W.* 6.165–68, 177–85, 190–92, 228–35, 250–84, 316, 346, 353–55, 407, 434). Almost poetically, Josephus says, "You would indeed have thought that the Temple Mount was boiling over from its base, being everywhere one mass of flame" (*J.W.* 6.275). And Jesus' admonition to pray that the destruction "not happen in winter" (see Mark 13:18) would be irrelevant and curious in light of the fact that the city was captured and the temple burned in August and September.[16]

Josephus himself also claims to have predicted the destruction of the temple and the defeat of the Jewish rebels:

> But as . . . Josephus overheard the threats of the hostile crowd, suddenly there came back into his mind those nightly dreams, in which God had foretold to him the impending fate of the Jews and the destinies of the Roman sovereigns. . . . He was not ignorant of the prophecies in the sacred books. (*J.W.* 3.351–52)

This prophecy clarifies Josephus's occasional fatalistic statements: "That building, however, God, indeed long since, had sentenced to the flames" (*J.W.* 6.250). But what "prophecies in the sacred books" did Josephus have in mind? He relates two of them, albeit in very cryptic terms:

> Who does not know the records of the ancient prophets and that oracle which threatens this poor city and is even now coming true? For they foretold that it would then be taken whenever one should begin to slaughter his own countrymen. (*J.W.* 6.109)

> Thus the Jews, after the demolition of Antonia, reduced the temple to a square, although they had it recorded in their oracles that the city and the sanctuary would be taken when the temple should become foursquare. (*J.W.* 6.311)

What prophecies Josephus had in mind is difficult to decide. He may have seen in prophecies that originally concerned the destruction of First Temple further prophecies for the temple of his own day. We actually have an example of this in the remarkable activity of one Jesus, son of Ananias, who for seven and a half years proclaimed the doom of Jerusalem and its temple. According to Josephus:

> Four years before the war . . . one Jesus, son of Ananias, . . . standing in the temple, suddenly began to cry out:
>
> "A voice from the east,
> A voice from the west,
> A voice from the four winds,
> A voice against Jerusalem and the Sanctuary,
> A voice against the bridegroom and the bride,
> A voice against all people." (*J.W.* 6.301)
> "Woe to Jerusalem!" (*J.W.* 6.306)
> "Woe once more to the city and to the people and to the
>   Sanctuary, . . .
>   and woe to me also" (*J.W.* 6.309)

We again hear an allusion to Jeremiah 7, this time to verse 34 ("I will make to cease . . . the voice of gladness, the voice of the bridegroom and the voice of the bride. . . ."). As in the earlier demonstration by Jesus of Nazareth, the allusion to Jeremiah was rightly understood as a threat against the temple. Josephus tells us that the Jesus of his time, a "rude peasant," was arrested by leading citizens and severely beaten. When he continued to cry out as before, he was taken before the Roman governor, Albinus, who had him "flayed to the bone with scourges" (*J.W.* 6.302–4). The governor decided that the man was a maniac, and so he released him (6.305). Jesus continued to proclaim his foreboding oracle until he was killed by a siege stone catapulted over the city wall (6.309). Later I will give more about this interesting character and what motivated him.

In not especially early rabbinic tradition we are told that at least two early rabbis predicted the destruction of the Herodian Temple:

> Forty years before the destruction of the temple the western light went out, the crimson thread remained crimson, and the lot for the Lord always came up in the left hand. They would close the gates of the temple by night and get up in the morning and find them wide

open. Said Rabban Yohanan ben Zakkai to the Temple, "O Temple, why do you frighten us? We know that you will end up destroyed. For it has been said, 'Open you doors, O Lebanon, that the fire may devour your cedars!' [Zech. 11:1]." (*y. Sotah* 6.3; cf. *b. Yoma* 39b; *Lam. Rab.* 1:5 §31)

Rabbi Zadok observed fasts for forty years in order that Jerusalem might not be destroyed, [and he became so thin that] when he ate anything the food could be seen [as it passed down his throat]. (*b. Gittin* 56a)

Zadok, Yohanan ben Zakkai, and other rabbis, we are told, tried to persuade the rebels to surrender to the Romans. Nearly murdered for his failure to support the rebellion, Yohanan finally escaped the city, being carried out in a coffin (*Lam. Rab.* 1:5 §31; *b. Git.* 56a–b; *'Abot R. Nat.* [A] 4:5). According to the tradition in *Lamentations Rabbah*, Zadok's life was spared at Yohanan's request. How much (if any) of this is historical is hard to say.

Examination of these traditions and oracles that speak of the coming destruction of the Herodian Temple reveals that they are almost always based upon the language and oracles of the classical prophets of the Old Testament. This observation also applies to the predictions of Jesus. Virtually every phrase reflects the language and imagery of the prophets who spoke of the destruction of the Solomonic Temple. Indeed, the destruction of the First Temple seems to have laid the groundwork for the emergence of a typology, which at times could be exploited by critics of the temple establishment.

Review of these traditions leads me to the following four conclusions:

1. As did many others, Jesus of Nazareth predicted the destruction of the Herodian Temple. This tradition is well attested and is corroborated in a variety of ways in the New Testament Gospels.

2. As did many others, Jesus employed the language of the classical prophets, particularly Jeremiah and Ezekiel, whose oracles were concerned with the Babylonian destruction of the Solomonic Temple, in predicting the Herodian Temple's destruction. Moreover, Jesus even alluded to some of the same complaints voiced by the prophets of old (e.g., Jer. 7:11).

3. There is substantial evidence of corruption in the Herodian Temple establishment. Furthermore, there is evidence of sectarian and peasant resentment toward the ruling establishment (i.e., ruling priests, Roman

authorities). Jesus' action in the temple (the so-called "cleansing") was in all probability related to, and indeed possibly the occasion for, a prophetic word against the temple.[17]

4. The fact that the first-century temple was constructed by Herod may have been a factor in anticipating its destruction. Built by Herod and administered by corrupt non-Zadokite ruling priestly families, the temple—in the minds of some—faced certain destruction.

We may be skeptical of some of these prophecies and suspect them of being little more than *vaticinia ex eventu* ("prophecies from the event"), but to classify all of them this way strikes me as special pleading. There are simply too many of them, and most of them show no knowledge of what actually happened in the summer of 70 CE. We are encouraged to accept them as genuine, for the details of the prophecies simply do not match well the details of the actual event.

A Family Feud

What we have is a generation, of approximately forty years, of competition between the family of Jesus on the one hand, and the family of Annas and their aristocratic allies on the other hand. This tumultuous history begins with Jesus' entry into Jerusalem in the year 30 (or perhaps 33) CE. After sharply criticizing the temple establishment, Jesus is himself confronted by the establishment. Before the week concludes, Jesus is brought before Annas, former high priest, and his son-in-law Caiaphas, current high priest (Matt. 26:57; John 18:13–14, 24, 28; Josephus, *Ant.* 18.63–64, "the first men among us"). Jesus is condemned and sent to the Roman governor Pontius Pilate, who orders Jesus' death by crucifixion.

The Easter event transformed the remnants of the movement into what became the church. The principal disciples of Jesus began proclaiming the good news of the resurrection of Jesus and soon encountered aggressive opposition from the ruling priests (Acts 4:1–4). Peter and others are brought before the Jewish rulers, among them "Annas the high priest and Caiaphas and John and Alexander, and all who were of the high-priestly family" (Acts 4:6). Here once again high priest (emeritus) Annas and his son-in-law Caiaphas, current high priest, confront the Jesus movement. With them is a priest called "John" (or "Jonathan"), one of the sons of Annas, who in 37 CE served as high priest briefly after Caiaphas was deposed (Josephus, *Ant.* 18.95). The ruling priests order Peter and his colleagues to cease speaking of Jesus, but they remain defiant (Acts 4:14–22). They continue to preach, and the church continues to grow.

High Priest Annas and His Family

Annas son of Seth (6–15 CE)
Eleazar son of Annas (16–17 CE)
Joseph, called Caiaphas, son-in-law of Annas (18–37 CE)
Jonathan son of Annas (37 CE)
Theophilus son of Annas (37–41 CE)
Matthias son of Annas (?)
Annas son of Annas (62 CE)

(See Luke 3:2; John 18:13–14; Acts 4:6; Josephus, *Ant.* 18.26, 33–35, 95; 20.197–200.)

The opposition to the church, however, also continues. Not long after the council (Sanhedrin) had warned Peter, the deacon-turned-evangelist Stephen suffers martyrdom. Criticized by members of the Synagogue of the Freedmen (Acts 6:9), Stephen is brought before the council (6:12–15), which includes "the high priest" (7:1), who can only be Caiaphas. Stephen is stoned to death (7:58–60). After the brief administration of Jonathan, son of Annas, another son of Annas named Theophilus is appointed to the high priesthood in 37 CE. At the beginning of his administration, Agrippa I, grandson of Herod the Great, acquired the tetrarchies of Philip and Lysanius. After the death of Caligula in 41 CE, Emperor Claudius appointed Agrippa I over the whole of Israel as "king of the Jews." It was during his reign, perhaps influenced by Theophilus and his family, that Agrippa I puts to death James the son of Zebedee and arrests Peter (Acts 12:1–5). After his escape from prison, Peter removes himself from Jerusalem, and James the brother of Jesus becomes the leader of the church (12:17).

James manages to remain alive and active in Jerusalem for about twenty years. But with the sudden death of the Roman governor Festus, recently appointed Annas (or Ananus), son of Annas, seized the opportunity to have James and some others (likely Christians) put to death by stoning. When Albinus the new governor arrived, he removed Annas (Josephus, *Ant.* 20.197–203). What happens next is very interesting. Not long after the death of James and arrival of Albinus, one Jesus ben Ananias entered Jerusalem (perhaps in 63 CE) and began uttering an oracle of woe based on Jeremiah 7. Not surprisingly, the ruling priests were outraged, wanted the man put to death, and no doubt would have killed him had it not been for the Roman governor. Albinus interrogated the man, whipped him, and then released him (Josephus, *J.W.* 6.300–309).

One must wonder if Jesus ben Ananias was a Christian prophet who took up his oracle in protest against the killing of James and, like Jesus of Nazareth some thirty years earlier, applied the grim Jeremiah 7 to his aristocratic priestly contemporaries. In any event, Josephus tells us that this man proclaimed the doom of the city and sanctuary for seven years and then died during the siege in the summer of 70 CE. With the death of Jesus ben Ananias, the capture of the city of Jerusalem, and the destruction of the temple, the first generation of the church came to a sudden and violent conclusion. It was a generation that began and ended amid conflict with the ruling priests. It was a conflict that began and ended amid prophecies inspired by Jeremiah 7.

In the remainder of this book, I want to follow this interesting thread, fleshing out various components along the way. My treatment is admittedly quite selective; a number of important issues are passed over. My goal is to explore more fully the dynamics of the conflict between Jesus and his followers on the one hand, and Annas and his followers on the other hand. I believe that better understanding of these dynamics will help us understand better the history and achievement of the Christian church in Jerusalem in that crucial first generation.

I bring this introduction to a close with a quick preview of the chapters that follow. In chapter 1 I ask a fundamental question: Did Jesus intend to found the Christian church? The general public would probably answer in the affirmative; most biblical scholars and historians would answer in the negative. Apart from careful qualification, neither answer is correct. There can be little doubt that Jesus envisioned the creation of a community or society, but it is most unlikely that he envisioned something outside of or over against Israel itself. So what exactly then did Jesus envision? The answer to this question will help us understand the dynamics of the first generation of his movement, including its relationship to the temple establishment.

Chapter 2 inquires into Jesus' proclamation of the kingdom of God and asks in what way, if at all, the "kingdom of God" relates to the Christian church. We shall find that Jesus' concept of the kingdom is deeply rooted in Israel's ancient Scripture, especially in the book of Isaiah. The coming kingdom of God brings to an end the human kingdoms of oppression and injustice. That Israel's Gentile oppressors face judgment is indeed good news for Israel, but in Jesus' conception of the kingdom, even Israel itself is subject to a critical review. Jesus will challenge assumptions of election, warning that even the "sons of the kingdom" face judgment unless they repent. Jesus knows too that this message of judgment will eventuate in his death and that through his death a repentant remnant, his community or church, will be established. In his teaching and example are hints that this remnant will include Gentiles.

Chapter 3 looks at the role of James the brother of Jesus as leader of the new movement in Jerusalem. A number of questions will be explored, such as why James, who was not one of his brother's original disciples, rose to such prominence in the church; how it was that James could remain in Jerusalem, when Peter found it necessary to flee; and how James related to Paul—according to their letters and according to the book of Acts—and in what ways they may have differed over "works of the law."

Chapter 4, which more or less serves as an excursus, explores further the apparent tension between Paul and James on the matter of law and works. At the heart of this debate is the question of why "works" are in view in these respective authorities. We will examine the zealot model, typified by the priest Phinehas; the teaching on works of law found in the *Halakic Letter* from Qumran (4QMMT = 4Q394–99); and the dominical commandment to love one's neighbor as one's self.

Chapter 5 examines the conflict between the families and followers of Jesus and Annas the high priest. This conflict is traced from the initial encounter between Jesus and Caiaphas, the son-in-law of Annas, onward to the murder of James, the brother of Jesus, at the hands of Annas, son of Annas the elder. Here I will also suggest that the "rude peasant," one Jesus ben Ananias, who warned of approaching judgment, was a member of the Jesus movement and rose up in protest of the murder of James. With the death of ben Ananias and the destruction of the temple, the first generation of the Jesus movement comes to an end.

The book could have concluded with chapter 5. But I believe it is important to examine the post-70-CE period in order to gain a better perspective of the problems and trends that emerged in the first generation and came to fuller expression in following generations. Accordingly, chapter 6 traces the aftermath of the Jewish rebellion, an aftermath that saw the church move away from its Jewish roots and Jewish leadership in Jerusalem. I look at the growing estrangement between the followers of Jesus and the synagogue, as we see it in Matthew, John, Revelation, Ignatius, and Justin Martyr. The chapter concludes with the Bar Kokhba revolt (132–135 CE) and the bitter polemic between Jews and Christians that ensued.

I have also added an appendix that further explores the factors—both historical and theological—that led to the rift between the Jesus movement and the synagogue. I hope to clarify what it really was that drove the wedge between the Jewish community that had reservations about the messianic credentials of Jesus and the Jesus community, which in its first century or so held in very high regard the Scriptures of Israel and the heritage of the Jewish people.

Chapter One

Did Jesus Intend to Found a Church?

Did Jesus intend to found the Christian church? This interesting question can be answered in the affirmative and in the negative. It depends on what precisely is being asked. If by church one means an organization and a people that stand outside of Israel, then the answer is no. If by a community of disciples committed to the restoration of Israel and the conversion and instruction of the Gentiles, then the answer is yes.[1] So what exactly did Jesus found?

The word usually translated "church" in the Greek New Testament is *ekklēsia*. In the New Testament the word occurs some 114 times. But it also occurs some 100 times in the Septuagint, the Greek translation of the Hebrew Bible. Most of the occurrences of *ekklēsia* in the Septuagint translate forms of *qahal*, whose basic meaning as a noun is "assembly" or "congregation" and as a verb is "to assemble." The Christian word "church" comes from the Greek adjective, *kyriakos*, which means "of the Lord" or "the Lord's" (cf. 1 Cor. 11:20, "the Lord's supper"; Rev. 1:10, "on the Lord's day"). Accordingly, "church" is an anglicized and abbreviated form of *hē ekklēsia hē kyriakē*, "the Lord's assembly."

The Language of Assembly in Jesus

The word *ekklēsia* occurs three times in the Gospels, all three in the Gospel of Matthew. After Peter identifies Jesus as the Messiah, Son of God, Jesus declares: "And I tell you, you are Peter, and on this rock I will build my church [*ekklēsia*], and the powers of death shall not prevail against it" (Matt. 16:18). Two chapters later, in the discourse on community discipline, Jesus instructs his disciples regarding one who has sinned and initially refuses to hear out the offended party: "If he refuses to listen to them, tell it to the church [*ekklēsia*]; and if he refuses to listen even to the church [*ekklēsia*], let him be to you as a Gentile and a tax collector" (18:17).

How much of this material derives from Jesus and, assuming that some of it does, in what form Jesus originally uttered it—these matters are not easy to determine. The first part (Matt. 16:17–19), Jesus' response to Peter's confession, may have been added to the tradition that Matthew found in Mark 8:27–30. Then again, Mark 8:27–30 may represent an abridged version of a longer, fuller, more primitive version of the story. In favor of the latter view is the presence of a number of Semitisms, as well as vocabulary that Matthew does not use elsewhere.[2] The second and third references to the "church," in Matthew 18:17, are part of tradition (i.e., Matt. 18:15–17) that probably derives from Q (cf. Luke 17:3–4), a source preserving Jesus' teachings, on which both evangelists Matthew and Luke drew.

At least it seems that Jesus envisioned and spoke of an assembly, or community, of disciples, who adhere to his teaching and embrace his mission. And I think what he envisioned was more than merely a band of disciples, such as gathered around several rabbis in his approximate time. Jesus' assembly, his *qahal* or *ekklēsia*, was perhaps somewhat analogous to the *yahad* (*yaḥad*), or "community," we hear about in some of the Qumran scrolls. In the scrolls, which are sometimes dubbed "sectarian," in the sense that they were composed by the men of Qumran (probably to be identified with the Essene sect), we encounter dozens of references to the community. These men are said to constitute the "community of God" (1QS 1.12), a "community whose essence is truth, genuine humility, love of charity, and righteous intent" (1QS 2.24), and the like. This community was guided by the prophetic command of Isaiah 40:3, "In the wilderness prepare the way of the LORD . . ." (1QS 8.13–14). Indeed, just like the early Christian movement, the men of Qumran called their movement "the Way" (1QS 9.17–18; 10.21; cf. Acts 9:2; 19:9, 23; 22:4; 24:14, 22), an unmistakable allusion to the passage from Isaiah. The Qumran community also called itself a *qahal*, or "assembly" or "congregation," many times in the *Damascus Covenant* (= *Damascus Document* [CD] 7.16–17; 12.5–6; 14.17–18), the *War Scroll* (1QM 4.10; 14.5), and other sectarian texts (e.g., 1QSa 1.4, 25; 2.4). If the Hebrew scrolls from Qumran had been translated into Greek, it is probable that the occurrences of *qahal* would have appeared as *ekklēsia*.

Qumran's community was organized. There was a Righteous Teacher, whose instruction was authoritative (CD 1.11; 20.14, 28, 32; 1QpHab

Figure 1.1. Community Compound at Wadi Qumran. The ruins at Wadi Qumran, west of the Dead Sea, were excavated in the 1950s by Roland de Vaux. Further work in the 1990s under the direction James F. Strange resulted in the discovery of an ostracon (a potsherd that bears writing) on which property (given to the Qumran community?) is listed. Pictured above is an artistic reconstruction of the community compound. Courtesy of Israelphotoarchiv©Alexander Schick bibelausstellung.de.

1.13; 7.4; 4Q165 frags. 1–2, line 3). There was a group of "twelve" men (nonpriests), who were important in the *Yahad* (1QS 8.1; 4Q259 2.9), as well as twelve "commanders" (4Q471 frag. 1, line 4) and twelve ruling priests (1QM 2.1; 4Q471 frag. 1, line 2). The twelve tribes/sons of Israel are frequently mentioned (1QM 3.14; 5.1; 4Q365 frag. 12b, 3.12; 11Q19 21.2–3; 23.3, 7; 11Q20 6.11). All of this has a counterpart in the Jesus circle: Jesus appoints twelve men, whom he calls apostles (Matt. 10:2; Mark 3:14; Luke 6:13); he speaks of the twelve sitting "on twelve thrones, judging the twelve tribes of Israel" (Matt. 19:28 = Luke 22:28–30). More will be said below about the importance of the twelve typology.

Qumran speculated about the seating arrangements when the Messiah appeared. They believed they knew who would sit with the Messiah and what types of persons would be excluded from this exalted company (e.g., the lame, blind, and persons with other physical defects; cf. 1QSa 2.3–9). The disciples of Jesus bickered over who would sit in the places of honor (Matt. 20:20–28; Mark 10:35–45; Luke 22:24–27) and Jesus himself, in his well-known parable of the Banquet (Luke 14:15–24, esp. v. 21), implied that the lame, blind, and physically defective in fact would sit in the places of honor.

The coherence of community and organizational language is remarkable, to be sure, but it does not require us to think that Jesus "got his ideas from Qumran" or that he had at one time been an Essene. It shows that Jesus and the men of Qumran belong to the same culture but not to the same community. The coherence also reveals the presence of traces of community, even community structure, in the Jesus circle prior to Easter and the launch of the church.

We see no radical, non-Jewish changes in the organization of the Jesus movement in its early years. In the book of Acts (at 6:1–6), the appointment of deacons (from the Greek *diakonein*, "to serve") to assist the apostles is completely in step with Jewish culture. The continuity with Jewish traditions of community and social organization is reflected in the language of Paul, Peter, James, and others, as we shall see in the following sections.

The Language of Assembly in Paul

The word *ekklēsia*, in reference to the Christian assembly, occurs many times in the book of Acts and many times in Paul's Letters. In his letter to the Christians in Rome, Paul speaks of "the churches of the Gentiles" (Rom. 16:4) and "the churches of Christ" (16:16). In his letters to the Christians of Corinth, the address reads: "To the church of God which is at Corinth" (1 Cor. 1:2; 2 Cor. 1:1); also in his Letter to the Galatians: "To the churches of Galatia" (1:2); and in the Thessalonian correspondence: "To the church of the Thessalonians" (1 Thess. 1:1; 2 Thess. 1:1). Eleven of the thirteen letters that bear the name of Paul as sender refer to the church, the *ekklēsia*, with some 60 or 61 occurrences in all, or just over half of all occurrences of the word in the writings of the New Testament. Indeed, most of the 23 occurrences of *ekklēsia* in the book of Acts involve the missionary activities of Paul. From these data we may justly infer that the language and concept of the church were of major importance to Paul, the apostle to the Gentiles.

The nominal and verbal forms of *qahal* occur some 65 times in the Dead Sea Scrolls. One occurrence offers a striking parallel with Paul's usage. In the *War Scroll* some banners are to have inscribed on them the words "The Assembly of God [*qahal 'el*]" (1QM 4.10). In Greek this would be rendered *ekklēsia tou theou*, that is, "assembly/church of God." Comparison of Paul's ecclesiastical or organizational language with the scrolls from Qumran reveals several interesting parallel points. Paul speaks of actions taken "by the many [*hypo tōn pleionōn*]" (2 Cor. 2:5–6), which approximates references to the "many" or "general membership" in the *Community Rule* (e.g., 1QS

6.11b–12, "During the session of the general membership [*harabim*] no man should say anything except by the permission of the general membership [*harabim*]"). In Philippians 1:1 Paul mentions "bishops" or "overseers" (*episkopoi*), which has its equivalent in the very passage in the *Community Rule* that has just been mentioned: ". . . who is the overseer [*hamebaqqer*] of the general membership [*harabim*]" (1QS 6.12). The Hebrew's *mebaqqer* appears to be the equivalent of Paul's *episkopos*.

There are also several important theological parallels between Paul's language and the language of the Scrolls. Paul speaks of the "righteousness of God" (Rom. 1:17; 3:21: *hē dikaiosynē theou*); so do the Scrolls (1QS 1.21; 10.23: *tsedekot 'el*; 1QS 10.25; 11.12: *tsedeket 'el*). Paul speaks of the "grace of God" (Rom. 5:15; 1 Cor. 3:10: *hē charis tou theou*); so do the Scrolls (1QS 11.12, *hasdei 'el*). Paul also speaks of the "works of the Law" (Rom. 3:20, 28; Gal. 2:16; 3:2, 5, 10: *erga nomou*); so do the Scrolls (1QS 6.18, *ma'esey betorah*; 4Q398 frags. 14–17, 2.3 = 4Q399 frag. 1, 1.11: *ma'esey hatorah*). And Paul speaks of the "new covenant" (2 Cor. 3:6, *kainē diathekē*); so do the Scrolls (CD 19.33–34; 20.12; 1QpHab 2.3: *berith hahadashah*).[3]

From this brief survey we see that Paul's ecclesiastical language is indebted not to some foreign Hellenistic terminology but to the language of his people—the Jewish people, a language that is reflected in some cases in the old Scriptures and in other cases in the more or less contemporary writings from Qumran. The use of *ekklēsia* in the Septuagint, Philo, Josephus, and various writings from the New Testament period (e.g., Jdt. 6:16; 7:29; *T. Job* 32:8; *Pss. Sol.* 10:6) bears this out.

The use of the word "church" and related terminology by the early followers of Jesus gives no indication that this new community thought of itself as standing outside of Israel. But the preference for and repeated use of "church" (*ekklēsia*), instead of "synagogue" (*synagōgē*), make clear that the assemblies of Christians—almost always made up of Jews and Gentiles—normally functioned outside the established synagogues. This seems clear in Paul's Letters and in the narratives of his missionary travels and activities recounted in the book of Acts.

The Language of Assembly in Peter and James

The language and orientation of the Letters of Peter and James, however, are noticeably different from what we have seen in Paul. Although I cannot here debate questions of date and authorship of these letters, I take the position that both James and 1 Peter are authentic and early letters, the former dating to the late 40s or early 50s, and the latter dating to the

early 60s. Both letters reflect an unmistakably Jewish, Palestinian
even if the latter, that is, the Letter of Peter, was composed in or near
Rome.

First Peter is addressed "to the exiles of the Dispersion" (or "Diaspora"), who are "chosen and destined by God the Father and sanctified
by the Spirit" (1 Pet. 1:1–2a). Such language is right at home in the world
of Jewish thought and self-understanding. The word "exile" (also "alien"
or "sojourner") is *parepidēmos*, that is, the foreigner who resides alongside
a people not one's own. In the Greek translation of the Hebrew Bible,
the great patriarch Abraham applies this term to himself when he says, "I
am a resident alien and a sojourner [*paroikos kai parepidēmos*] among you"
(Gen. 23:4 AT). The psalmist alludes to this passage and to the history of
the great patriarchs, all of whom were sojourners, when he cries out to
God in prayer: "Listen to my prayer, O Lord, and to my petition give ear;
do not pass by my tears in silence, because I am a sojourner [*paroikos*] with
you, and a visiting stranger [*parepidēmos*], like all my fathers" (Ps. 38:13
LXX, NETS = 39:12 RSV).

Peter also describes his readers, his fellow aliens, as "of the Dispersion,"
or "Diaspora." The Greek word *diaspora* occurs about one dozen times
in the Greek translation of the Hebrew Scriptures, including occurrences
in some books of the Apocrypha that may have originated in the Greek
language. Scripture reassures the people of Israel that the scattered will be
gathered: "If your dispersion be from an end of the sky to an end of the sky,
from there the LORD your God will gather you" (Deut. 30:4 AT; Neh. 1:9;
Ps. 147:2). The prophet Jeremiah warned a sinful and disobedient people:
"Send them away from my presence and let them go! . . . I will disperse
them in a dispersion in the gates of my people" (Jer. 15:1, 7 AT). But a
forgiving God promises to restore "the tribes of Jacob and to turn back
the dispersion of Israel" (Isa. 49:6 AT). This same hope is expressed in the
struggle against Antiochus IV, where we hear the prayer: "Gather together
our scattered people, set free those who are slaves among the Gentiles
[nations], look on those who are rejected and despised, and let the Gentiles
[nations] know that you are our God" (2 Macc. 1:27). Thus also prays the
author of the *Psalms of Solomon*: "Gather together the dispersion of Israel
with pity and kindness, for your faithfulness is with us" (8:28).

Peter's description of his addressees as "exiles of the dispersion" would
immediately bring to the minds of his readers and hearers—most of whom
we should assume were Jewish—these themes and images expressed in
Israel's sacred writings. Just as surely as the patriarchs long ago were dispersed among the nations, away from the land promised by God, living

Excavated Pre-70-CE Synagogues

Capernaum (probable: basalt foundations beneath limestone
    synagogue superstructure)
Gamla
Herodium
Jericho
Magdala
Masada
Modiʻin (or Modein)
Qiryat Sefer
Shuafat (unconfirmed)

as exiles and sojourners, so those who hope in Jesus the Messiah are
scattered about in the districts of Asia Minor, far away from the land of
Israel. Implicit in this typology is the hope, expressed in the prophets,
that someday God will gather his scattered people.

The Judaic character of the Letter of James is quite evident. The letter
begins with these words: "James, a servant of God and of the Lord Jesus
Christ, To the twelve tribes in the Dispersion: Greeting" (1:1). There are
several features of interest. First, James's self-designation as "a servant
of God" (*theou . . . doulos*) echoes the language of Scripture. We think of
Jonah the prophet, who answers the frightened sailors: "I am a servant of
the Lord [*doulos kyriou*], and I worship the Lord" (Jonah 1:9 LXX). We
recall Jeremiah's prophecy of a repentant Israel that will declare, "Behold,
we shall be your servants [*douloi hēmeis esometha soi*], because you are the
Lord God" (Jer. 3:22b LXX). We are also reminded of the confession of
the Judeans, who are rebuilding the temple of Jerusalem, when queried
by the king's officer: "We are the servants of the God [*douloi tou theou*] of
heaven and earth, and we are rebuilding the house that was built many
years ago" (Ezra 5:11). And of course Moses the lawgiver is called the
"servant of God" (Neh. 10:30 LXX = 10:29 RSV).

As in Peter's letter, James refers to the "dispersion," or Diaspora. However, unlike Peter, who refers to several specific geographic and political
regions, James offers no qualification. He refers to the Dispersion in its
totality and thus writes to all believers who live outside the land of Israel.
In this sense he reflects more exactly the prophetic vision and hope—
often implicit in Jewish literature—that all of God's people, wherever

Figure 1.2. Synagogue at Magdala. In 2009 a synagogue, dated to the first century BCE, was discovered at Migdol (or, in the Aramaic of the time of Jesus, Magdala), on the northwest shore of the Sea of Galilee. It was excavated by Dina Avshalom-Gorni and Arfan Najar. Photograph courtesy of Israelphotoarchiv©Alexander Schick bibelausstellung.de.

they may reside, will someday be gathered. In this respect, the Letter of James strikes a more universal note than the more narrowly focused Petrine letter.

Of great interest is James's address "to the twelve tribes" (*tais dōdeka phylais*). Although we should assume that the primary audience in view comprises Jews who share James's faith in and commitment to the "Lord Jesus Christ," or in less Hellenistic terms, "the Lord Jesus the Messiah," it is possible that a wider audience is in view. James may well have been addressing all Jews willing to hear him, as a religious voice of authority emanating from Jerusalem. It will be argued in chapters 3 and 5 that for more than twenty years, James competed with the religious leadership of Jerusalem for the hearts and minds of the Jewish people. James was not interested in founding a church as an institution outside of Israel. In any case, we must underscore the interesting fact that James addressed his letter to the "twelve tribes" and not to members of a church, in which are present Gentiles as well as Jews. In other words, James begins his letter in a manner that is conspicuously different from Paul's Letters.

The concept of "twelve tribes" goes right to the heart of the story portraying the origin of the people of Israel. The twelve tribes spring from the twelve brothers, the twelve sons of the patriarch Jacob, son of Isaac and grandson of Abraham, as the brothers themselves say: "We, your servants, are twelve brothers, the sons of one man in the land of Canaan" (Gen. 42:13; cf. 42:32). As death approached, Jacob gathered his sons for their respective blessings. The narrator introduces the scene thus: "All these are the twelve tribes of Israel" (Gen. 49:28).

Not surprisingly, the concept of twelve sons and twelve tribes took on symbolic significance.[4] We see this in the design of the holy garments to be worn by the high priest: "There shall be twelve stones with their names according to the names of the sons of Israel; they shall be like signets, each engraved with its name, for the twelve tribes" (Exod. 28:21; cf. 39:14). The symbolism of the twelve tribes is underscored in dramatic fashion as they prepare to cross the Jordan River and enter the promised land. Joshua is commanded to erect a monument at the site of the crossing, a monument made of twelve stones, "according to the number of the tribes of the people of Israel" (Josh. 4:8). The prophet Ezekiel recalls this symbolism in his vision of the restoration of Israel, when the promised land is recovered: "These are the boundaries by which you shall divide the land for inheritance among the twelve tribes of Israel" (Ezek. 47:13).

James's address to the "twelve tribes in the Dispersion/Diaspora" could hardly fail to evoke the traditions and hopes expressed in these Scriptures. James's manner of speaking suggests, moreover, that he conceives of the Jesus community as standing fully in continuity with Israel. There is no hint of opposition from "the Jews" or of disagreement with "Judaism," as seen, for example, in Paul's reference to his "former life in Judaism" (Gal. 1:13–14). But in speaking this way, James has not jumped over Jesus, as it were, and reached back to the ancient Scriptures of Israel. On the contrary, James has given expression to an important typology that lies at the very heart of the Jesus movement itself.

The Typology of the Twelve Tribes

The typology of the twelve tribes of Israel is seen in Jesus' appointment of twelve disciples, initially to be with him, but in time to be "sent out" (*apostellein*) as "apostles" (*apostoloi*) who proclaim his message of God's rule, as we see in the four New Testament Gospels (cf. Matt. 10:1–2,

5; 11:1; Mark 3:14; 4:10; 6:7; Luke 6:13; 9:1, 12; 18:31; John 6:67, 70; 20:24). But the typology is also attested in an important saying preserved in somewhat different forms in Matthew and Luke:

> Truly, I say to you, in the new world, when the Son of man shall sit on his glorious throne, you who have followed me will also sit on twelve thrones, judging the twelve tribes of Israel. (Matt. 19:28)

> You are those who have continued with me in my trials; and I assign to you, [29]as my Father assigned to me, a kingdom, [30]that you may eat and drink at my table in my kingdom, and sit on thrones judging the twelve tribes of Israel. (Luke 22:28–30)

This saying of Jesus draws upon two important passages from Scripture: Daniel 7:9–14 and Psalm 122:1–5. The first passage constitutes a vision in which thrones of judgment are set up, God takes his seat, and a figure "like a son of man" is presented and receives authority and an everlasting kingdom. The second passage celebrates worship in the temple in Jerusalem, where "the tribes go up," where "thrones for judgment" have been set up, "thrones of the house of David." These interesting passages are brought together in an old rabbinic midrash that inquires into the significance of the plural "thrones" in Daniel 7:9. It is decided that one of the thrones is for God himself, and the others are for the "elders of Israel," who will judge the peoples of the earth (*Midr. Tanh. Qedoshim* §1, on Lev. 19:1–2).

The parallels are remarkable. Both Jesus and another rabbinic authority have linked two passages that speak of thrones and judgment and have understood them in approximately the same manner. For Jesus, the "elders" who will "sit on the thrones judging" will be his twelve disciples. For the later rabbinic authority, the "elders" are others, who will judge not the tribes of Israel but the Gentiles. Jesus' interpretation is older, it seems to me, for it corresponds more closely with the original idea of Psalm 122:5. The judgment of which this psalm speaks is not punitive, and it is not directed against Gentiles (as in the old rabbinic midrash); it is administrative and judicial, and it is for the benefit of the people of Israel. The analogy would be that of the ancient judges of Israel (as in the book of Judges), who administered and defended the tribes of Israel.

Jesus' appointment of twelve disciples and his eschatological saying in which he envisions his disciples' serving as princes and administrators over the twelve tribes of Israel strongly suggest that the restoration of Israel is in view. On the basis of these traditions alone, we may rightly conclude that Jesus foresaw and intended no break with Israel. His intention was not to bring into existence an organization that would stand outside of and perhaps even over against the people of Israel and its legacy of patriarchs, promises, and prophecies. But more needs to be said about the symbolism of twelve.

Jesus' twelve symbolism harks back to John the Baptist, whose baptizing activities and calls for repentance were part of a Joshua typology that from time to time was given expression in Israel in the final decades of the Second Temple period. Crossing the Jordan River, traditionally understood to divide the foreign land to the east from the promised land to the west, set in motion a symbolic typology that in the time of Jesus inspired calls for renewal and promised signs that strike us moderns as quite strange. Two of the most interesting examples are seen in Theudas and the unnamed Jewish man from Egypt. With regard to the first individual, first-century historian and apologist Josephus says:

> A certain impostor named Theudas persuaded the majority of the populace to take up their possessions and follow him to the Jordan River. He stated that he was a prophet and that at his command the river would be parted and would provide easy passage. With this talk he deceived many. (*Ant.* 20.97–98)

Josephus goes on to say that the Roman governor Fadus (44–46 CE) dispatched the cavalry, which scattered Theudas's following and killed many. The would-be prophet was himself captured and beheaded. His summons to his following to "take up their possessions and follow him to the Jordan River," which they would then cross (back into Israel, not away from Israel), is an unmistakable allusion to the crossing of the Jordan under the leadership of Joshua (cf. Josh. 3:14–17). In all probability Theudas (Acts 5:36) understood himself as the promised "prophet like Moses" (cf. Deut. 18:15–19; cf. also 1 Macc. 4:45–46; 9:27; 14:41), who, like Joshua, would lead the righteous of Israel in a new conquest of the promised land.

With regard to the Jewish man from Egypt (Acts 21:38), Josephus says:

> At this time there came to Jerusalem from Egypt a man who said that he was a prophet and advised the masses of the common people to go out with him to the mountain called the Mount of Olives, which lies opposite the city. . . . For he asserted that he wished to demonstrate from there that at his command Jerusalem's walls would fall down,

through which he promised to provide them an entrance into the city. (*Ant.* 20.169–70)

The Roman governor Felix (52–60 CE) promptly dispatched the cavalry, which routed and dispersed the Egyptian's following, though the Egyptian himself escaped and was never heard from again. Once again, Joshua typology was apparently at work, with the Egyptian's promise of the collapse of the walls an unmistakable allusion to what befell Jericho after the people of Israel entered the promised land (cf. Josh. 6:20). Here we probably have another example of restorative theology based on exodus/conquest typology, in which a number of Palestinian Jews hoped to effect political and economic change in their country.

John the Baptist's appearance at the Jordan River, where he summons Israel to repent and warns of coming judgment, should be interpreted in the light of the Joshua and Jordan typology we see at work in Theudas and the anonymous Jewish man from Egypt. How this typology was acted out varied, of course, from one individual to another. There is no evidence that John attempted to raise an army or promised a spectacular sign, such as the parting of the river or the collapse of the walls of Jerusalem, but his location at the Jordan, his demand for repentance, his

Roman Governors of Israel in Jesus' Time and the Church's First Generation

Prefects of Samaria and Judea
Valerius Gratus (15–19/25 CE)
Pontius Pilate 19/25–37 CE)
Marcellus (37 CE)
Marullus (37–41 CE)

Procurators of All Israel
Fadus (44–46 CE)
Tiberius Alexander (46–48 CE)
Ventidius Cumanus (48–52 CE)
Felix (52–60 CE)
Porcius Festus (60–62 CE)
Albinus (62–64 CE)
Gessius Florus (64–66 CE)

warning of judgment, his criticism of Antipas the tetrarch, and his violent end—execution by beheading, by order of Antipas—clearly places him in the company of men like Theudas (who also was beheaded) and the Egyptian Jew (who would have been beheaded if he had been captured), even if his strategy and proclamation differed in important ways.

But in what way did John's Jordan-Joshua typology manifest itself? One important aspect of the symbolism associated with the crossing of the Jordan River was the monument of twelve stones, which represented the twelve tribes of Israel. God commands Joshua:

> Take twelve men from the people, from each tribe a man, [3]and command them, "Take twelve stones from here out of the midst of the Jordan, from the very place where the priests' feet stood, and carry them over with you, and lay them down in the place where you lodge tonight." [4]Then Joshua called the twelve men from the people of Israel, whom he had appointed, a man from each tribe. . . . [8]And the men of Israel did as Joshua commanded, and took up twelve stones out of the midst of the Jordan, according to the number of the tribes of the people of Israel, as the LORD told Joshua; and they carried them over with them to the place where they lodged, and laid them down there. [9]And Joshua set up twelve stones in the midst of the Jordan, in the place where the feet of the priests bearing the ark of the covenant had stood; and they are there to this day. . . . [20]And these twelve stones, which they took out of the Jordan, Joshua set up in Gilgal. [21]and he said to the people of Israel, "When your children ask their fathers in time to come, 'What do these stones mean?' [22]then you shall let your children know, 'Israel passed over this Jordan on dry ground,' . . . [24]so that all the peoples of the earth may know that the hand of the LORD is mighty." (Josh. 4:2–4, 8–9, 20–22, 24)

Twelve stones are retrieved from the midst of the Jordan River, "according to the number of the tribes of the people of Israel." Then they are carried across the river and placed as a monument to the crossing of the river "on dry ground," so that Israel's descendants and "all peoples" will "know that the LORD is mighty."

John the Baptist may very well be pointing to the symbolism of "these stones" (*hoi lithoi houtoi*, Josh. 4:21 LXX) when he scolds those who approach him: "Do not presume to say to yourselves, 'We have Abraham as our father'; for I tell you, God is able from *these stones* [*ek tōn lithōn toutōn*] to raise up children to Abraham" (Matt. 3:9 = Luke 3:8; emphasis added). The proximity of "these stones" to the Jordan River and the role they play in Joshua typology, as well as the comparison to "children to Abraham," strengthen the likelihood that the stones to which John makes reference are not simply stones that happen to be lying about, but a specific group (or monument) of twelve stones that represent the twelve tribes of the people ("sons") of Israel.

The stone symbolism reappears in the Elijah narrative: "Elijah took twelve stones, according to the number of the tribes of the sons of Jacob, to whom the word of the LORD came, saying, 'Israel shall be your name'; and with the stones he built an altar in the name of the LORD" (1 Kgs. 18:31). In fact, later eschatological speculation links Elijah to the restoration of the tribes, as we see in the Wisdom of Ben Sira:

> You who were taken up by a whirlwind of fire, in a chariot with horses of fire; [10]you who are ready at the appointed time, it is written, to calm the wrath of God before it breaks out in fury, to turn the heart of the father to the son, and to restore the tribes of Jacob. (Sir. 48:9–10)

Accordingly, John's appearance in the wilderness, in the vicinity of the Jordan River, calling for repentance, speaking of "these stones," and dressed in a way that recalls the prophet Elijah—all these are coherent elements of a unified typology, whose point of origin was the crossing of the Jordan River under the leadership of Joshua, and whose purpose was preparation for the restoration of Israel, the people of God. John's reference to "these stones" probably was meant to recall the twelve stones erected as a monument by Joshua. If so, then Jesus' appointment of twelve apostles, who traveled throughout Israel, calling on the people to repent in light of the dawning of God's rule, should be understood as an extension of John's typology.[5]

Thus, what we see is an unbroken chain of restoration hope, symbolized by language and imagery of twelve, that is, the twelve tribes of Israel. Israel's ancient Scriptures spoke of the gathering and restoration of the twelve tribes; John symbolized this hope by locating his preaching and baptizing at the Jordan, where the twelve tribes under the leadership of Joshua crossed into the promised land, and where Joshua built a monument of twelve stones, signifying the crossing of the twelve tribes. John alludes to these stones in his call for repentance and warning not to presume on the basis of genetic descent from the great patriarch Abraham. Jesus continued the twelve typology and its symbolism of restoration by appointing twelve apostles. And finally, Jesus' brother James assumes this restoration typology, or at least echoes it, by speaking of Israel as the "twelve tribes in the Dispersion." In all of this we see no break with Israel, no attempt to create a movement or organization that stands outside of or opposed to the Jewish people.

Paul, the Church, and Israel

I have noted the contrast between Paul's typical letter addresses and the address we find in the Letter of James. I wonder if Paul's language and tone are different from those of James because Paul was the energetic "apostle to the Gentiles" (Rom. 11:13; Gal. 2:8)? If Paul did not think conversion to Judaism was necessary for Gentiles to join the assembly of Messiah Jesus (as he so vehemently argues in Galatians), then we should hardly expect to hear him address his readers as the "twelve tribes of the Dispersion." Even so, Paul shared the hope of Jesus and Jesus' brother James, the hope for Israel's redemption.

This hope is given eloquent expression in Paul's speech before Herod's great-grandson Agrippa II, as presented in the book of Acts: "I stand here on trial for hope in the promise made by God to our fathers, [7]to which our twelve tribes hope to attain, as they earnestly worship night and day. And for this hope I am accused by Jews, O king!" (Acts 26:6–7). Some will object that this speech reflects the theology of the author of Acts and not necessarily that of Paul. On the contrary, however the author may have edited Paul's words, the speech that we have in Acts truly represents the thought of the apostle, as we see in his warning to Gentile believers who may be tempted to think that Israel no longer has a future. In his letter to the Christians of Rome, Paul has this to say:

> Lest you be wise in your own conceits, I want you to understand this mystery, brothers: a hardening has come upon part of Israel, until the full number of the Gentiles come in, [26]and so all Israel will be saved; as it is written, "The Deliverer will come from Zion, he will banish ungodliness from Jacob"; [27]"and this will be my covenant with them when I take away their sins." [28]As regards the gospel they are enemies of God, for your sake; but as regards election they are

beloved for the sake of their forefathers. [29]For the gifts and the call of God are irrevocable. (Rom. 11:25–29)

Paul's emphatic affirmation of Israel's continuing election is categorical. Regrettably, Christian exegesis sometimes confuses Israel with the church. However, Paul's words cannot be any clearer. A "hardening has come upon part of Israel," that is, a spiritual obduracy has come upon ethnic Israel (not upon the church, whose membership grows with an increasing influx of Gentile converts!). Here Paul echoes the language of Israel's classical prophets Isaiah, Jeremiah, and Ezekiel, who in their own ways speak of Israel's spiritual blindness, deafness, and hardheartedness to God's law and will. Yet this obduracy is only partial and temporary: it will last "until the full number of the Gentiles come in." But when that full number has come in, "all Israel will be saved," as Isaiah the prophet has promised. The "all Israel" of which the apostle speaks is ethnic Israel, not the church. The apostle Paul believed with all his heart that Israel still has a future, that Israel remains God's chosen people, and that someday not a remnant but "all Israel will be saved."

But we must ask if Paul has created a new institution, a new organization, something that stands over against Israel, something that Jesus himself never anticipated. From time to time learned tomes and popular books have asserted that the Christian church is largely Paul's creation, that Jesus himself never intended for such a thing to emerge.

Jesus and the Remnant of Israel

Frankly, I think the hypothesis of Paul as creator of the church or inventor of Christianity is too simplistic. A solution that is fairer to the sources, both Christian and Jewish, is more complicated. The solution also takes us back to where we began—with the meaning of the word "church," or *ekklēsia*.

In sayings that admittedly reflect Matthean editing, Jesus affirms Peter's confession of his master as the Messiah, Son of God: "And I tell you, you are Peter, and on this rock I will build my church, and the powers of death shall not prevail against it" (Matt. 16:18). In a later collection of sayings relating to community regulations and discipline, Jesus tells his disciples: "If he [an offender] refuses to listen to them, tell it to the church; and if he refuses to listen even to the church, let him be to you as a Gentile and a tax collector" (Matt. 18:17). What is this "church" of which Jesus speaks? Is he speaking of the local house churches scattered

about in the Roman Empire? Or is he speaking of a community of people, within Israel, that has responded to his and John's call to repentance
and the reception of God's rule? We can answer this question, at least in
part, by comparing Jesus with his contemporaries.

One thinks of John's fiery preaching of judgment, his warning that the
ax has been laid against the root of the trees, and that the winnowing fork
will separate wheat from chaff (Matt. 3:10, 12; Luke 3:9, 17). Does this not
assume that only a remnant of Israel will be redeemed? Is this not the same
idea expressed in some of the prophets? One thinks of Isaiah: in his glorious vision of God enthroned in the temple, the prophet is told to proclaim
a message of obduracy and judgment: "Go, and say to this people: 'Hear
and hear, but do not understand; see and see, but do not perceive.' [10]Make
the heart of this people fat, and their ears heavy, and shut their eyes; lest
they see with their eyes, and hear with their ears, and understand with their
hearts, and turn and be healed" (Isa. 6:9–10). This is hardly a message that
Isaiah desires to proclaim. He asks the Lord "How long?" That is, how
long must he preach such a dismal message? And the Lord answers: "Until
cities lie waste without inhabitant, and houses without men, and the land
is utterly desolate, and the LORD removes men far away, and the forsaken
places are many in the midst of the land" (vv. 11–12). Isaiah is to preach his
word of judgment until judgment has run its course. His only consolation
is that a remnant will survive, a "holy seed" (v. 13).

Likewise the men of Qumran believe only a remnant of Israel will be
saved from the day of wrath that is coming. The corrupt priesthood will
be swept away. Sinners will be destroyed, and the Roman army, along
with its hated emperor, will be annihilated. The righteous, repentant
men of Qumran, the Essenes, will restore the priesthood, reform worship in Jerusalem, and with God's help and the raising up of the Messiah,
lead Israel into a time of unprecedented glory.

Some of Jesus' teaching fits into this framework in a general way. Many
of his parables and proverbial sayings presuppose a separation of the wicked
and the righteous. Only some of the soil in the parable of the Sower (Mark
4:3–9) produces fruit. When the disciples ask about the meaning of the
parables, Jesus enigmatically states: "To you has been given the secret of
the kingdom of God, but for those outside everything is in parables; [12]so
that they may indeed see but not perceive, and may indeed hear but not
understand; lest they should turn again, and be forgiven" (Mark 4:11–12).
Whatever its original setting, the saying obviously alludes to Isaiah 6:9–10
and clearly states that some understand the mystery of God's rule, yet others do not understand and instead remain obdurate.

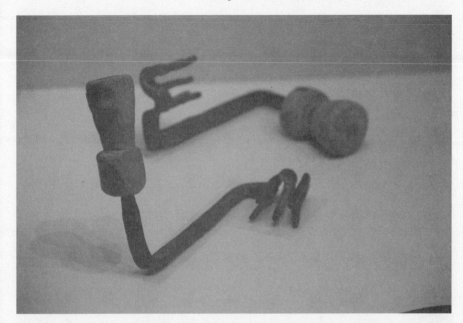

Figure 1.3. Keys. In late antiquity door keys were very large and often served both as keys and as door knobs or handles. Keys to some of the temple gates would have looked like the keys pictured here. Jesus promised Peter and the church that he will given him the "keys of the kingdom of heaven" (Matt. 16:19; 18:18). Photograph courtesy of Israelphotoarchiv©Alexander Schick bibelausstellung.de.

Jesus warns his followers to "enter by the narrow gate; for the gate is wide and the way is easy, that leads to destruction, and those who enter by it are many. [14]For the gate is narrow and the way is hard, that leads to life, and those who find it are few" (Matt. 7:13–14; cf. Luke 13:24). Jesus' saying is hardly unique, for we have close parallels in Scripture (e.g., Deut. 30:15, 19; Jer. 21:8), in the Dead Sea Scrolls (1QS 3.20–21), and in rabbinic literature (*m. 'Abot* 2.12–13; *b. Ber.* 28b). Jesus often speaks of the first as "last" and the last as "first" (e.g., Matt. 19:30; Mark 9:35; Luke 13:30). Reversal of fortunes is seen in some of his parables (e.g., Luke 16:19–30, where the poor man is received into paradise, and the wealthy man is condemned to Hades). Jesus warns that some Israelites who are near will be cast out, and others who are from afar will sit with the patriarchs in the kingdom of God (Matt. 8:11–12; Luke 13:28–30).

So what then did Jesus mean by referring to his "church," his *qahal*? In view of his teachings, some of which we have briefly surveyed, his church or assembly is a community of disciples, who have taken upon themselves his yoke (Matt. 11:29–30) and have embraced his teaching.

Jesus did not wish to lead his disciples out of Israel, but to train followers who will lead Israel, who will bring renewal to Israel, and who will
instruct Gentiles in the way of the Lord. Jesus longed for the fulfillment
of the promises and the prophecies, a fulfillment that would bless Israel
and the nations alike.

This was Paul's vision too. Earlier in this chapter I spent time discussing the Letters of Peter and James because these men were the principal leaders of the church in Jerusalem. Their teaching (which I scarcely
reviewed, limiting myself instead to the way they addressed the readers
of their respective letters) clearly stands in continuity with the traditions
and self-understanding of Israel. Paul refers to Peter and James as the
"pillars" (Gal. 2:1, 9, "I went up to Jerusalem. . . . James and Cephas and
John, who were reputed to be pillars"). It may be that "pillars" alluded to
the Jerusalem temple (Rev. 3:12), perhaps suggesting that the true worship of God was to be found in James and Peter, not in the Sadducean
priesthood, whose corruption and abuse of power occasioned much criticism in Jewish literature in late antiquity.[6]

There is no indication, either in the Letters of Peter, James, and Paul,
or in the traditions known of these men outside these letters, that the
church, or assembly, of Jesus was thought to be divorced from Israel.
The church of Jesus was estranged from and at odds with the ruling
priestly establishment in Jerusalem, but it did not feel estranged from
Israel itself. The estrangement of the church from Israel was not the
result of Jesus' teaching or Paul's teaching. Rather, the parting of the
ways, as it has been called in recent years, was the result of a long process. This process was hastened and exacerbated by difficulties experienced by the Jewish people as a result of the three disastrous Jewish
rebellions in 66–70 CE, 115–117, and 132–135. Some of this history will
be discussed later in this book.

Conclusion

I conclude by noting that the word synagogue (*synagōgē*) occurs in the
Letter of James. The RSV translates it not as "synagogue" but as "assembly": "For if a man with gold rings and in fine clothing comes into your
assembly, and a poor man in shabby clothing also comes in . . ." (2:2).
Commentators dispute what is meant here. Is James referring to a synagogue, whose congregation is entirely Jewish, some of whom believe in
Jesus and others do not? Or has James simply used a familiar term to
mean no more than an assembly or group of people? Later in his letter

the word *ekklēsia* occurs, where those who are sick are urged to "call for the elders of the church" (5:14).

What we may have here in the Letter of James, written perhaps fifteen years or so after the death of Jesus, is a glimpse of the life of the Christian community in a very early stage, when there was little distinction between *synagōgē* and *ekklēsia*, a time when a leader of the Jesus movement could live in Jerusalem and compete for the hearts and minds of his fellow Jews, not in order to lead them out of Israel, but to lead them toward the fulfillment of what God had promised Israel.

In chapter 3 we shall explore further what James taught and how he led his brother's movement. We will keep in mind the question that has been posed in this chapter: Did Jesus intend to found the church? And if so, in what sense? But before we address this question, we must take a fresh look at the proclamation of Jesus, the arrival of the kingdom of God, and its implications for Israel.

Chapter Two

From Kingdom of God to Church of Christ

In chapter 1 we asked if Jesus intended to found the Christian church. In the present chapter we must inquire into the transition from Jesus' proclamation of the kingdom of God to the emergence of the Christian church. In the following chapter we shall look at the nature of this church.

The shift from kingdom of God to church of Christ corresponds to the shift from the Jesus who proclaims (the kingdom), to the Jesus who is proclaimed (by the church). Historically New Testament scholars have treated this question as a great problem, claiming, for example, that Jesus did not foresee the church. In my view, however, the transition from kingdom proclamation to the church is neither strange nor unanticipated. Within the framework of the kingdom proclamation are found the very seeds of the new community that in the post-Easter setting will spring up as the church.

Proclaiming the Kingdom of God

Jesus proclaimed the kingdom of God, something almost no one disputes. What precisely Jesus envisioned this kingdom to be is another question. In the last quarter of the twentieth century, a group of scholars, mostly North American, tried to persuade us that the "kingdom" Jesus envisioned was of a Hellenistic character, whose chief purpose was to promote equality and egalitarian principles. Mainstream scholarship rightly rejected this theory, viewing the kingdom proclamation as rooted in Israel's sacred story and especially in the book of Isaiah. The evidence for this position is compelling.

The evangelist Mark sums up Jesus' proclamation as follows:

> Now after John was arrested, Jesus came into Galilee, preaching the gospel of God, [15]and saying, "The time is fulfilled, and the kingdom of God is at hand; repent, and believe in the gospel." (Mark 1:14–15)

On one occasion, in his itinerant preaching, Jesus is remembered to have appealed to Isaiah 61:1–2, as in Luke 4:

> And he came to Nazareth, where he had been brought up; and he went to the synagogue, as his custom was, on the sabbath day. And he stood up to read; [17]and there was given to him the book of the prophet Isaiah. He opened the book and found the place where it was written, [18]"The Spirit of the Lord is upon me, because he has anointed me to preach good news to the poor. He has sent me to proclaim release to the captives and recovering of sight to the blind, to set at liberty those who are oppressed, [19]to proclaim the acceptable year of the Lord." [20]And he closed the book, and gave it back to the attendant, and sat down; and the eyes of all in the synagogue were fixed on him. [21]And he began to say to them, "Today this scripture has been fulfilled in your hearing." (Luke 4:16–21)

Allusions to Isaiah 61 appear elsewhere in Jesus' teaching (e.g., Matt. 5:4; 11:4–5 = Luke 7:22). Indeed, Isaiah seems to have been one of Jesus' favorite books of Scripture, for he quotes it, paraphrases it, and alludes to it many times, often through the lens of the emerging Aramaic tradition that in time was committed to writings known as the Targumim.[1]

The core message of Jesus, "the kingdom of God is at hand," echoes the good news of Isaiah, as in 61:1: God "has anointed me to preach good news to the poor" (NIV). Not only does Isaiah speak of "good news" ("good tidings," "gospel"); the prophet also says it is the task of the one who has been "anointed," from which we have the word "messiah." Moreover, the proclaimer of the good news has been anointed by the "Spirit of the Lord GOD." As we shall see shortly, this is why it was so important for Jesus to validate his proclamation by appeal to works of power, especially his casting out evil spirits. These works of power were demonstrations that the "Spirit of the LORD" was truly upon him.

The message of Jesus does not simply echo the language of Hebrew Isaiah; it appears to echo the language of Aramaic Isaiah, which in later generations was preserved in the written Targumim (Targums). Compare the following passages from Hebrew and Aramaic Isaiah (with significant departures from the Hebrew noted in italics):

> . . . for the LORD of hosts will reign on Mount Zion and in Jerusalem, and before his elders he will manifest his glory. (Hebrew Isa. 24:23b)

> . . . for *the kingdom of* the Lord of hosts will *be revealed* on Mount Zion and in Jerusalem and before the elders of his people in glory. (Aramaic Isa. 24:23b)

> . . . so the LORD of hosts will come down to fight upon Mount Zion and upon its hill. (Hebrew Isa. 31:4b)

> . . . so *the kingdom of* the Lord of hosts will *be revealed to settle* upon Mount Zion and upon its hill. (Aramaic Isa. 31:4b)

> Get you up to a high mountain, O Zion, herald of good tidings; lift up your voice with strength, O Jerusalem, herald of good tidings, lift it up, do not fear; say to the cities of Judah, "Here is [Behold] your God!" (Hebrew Isa. 40:9)

> Get you up to a high mountain, *prophets who* herald good tidings to Zion; lift up your voice with force, you who herald good tidings to Jerusalem, lift up, fear not; say to the cities of the house of Judah, "*The kingdom of* your God *is revealed*!" (Aramaic Isa. 40:9)

> How beautiful upon the mountains are the feet of him who brings good tidings, who publishes peace, who brings good tidings of good, who publishes salvation, who says to Zion, "Your God reigns." (Hebrew Isa. 52:7)

> How beautiful upon the mountains *of the land of Israel* are the feet of him who announces, who publishes peace, who announces good tidings, who publishes salvation, who says to the congregation of Zion, "*The kingdom of* your God *is revealed*." (Aramaic Isa. 52:7)[2]

In the Aramaic all of these passages speak of the *revelation* of the kingdom of God (or Lord). In Isaiah 24:23 and 31:4 the Hebrew refers only to "the LORD of Hosts." In the first Hebrew passage the Lord "will reign," and in the second he "will come down to fight." In the Aramaic version both are transformed to read, "the kingdom of the Lord of Hosts will be revealed." In Isaiah 52:7 the confession "Your God reigns" is expanded to read, "The kingdom of your God is revealed," while in 40:9 the mere summons "Behold your God" alone is sufficient to warrant the same expansion.

Common to all of these passages is the idea that God is king, something confessed elsewhere in Scripture, especially in the Psalms (5:2; 44:4; 47:6–7; 68:24; 74:12; 84:3; 95:3; 145:1). In this connection we should not forget what Samuel told ancient Israel, when the people clamored for a king so that they might be like the nations: "The LORD your God [is] your king" (1 Sam. 12:12).[3]

The passages from Isaiah that have been cited depict God in his kingly activities. In 24:23 the Lord reigns on Mount Zion. Mount Zion is his throne. In 31:4 God fights on Mount Zion, as, it is implied, a king would fight to defend his kingdom. In 40:9 the cities of Judah are bidden to hear the good news of the presence of their God, much as messengers go before the king to announce his arrival. In 52:7 the good news of peace and salvation is summed up in the announcement that "God reigns," implying that his enemies have been vanquished. Just as the messenger speeds ahead to tell the anxious and waiting people the glad tidings that their monarch has been victorious, so the messenger of Isaiah announces to Israel that God has defeated his enemies and rules in power and glory.

The Aramaic paraphrases of these four passages have not significantly altered the original meaning of Hebrew Isaiah: they have made explicit what the Hebrew passages imply. In his mighty actions, the kingdom, or rule, of God will be revealed. It is this good news—the rule of God—that Jesus proclaims in his time. The awaited and longed-for revelation of the rule of God has now at last arrived, or in the words of Jesus: "The kingdom of God is at hand; repent, and believe in the gospel [good news]" (Mark 1:15).

The language of the revelation of the kingdom of God is not unique to Isaiah. It also is given expression elsewhere in the Aramaic versions of the Prophets. Again, the major departures from the Hebrew will be noted in italics:

Saviors shall go up to Mount Zion to rule Mount Esau; and the kingdom shall be the LORD's. (Hebrew Obad. 21)

Saviors shall go up to Mount Zion to judge the citadel of Esau; and the kingdom of the Lord *shall be revealed over all the inhabitants of the earth.* (Aramaic Obad. 21)

The Hebrew version's prophecy that the "kingdom shall be the Lord's" becomes in the Aramaic, "the kingdom of the Lord shall be revealed." This kingdom of the Lord, the expansive paraphrase declares, will be "over all the inhabitants of the earth." It is not simply a new Israelite kingdom, a kingdom limited to the geography of Israel. Rather, the kingdom of the Lord is a universal kingdom under whose authority all of humanity will someday find itself.

Similar themes are expressed in Zechariah 14:9, where we are again told that the kingdom of the Lord has universal scope:

And the Lord will become king over all the earth; on that day the Lord will be one and his name one. (Hebrew Zech. 14:9)

And *the kingdom of* the Lord *will be revealed* upon *the inhabitants of* the earth; at that time *they shall serve before* the Lord with one accord, *for his name is established in the world; there is none apart from him.* (Aramaic Zech. 14:9)

Zechariah speaks of the oneness of the Lord: "on that day the Lord will be one and his name one." The Lord will rule the earth and preside over all inhabitants, but he will not share this rule with other deities. He is the Lord, he is one, and his name is one. The prophet's affirmation clearly echoes the well-known Shema (*shema‵*): "Hear, O Israel: The Lord our God is one Lord" (Deut. 6:4).[4] The last clause, "There is none apart from him," probably alludes to Deuteronomy 4:39 ("There is none else" [KJV]). The Aramaic version extends the theme of oneness by adding that the earth's inhabitants "shall serve the Lord with one accord" (lit., "one shoulder"). All of humanity will recognize the Lord and will serve him faithfully.

The theme of God's kingdom being revealed to the inhabitants of the land also appears in Ezekiel, though with a different nuance:

Your doom has come to you, O inhabitant of the land; the time has come, the day is near, a day of tumult, and not of joyful shouting upon the mountains. (Hebrew Ezek. 7:7)

The kingdom was been revealed to you, O inhabitant of the land! The time of misfortune has arrived, the day of tumultuous confession is near, and there is no escaping to the mountain strongholds. (Aramaic Ezek. 7:7)[5]

Behold, the day! Behold, it comes! Your doom has come, injustice has blossomed, pride has budded. (Hebrew Ezek. 7:10)

Behold, the day of retribution! Behold, it is coming! *The kingdom has been revealed! The ruler's rod* has blossomed! Wickedness has sprung up. (Aramaic Ezek. 7:10)

In these passages from Ezekiel, the arrival of the kingdom (note that in the verses from Aramaic Ezekiel, the kingdom is not qualified with the words "of God" or "of the Lord") is associated with judgment. The prophet has pronounced judgment not only on tiny Israel but also on the whole land, implying judgment upon the major Middle Eastern empires. As in Amos 5:18, the approaching judgment is not an occasion for joy but of terror.[6] The threat of judgment is enhanced in Aramaic Ezekiel 7:10 with the replacement of "injustice" with "the ruler's rod." In the Aramaic paraphrase the time of fearful judgment will take place when the kingdom of God is revealed.

In the final passage the awaited Messiah and the kingdom of God are linked:

. . . and the LORD will reign over them in Mount Zion from this time forth and for evermore. [8]And you, O tower of the flock, hill of the daughter of Zion, to you shall it come, the former dominion shall come, the kingdom of the daughter of Jerusalem. (Hebrew Mic. 4:7b–8)

The kingdom of the Lord will *be revealed upon* them on Mount Zion from now and forever. [8]And you, *O Messiah of Israel, who have been hidden away because of the sins of the congregation of Zion, the kingdom shall come to you,* and the former dominion shall *be restored to* the kingdom of the *congregation* of Jerusalem. (Aramaic Mic. 4:7b–8)[7]

We again encounter the familiar refrain, "The kingdom of the Lord will be revealed," inspired by the Hebrew version's "the LORD will reign" (as also in Hebrew Isa. 24:23). This time, however, the Messiah himself is introduced, as the Hebrew's "O tower of the flock" becomes in Aramaic "O Messiah of Israel." The Messiah of Israel, we are told, has been "hidden away because of the sins" of Israel. Redemption will come when Israel repents. Repentance is greatly emphasized in Aramaic Isaiah.

It is not surprising that the Aramaic paraphrases of the Prophets, especially Isaiah, emphasize the necessity for repentance. Calling the nation to repent was the chief occupation of the prophets. In the Aramaic version of the Prophets, however, repentance often entails returning to the law of Moses. In Aramaic Ezekiel 7 the revelation of the kingdom means judgment. Elsewhere the revelation of the kingdom means redemption of Israel's righteous remnant. For example, Hebrew Isaiah 10:21 promises a shattered Israel that "a remnant will return, the remnant of Jacob, to the mighty God." Aramaic Isaiah agrees, but not without an important qualification: "The remnant *that have not sinned and that have repented from sin*, the remnant of *the house of* Jacob, shall return . . ." (with italics indicating additions to the text). This repentant remnant may expect deliverance at the hands of the Messiah, as it again says in the Aramaic: "And it will come to pass in that time his stroke shall pass from you, and his yoke from your neck, *and the Gentiles will be shattered before the Messiah*" (with italics indicating changes to the text).[8]

Elsewhere in Aramaic Isaiah the Messiah plays a role in the return of the remnant and the gathering of exiles (4:2; 53:8). When God brings home the remnant that has repented, he will purify, cleanse, and acquit them, that "they may see the kingdom of their Messiah" (53:10). Indeed, the Messiah will himself "seek forgiveness" for the sin of the remnant and "pardon for the sins of many" (53:11–12).

Rabbinic authorities recognized the importance of repentance, some believing that repentance was a necessary precondition for redemption and the appearance of the kingdom. Not surprisingly, Isaiah 59:20 was appealed to: "And he will come to Zion as Redeemer, to those in Jacob who turn from transgression, says the LORD." (In the Aramaic the wording is altered somewhat, but the meaning is essentially the same.) According to Rabbi Jonathan: "Great is repentance, because it brings about redemption, as it is said, 'And he will come to Zion as Redeemer, to those in Jacob.' Why will a redeemer come to Zion? Because of those that turn from transgression" (*b. Yoma* 86b). The antiquity of this exegesis seems to be confirmed by Paul's appeal to Isaiah 59:20, when he confidently asserts that not just a remnant will be saved, but when the Redeemer comes, "all Israel will be saved" (Rom. 11:25–28).

Figure 2.1. Sea of Galilee, looking west, with the cliffs of Arbel in the background. Photograph courtesy of Israelphotoarchiv©Alexander Schick bibelausstellung.de.

Similarly, the Jewish sages taught that the kingship of God had to be embraced before blessings could be expected: "First of all accept him as king over you, then seek mercy from him" (*Sifre Num.* §77 [on Num. 10:1–10]). Not until Israel makes God king will God humble Israel's enemies.

It is not surprising, then, to find Jesus' announcement of the kingdom of God prefaced by a call to repentance (by John and then by Jesus himself). The appearance of the kingdom of God is good news, to be sure, but it also brings with it judgment—judgment upon evil, both Jew and Gentile. Hence the urgent call for repentance. Both dimensions—good news and warning of judgment—are seen in Jesus' teaching and activities, which will be discussed shortly.

Before concluding this part of the discussion, it is necessary to say a few things about the kingdom ideas in the book of Daniel, another part of Scripture that was very important for Jesus. In a series of visions, Daniel foresees the coming heavenly kingdom that will bring to an end the era of human wickedness and oppressive human kingdoms. In chapter 2,

Roman Emperors, from Jesus to Bar Kokhba

Augustus (31 BCE–14 CE)
Tiberius (14–37 CE)
Caligula (37–41)
Claudius (41–54)
Nero (54–68)
Galba, Otho, Vitellius (68–69)
Vespasian (69–79)
Titus (79–81)
Domitian (81–96)
Nerva (96–98)
Trajan (98–117)
Hadrian (117–138)

Daniel describes Nebuchadnezzar's dream of the great statue, composed of metals (with an admixture of clay for the feet), whose values diminish from head to feet (2:31–35). In chapter 7, Daniel sees the vision of the four beasts that come up from the sea, resembling a lion, a bear, a leopard, and the terrible beast with teeth of iron and ten horns (7:2–8).

The tradition of a succession of four kingdoms is very old, and the identifications of the kingdoms vary. Precisely which four are in view in Daniel 2 and 7 is debated. The four kingdoms in Daniel may be the Babylonians, Medes, Persians, and Greeks (Alexander the Great), of which the last divides into two major kingdoms (Seleucus in the north [Syria] and Ptolemy in the south [Egypt]) whose iron character is diluted with clay through intermingling with the locals. This is one interpretation; there are others. In the passage of time, the last kingdom came to be identified with the Roman Empire.[9] For our purposes these identifications are not important. What is important is what happens after the four kingdoms.

What brings the human kingdoms to an end is the everlasting kingdom that God will establish. In reference to the image in Daniel 2, we are told: "And in the days of those kings the God of heaven will set up a kingdom which shall never be destroyed, nor shall its sovereignty be left to another people. It shall break in pieces all these kingdoms and bring them to an end, and it shall stand for ever" (2:44). Every kingdom has been set up by God, including those to be destroyed. All power exercised by human kings has been assigned to them by God. God will remove their power and give it to an everlasting kingdom.

The implicit logic compels the reader to acknowledge the power and sovereignty of Israel's God. Because it is God who has established all of the kingdoms, including those that brought the kingdom of Israel (or Judah) to an end, it is within his sovereign power to raise up a final kingdom, which will permanently displace the pagan kingdoms. Israel will once again receive the kingdom. In the colorful imagery of the monarch's dream, what brings about this destruction is the "stone . . . cut from the mountain by no human hand" (Dan. 2:45). This stone will not only shatter the inferior base of the image, its feet of iron and clay, but will also break to pieces every part of the image, including the metals of quality. The image signifies a steady decline in the quality of the kingdoms— a golden kingdom destroyed Judah, a silver kingdom will destroy the golden one, a bronze one will destroy the silver, and an iron one will destroy the bronze, with the iron kingdom (legs) degenerating into a mixture of iron and clay (feet). The divinely prepared stone will bring an end to this downward cycle and will found an everlasting kingdom, a kingdom described as a great mountain (2:35). It was a vision that many in Israel in Jesus' day longed to see fulfilled. But not everybody shared this longing.

The Fate of the Kingdom Proclaimer

The four beasts of Daniel's night vision come to an end when the court of heaven convenes and God, the Ancient of Days, takes his seat (Dan. 7:9–10). Although not described, judgment upon the four kingdoms is assumed. The loud, boasting fourth beast is "slain and its body destroyed and given over to be burned with fire" (7:11b). With the destruction of the fourth beast (Alexander's empire?), the smaller, less dangerous beasts (or kingdoms) continue a little longer but with diminished power (7:12). In the end, though, they too are doomed because a new kingdom is coming, ruled by "one like a son of man":

> I saw in the night visions, and behold, with the clouds of heaven there came one like a son of man, and he came to the Ancient of Days and was presented before him. [14]And to him was given dominion and glory and kingdom, that all peoples, nations, and languages should serve him; his dominion is an everlasting dominion, which shall not pass away, and his kingdom one that shall not be destroyed. (7:13–14)

Originally the figure that resembles a "son of man," or human, in contrast to the four beasts, represented God's faithful people Israel. Israel will be given "dominion and glory and kingdom" and will be served by "all peoples, nations, and languages." The peoples will no longer dominate Israel, as they have since the days of the Babylonian Empire. Israel's kingdom, in contrast to the four kingdoms that have passed away, will never pass away but shall endure forever.

By the first century, however, the "son of man" figure came to be understood as an individual, perhaps even the Messiah himself. This interpretation is attested in *1 Enoch* 37–71 (the so-called Similitudes of Enoch) and 2 Esdras (= *4 Ezra*) 13. The former was probably composed around the turn of the Common Era; the latter was likely composed near the end of the first century CE. It seems that Jesus interacted with this interpretation.

Jesus appealed to both Daniel 2 and 7. The two passages tell us a lot about Jesus' understanding of himself and his mission. Daniel 2, particularly verses 44–45, which speak of the everlasting kingdom—likened to a stone carved by no human hand, which destroys the other kingdoms—is echoed in the charge brought against Jesus in the hearing before the high priest and his colleagues: "We heard him say, 'I will destroy this temple that is made with hands, and in three days I will build another, not made with hands'" (Mark 14:58). To be sure, this statement has been uttered by witnesses whose testimony is said to be false (14:56, 59), but Jesus' explicit prediction of the temple's doom (13:2), the similar saying attributed to him in the Gospel of John (2:19), and the mockery at the cross (Mark 15:29)—all strongly suggest that Jesus did actually say something about the doom of the temple establishment in words that probably intentionally alluded to Daniel 2:44–45.[10]

Daniel 7 lies behind important aspects of Jesus' teaching. His habit of referring to himself as "the Son of man" probably owes something to the vision of the "one like a son of man" in Daniel 7:13. Consistently using the definite "*the* Son of man," when in Daniel 7:13 it is indefinite ("*a* son of man"), is Jesus' way of specifying a particular figure and particular passage of Scripture. The idiom itself is common in the Aramaic language of Jesus' time and means no more than "human," as opposed to an angel or an animal. There is nothing about the idiom in Daniel 7:13 that is either technical or titular. All Jesus meant to do was call attention to the human figure described in Daniel 7, the figure who is brought before God and the heavenly council.[11]

This is why Jesus says to the scribes who question his presumption in declaring the paralyzed man's sins forgiven: ". . . that you may know that the Son of man has authority on earth to forgive sins" (Mark 2:10). Jesus speaks of authority *on earth* because the Son of man has received his authority from God *in heaven* (as depicted in Dan. 7:9–14). Having received his authority from heaven, Jesus now exercises it in his ministry on earth. This same heavenly authority lies behind Jesus' remarkable claim that "the Son of man is lord even of the Sabbath" (Mark 2:28).[12] To claim lordship over the Sabbath in a sense rivals God's authority, for it was God who sanctified the Sabbath (Gen. 2:2–3) and commanded his people to respect it (Exod. 20:8–11).

The most dramatic appeal to Daniel 7 occurs in Jesus' reply to the high priest, who demands, "Are you the Christ, the Son of the Blessed?" (Mark 14:61). Jesus replies: "I am; and you will see the Son of man seated at the right hand of Power, and coming with the clouds of heaven" (14:62). Jesus has blended elements from Daniel 7:13 ("Son of man . . . coming with the clouds of heaven") and Psalm 110:1 ("Sit at my right hand . . ."). Both passages envision thrones and sitting in judgment, so the passages are readily linked by common theme and vocabulary. Indeed, the passages are so linked in rabbinic interpretation (cf. *Midr. Pss.* 2.9 [on Ps. 2:7]). To be seated (which could imply being stationary) yet "coming with the clouds" (which implies movement) is not a contradiction;[13] it is an allusion to being seated on God's chariot throne (Ezek. 1 and 10). That Daniel 7 envisions the chariot throne is made clear in its description: God's "throne was fiery flames, its wheels were burning fire" (Dan. 7:9).[14]

The high priest understood the implications of Jesus' remarkable claim. He was enraged and regarded Jesus' astonishing words as blasphemy. His colleagues agreed, asserting that Jesus was worthy of death (Mark 14:63–64). Jesus was held in custody for the night, and the following morning the council agreed to hand Jesus over to Pilate so that he might be executed.

Forming a New Community

The book of Daniel provides part of the backdrop for Jesus' words and actions relating to his fate. These words and actions will play an important role in the development of a new community that, given time and circumstances, will eventually separate itself from the larger community of Israel. The emergence of the new community is closely tied to the fate of its founder.

Just as Daniel's son-of-man figure plays a role in deciding Jesus' fate when he is brought before the council, so this figure plays a role in Jesus' anticipation of this fate. Here I chiefly have in mind the so-called passion predictions in Mark 8:31; 9:31; and 10:32–34. The first one reads as follows: "And he began to teach them that the Son of man must suffer many things, and be rejected by the elders and the chief priests and the scribes, and be killed, and after three days rise again."[15] The epithet "the Son of man" alludes to Daniel 7:13, but the anticipation of suffering and rejection may allude to the conclusion of Daniel 7, in which we are told that the enemy of God "shall speak words against the Most High, and shall wear out the saints of the Most High, . . . and they shall be given into his hand for a time" (v. 25). The Hebrew equivalent of the Aramaic verb

Israel in Exile

Jesus uses traditions from Daniel, Zechariah, and the second half of Isaiah. All three of these books play a major role in Jesus' theology; and all three reflect periods of exile in the life and history of Israel. Daniel reflects an exilic perspective, ostensibly the Babylonian exile (sixth century BCE), but in reality the Seleucid period of oppression and terror (second century BCE). Zechariah stems from the exilic period and entertains hopes that Israel's kingdom will be restored under the leadership of the "two sons of oil" (4:14, lit.), Zerubbabel of Davidic descent and Joshua the high priest. Second Isaiah calls for a new exodus and a new Israel, which he dubs the Servant of the Lord. Jesus' utilization of these books, indeed his being informed and shaped by them, is very revealing. It strongly suggests that Jesus identifies himself and his mission with an oppressed Israel in need of redemption, and that he himself is the agent of redemption. He is the Danielic "Son of man" to whom kingdom and authority are entrusted. He is the humble Davidic king of Zechariah's vision who enters the temple precincts, offers himself to the high priest, and takes umbrage at temple polity. And he is the eschatological herald of Isaiah who proclaims the "gospel" of God's reign and the new exodus. All of this suggests that, among other things, Jesus understands his message and ministry as the beginning of the end of Israel's exile.[16]

bala', translated "wear out," can mean "afflict," as we see in 1 Chronicles 17:9 ("the wicked will not again afflict them" [AT]), while the verb used in the Greek translation of Daniel 7:25, *katatribein*, can mean "wear out" or "break," as we see in Josephus, who says the Romans "had broken their engines against the walls" (*J.W.* 4.127).

The anticipation that Jesus might suffer and die may also have been suggested by Daniel 9:26, which foretells that "an anointed one [or Messiah] shall be cut off, and shall have nothing; and the people of the prince who is to come shall destroy the city and the sanctuary. Its end shall come with a flood, and to the end there shall be war; desolations are decreed." It is not hard to see how this prophecy can fit with Jesus' expectations of suffering and death, to be followed eventually by the destruction of Jerusalem and the temple, accompanied by wars and desolation (as Jesus foretold in Mark 13).[17]

Jesus' anticipation of suffering is also seen in his calling his disciples to take up the cross: "If any one would come after me, let him deny himself and take up his cross and follow me. [35]For whoever would save his life will lose it; and whoever loses his life for my sake and the gospel's will save it" (Mark 8:34–35 NIV). This summons may well have been edited in the aftermath of the passion, but its authenticity is quite probable. It reflects Jesus' style of teaching, yet it also stands in tension with what actually happened the day of Jesus' crucifixion. As it turned out, Jesus was unable to carry his cross: he needed assistance (Mark 15:21). The saying in 8:34, then, hardly seems to have been inspired by the events that overtook Jesus. (Why have Jesus say something that he himself was unable to live up to?) Moreover, the threat of crucifixion of those who live with integrity seems to have been proverbial.[18] That Jesus, surely aware of the danger he faces, would speak this way should hardly occasion surprise. Moreover, the saying in Mark 8:35 is typical of Jesus' use of hyperbole and vivid contrast (see Mark 9:35; 10:31, 43; Matt. 6:24 = Luke 16:13). This manner of speaking was not typical of the early church. And the Words of Institution, uttered at the Last Supper (Mark 14:22–25), clearly presuppose Jesus' impending suffering and death. This important tradition will be considered below.

Jesus invites people to join him. He challenges followers to take upon themselves the "yoke" of his discipleship (Matt. 11:29–30). He calls people to repent and believe in the good news of the kingdom of God (Mark 1:15; 6:12). He warns of coming judgment (Matt. 7:1–2; 11:20–24 = Luke 10:13–15; Mark 3:28–29; Luke 13:1–5; 16:19–31).[19] He teaches that only some will respond (Matt. 7:13–14; Mark 4:3–8, 14–20). He warns that many of the heirs apparent, the seemingly chosen, will in fact be excluded from the kingdom, while many people, those one would think have little chance, will be included (Matt. 8:11–12 = Luke 13:28–30; 14:15–24). All of this is consistent with the expectation of the formation of a new community.

The call for repentance and the realistic expectation that only a remnant would actually respond to the message provide the backdrop in the light of which we should understand the formation of the new community. The hints of a remnant are found in several places. In the parable of the Sower, or better, the parable of the Four Soils (Mark 4:3–8), only one type of soil proves fruitful. Jesus urges his followers to "enter by the narrow gate; for the gate is wide and the way is easy, that leads to destruction, and those who enter by it are many. [14]For the gate is narrow and the way is hard, that leads to life, and those who find it are few" (Matt. 7:13–14). Only a few enter the narrow gate; most pass through the wide gate, which leads to destruction. This is why Jesus explains to his disciples, "For many are called, but few are chosen" (Matt. 22:14), and elsewhere he soberly warns his contemporaries that "the sons of the kingdom will be thrown into the outer darkness" (Matt. 8:12 = Luke 13:28).

One thinks of the not-easily-understood utterance, placed between the parable of the Four Soils (Mark 4:3–8) and its explanation (4:14–20): "To you has been given the secret of the kingdom of God, but for those outside everything is in parables; [12]so that they may indeed see but not perceive, and may indeed hear but not understand; lest they should turn again, and be forgiven" (Mark 4:11–12). Here Jesus alludes to Isaiah 6:9–10, a passage in which God burdens the prophet Isaiah with the awful task of preaching judgment upon an obdurate and sinful people of Israel.

In keeping with his practice, Jesus has appealed to Isaiah as understood in Aramaic. In Hebrew the prophet is commanded: "Go and say to this people: 'Hear and hear, but do not understand. . . . '" The Hebrew version implies that the word of judgment applies to all of Israel. But the Aramaic reads, "Go and speak to this people who hear and hear but do not understand," thus limiting the word of judgment to those who refuse to hear and see. The utterance of Jesus seems to reflect this perspective. The secret of the kingdom of God has been disclosed to his disciples, but for those who are "outside" (those who refuse to respond to the proclamation of the kingdom), the truths of the kingdom are little more than riddles (another meaning, especially in Aramaic, of the word *mashal* that can also be translated "parables"). The implication is that only a remnant

Figure 2.2. Capernaum. Foundations and lower wall portions have been excavated at Capernaum, on the northwest shore of the Sea of Galilee, dating to first century BCE and first century CE. Photograph courtesy of Israelphotoarchiv©Alexander Schick bibelausstellung.de.

of Israel will be included in the kingdom. This is entirely consistent with Isaiah 6, which ends (at v. 13) with the promise of a surviving remnant.

In warning that many of the apparent elect, the physical descendants of Abraham, might be cast out, Jesus implies that others—perhaps even Gentiles—will be included. His assertion that "many will come from east and west and sit at table with Abraham, Isaac, and Jacob in the kingdom of heaven" (Matt. 8:11 = Luke 13:29) probably alludes to Psalm 107:2–3 ("the redeemed, . . . whom he has . . . gathered in from the lands, from the east and from the west, from the north and from the south") or Isaiah 43:5 ("I will bring your offspring from the east, and from the west I will gather you"), which no doubt was widely interpreted in reference to the Jewish Diaspora. But in Jesus' thinking, Gentiles may well have been in mind.

Openness to the inclusion of Gentiles is seen in the interesting exchange with the woman described as either Syrophoenician or Canaanite (Mark 7:26; Matt. 15:22). On behalf of her stricken daughter, she begs Jesus for help. Jesus tells her that his mission is directed primarily toward

Israel. (This is implied in Mark 7:27, but stated explicitly in Matt. 15:24; cf. Matt. 10:5–6.) He is not opposed to helping her; he is even willing to do so. It is simply a matter of priority and timing: The restorative blessings of the kingdom are extended first to the people of Israel, who are likened to children at the table eating their bread (an image probably related to the expectation of the eschatological banquet described in Isa. 25:6). The desperate woman does not dispute the point. Rather, building upon the metaphor, she declares that "even the dogs under the table eat the children's crumbs" (Mark 7:28; Matt. 15:27). In saying this, the woman implies that God's work in Jesus is so great that mere crumbs will be sufficient for her. Jesus is impressed with her response: "For this saying you may go your way; the demon has left your daughter" (Mark 7:29; cf. Matt. 15:28, "O woman, great is your faith! Be it done for you as you desire"). Israel may have the priority, but the grace of God is more than sufficient to meet the needs of Gentiles who make supplication. The same applies in the case of the centurion of Capernaum. When he declares that Jesus need not enter his house but only speak the word and his suffering servant will be healed, Jesus exclaims, "Truly, I say to you, not even in Israel have I found such faith" (Matt. 8:10 = Luke 7:9). Israel's privileged position remains (as the centurion seems to have understood), but Gentiles who respond in faith will not be ignored.

These encounters with Gentiles are consistent with Jesus' teaching elsewhere. In the temple precincts, on the occasion of his demonstration, Jesus declares: "Is it not written, 'My house shall be called a house of prayer for all the nations'? But you have made it a den of robbers" (Mark 11:17). Here Jesus quotes part of Isaiah's great oracle, in which Israel's temple and faith are to serve as a spiritual lighthouse to the world (Isa. 56:3–8), an oracle itself based upon Solomon's remarkably ecumenical prayer of dedication (1 Kgs. 8:41–43). But under the administration of Jesus' day, the temple establishment has become a "den of robbers" (Jer. 7:11) and hence faces the judgment of which Jeremiah long ago warned. Jesus' complaint and appeal to Isaiah 56 at the very least implies a concern for Gentiles, that they too might come to know the God of Israel.

Jesus' interest in Gentiles in part lies behind his teaching in which he contrasts Israel's lack of faith with the eagerness shown by Gentiles in the days of Solomon and the great prophets of old:

> The queen of the South will arise at the judgment with this generation and condemn it; for she came from the ends of the earth to hear

the wisdom of Solomon, and behold, something greater than Solomon is here. (Matt. 12:42 = Luke 11:31)

The men of Nineveh will arise at the judgment with this generation and condemn it; for they repented at the preaching of Jonah, and behold, something greater than Jonah is here. (Matt. 12:41 = Luke 11:32)

The same may well be implied in the woes that Jesus pronounces over Chorazin and Capernaum:

Woe to you, Chorazin! woe to you, Bethsaida! for if the mighty works done in you had been done in Tyre and Sidon, they would have repented long ago in sackcloth and ashes. [22]But I tell you, it shall be more tolerable on the day of judgment for Tyre and Sidon than for you. [23]And you, Capernaum, will you be exalted to heaven? You shall be brought down to Hades. For if the mighty works done in you had been done in Sodom, it would have remained until this day. [24]But I tell you that it shall be more tolerable on the day of judgment for the land of Sodom than for you (Matt. 11:21–24 = Luke 10:13–15)

The assertion that the people of Nineveh, Tyre, and Sidon would have repented if they had heard the preaching of Jesus and witnessed the mighty works that God was doing through him in towns like Chorazin and Capernaum implies that the Gentiles of Jesus' day, Gentiles such as the Syrophoenician woman and the centurion, may well be more receptive to the good news. Such teaching would have provided the theological precedent and framework for the development of the Gentile mission that we see in the book of Acts, in which rejection and persecution at the hands of Jewish leadership (Acts 4–8) drive the followers of Jesus toward Gentiles (Acts 8–14).

What we see unfolding in the book of Acts illustrates aspects of Jesus' teaching and experience. The refusal of Chorazin and Capernaum to repent finds its correspondence in the refusal of Jewish populations to repent in the book of Acts. These refusals contrast with the eagerness of Gentiles to embrace the good news and benefit from it. But Jewish refusal does not mean an end of the Jewish mission. This too is seen quite clearly in the book of Acts.

Every time Paul and his traveling companions enter a new city, they go directly to the synagogue and proclaim the good news of what God had done in Messiah Jesus (Acts 13:14, Antioch of Pisidia; 14:1, Iconium; 17:1, Thessalonica; 17:10, Beroea; 17:17, Athens; 18:4, Corinth; 18:19, Ephesus). This practice reflects Paul's understanding of the priorities of the gospel, which, he says, "is the power of God for salvation to every one who has faith, *to the Jew first* and also to the Greek" (Rom. 1:16, emphasis added; see also 2:9–10). Only when the Jews of a given city or synagogue refuse to hear Paul does he then go to the Gentiles. We see this in his response to the antagonism of the synagogue congregation in Antioch of Pisidia: "Since you thrust [the gospel] from you, . . . we turn to the Gentiles" (Acts 13:46). Attentive readers of Acts will assume that the rationale Paul gives here applies also to his experiences in other cities.[20]

Israel's priority in the early church's mission was directly rooted in the teaching and example of Jesus. Although he instructs his disciples, "Go nowhere among the Gentiles, and enter no town of the Samaritans, [6]but go rather to the lost sheep of the house of Israel" (Matt. 10:5–6), elsewhere he teaches his disciples that they will bear witness to "governors and kings" (Matt. 10:18 = Luke 21:12), which probably implies bearing witness to Gentiles (as is made explicit in Matt. 10:18). And the resurrected Jesus commands his followers to "make disciples of all nations" (Matt. 28:19; cf. Acts 1:8). Accordingly, the actions and teachings of Jesus provide a foundation on which his followers will build in the aftermath of Easter.

The Continuation of Jesus' Work

The death of Jesus brought an abrupt halt to his mission and his proclamation of the kingdom of God. Other Jewish prophets and would-be messiahs of late antiquity saw their respective ministries come to sudden and tragic ends. So, in a sense, this was nothing new; it had happened before and would happen again. But the end of Jesus' ministry, as it turned out, did not last long. The resurrection of Jesus "on the third day" after his crucifixion reignited his mission and launched, or perhaps I should say "relaunched," his community.

But the resurrection in itself is not a sufficient explanation of the church, as the community of Jesus came to be called. The Words of Institution (spoken at the Last Supper) and related teaching (Mark 10:41–45; 14:22–25) gave meaning to the death of Jesus, while his preaching, teaching, and activities provided the content for the church's theology and gave direction to the church's mission. The appointment of the Twelve originally signaled the restoration of Israel. The replacement of

Messianic Agitators and Prophets from Herod the Great's Death to Bar Kokhba's Rise

Judas son of Ezekias (4 BCE)
Simon (4 BCE)
Athronges (4–2 BCE)
John the Baptist (20s CE)
Jesus of Nazareth (28–30)
The Samaritan prophet (36)
Theudas (45)
The Jew from Egypt (56)
Jesus son of Hananiah (62/63–70)
Menahem son of Judas the Galilean (66)
John of Gischala (67–70)
Simon bar Giora (68–70)
Simon ben Kosiba, aka Bar Kokhba (132–135)

Judas Iscariot, the lapsed apostle, with another man restored the Twelve (Acts 1:15–26), implying that its mandate was a continuing one and at the same time provided an administrative structure around which the new community, the *qahal* or *ekklēsia*, the assembly of Jesus, the church, could reorganize and find its bearings. The church continued the work of Jesus through its summons to all people, both Jew and Gentile alike, to repent and to believe in God's Messiah, Jesus of Nazareth, risen from the dead, fulfiller of promises and prophecies.

The absence of Jesus surely created a problem for his new community. Who will lead it and continue its witness to Israel and its evangelistic outreach to the Gentiles? Who will provide direction as the new community wrestles with the problem of blending Jews and Gentiles into its membership? Initially leadership was provided by Peter, the most prominent member of the original disciples. Within a few years, however, James, the brother of Jesus, became the leader of church of Jerusalem. How and why this came about will be pursued in chapter 3.

Figure 2.3. Empty Tomb. The Christian movement was reignited with the discovery of the empty tomb, with its round stone door rolled aside, and appearances of the risen Jesus. Photograph courtesy of Israelphotoarchiv©Alexander Schick bibelausstellung.de.

Chapter Three

James as Leader of the Jesus Community

The emergence of James (or *Iakōbos*, Jacob), the brother of Jesus, as leader of the Jesus movement is something of a mystery. The name of James—not to be confused with two of the twelve disciples who also have this name—appears once in the New Testament Gospels. When Jesus returns to Nazareth, his hometown, and preaches in the synagogue, some of the villagers ask: "Is not this the carpenter, the son of Mary and brother of James and Joses and Judas and Simon, and are not his sisters here with us?" (Mark 6:3). Not only is there no hint that James was among Jesus' following; the Gospel of John also tells us that the brothers of Jesus did not believe in him and were not numbered among his disciples (John 7:3–5). Yet about halfway through the book of Acts (ca. 41–44 CE), Luke's second volume, narrating the early history of the church, James the brother of Jesus suddenly appears and seems to be the head of the Jesus movement in Jerusalem. How is this to be explained?

Part of the answer surely lies in James's experience of the risen Christ. In the earliest surviving written account of appearances of the risen Christ, Paul writes that Jesus "appeared to Cephas [Peter], then to the twelve. Then he appeared to more than five hundred brethren at one time, most of whom are still alive, though some have fallen asleep. Then he appeared to James, then to all the apostles" (1 Cor. 15:5–7). From this we infer that it was Jesus' appearance after the resurrection that transformed James into a believer.[1] Paul's language, moreover, seems to suggest that James was regarded as an apostle, though not one of the Twelve. His kinship with Jesus could explain his elevation to leadership, but that is only conjecture.[2]

In a Jewish Gospel known to Jerome, the great Christian scholar who possessed expertise in Greek and Hebrew, studied Hebrew in Bethlehem, and supervised the translation of both Testaments of Scripture into Latin (what eventually comes to be known as the Vulgate), we hear of an interesting tradition about James. We find this tradition in a quotation thought to have come from the *Gospel of the Hebrews*, a writing that scholars think was composed around 140 CE. We not only read more about the resurrection appearance of Jesus to his brother James; we also read that James was present at the Last Supper, the night in which Jesus was arrested. The quotation runs as follows:

> And when the Lord [Jesus] had given the linen cloth to the servant of the priest, he went to James and appeared to him. For James had sworn that he would not eat bread from that hour in which he had drunk the cup of the Lord until he should see him risen from among them that sleep. And shortly thereafter the Lord said: "Bring table and bread!" And immediately it is added: "He took the bread, blessed it and broke it and gave it to James the Just and said to him: 'My brother, eat your bread, for the Son of Man is risen from among them that sleep.'" (Jerome, *Vir. ill.* 2)[3]

This is an amazing piece of tradition. The first clause is tantalizing. What is the significance of the "linen cloth"? Is it part of the burial cloths with which the body of Jesus was wrapped? Who is the "servant of the priest"? We may have overlap with Johannine tradition. If so, then perhaps the priest's servant is Malchus (cf. John 18:10), and perhaps the linen cloth is either the cloth that covered Jesus' face or part of the other graveclothes with which he had been wrapped for burial (cf. John 20:5–7). Of greater importance is the prominence given to James. We are told that he "had sworn" to refrain from bread until Jesus was risen and that he had made this oath when "he had drunk the cup of the Lord." This surely alludes to the Last Supper and runs parallel to Jesus' vow not to drink wine (cf. Mark 14:25; Matt. 26:29; Luke 22:18) or eat the Passover (cf. Luke 22:16) until he may do so in the kingdom of God. But in Jerome's Jewish Gospel, it is James who makes a vow. It is James who observes the first post-Easter Eucharist, in the very presence of the risen Christ. The status of James is clearly enhanced in this version, as we might expect in a Gospel cherished, if not generated by, a Jewish community of believers.[4]

It is impossible to establish the authenticity of this intriguing tradition. It may well be nothing more than hagiography, that is, an example of pious imagination that with speculation attempts to answer the very question we have: How did James became a believer in his brother Jesus, and how did he rise to prominence among the leaders of the Jesus movement in Jerusalem?

Everything we know of him suggests that James was a capable, pious man, who provided the Jesus movement with effective leadership in Jerusalem, even when controversies with the priestly leadership resulted in the departure of the twelve apostles. With the departure of Peter, the original leader of the apostles, James emerged as the new leader. What kind of leader was he, and how did he relate to the other leaders of the Jesus movement, in Judea and outside Judea? To these questions we now turn.

James as Leader of the Jesus Community in Jerusalem

James's priority among leaders of the early church is attested in 1 Corinthians 15:7, cited just above. The sequence of appearances that Paul provides suggests that James was secondary to Peter (Cephas) and the "twelve" (= the eleven plus Matthias, the replacement appointed in Acts 1:23–26?). In Galatians 2:9 Paul refers to James as one of the "pillars [*styloi*]" of the church. "Pillar" here may carry temple connotations, for *stylos* occurs frequently in the LXX in reference to the pillars, or upright frames, in the tabernacle (e.g., Exod. 26:15–37; 27:10–17; 35:11, 17; 36:36, 38; 38:10–19; 39:33, 40; 40:18). For example, "Moses erected the tabernacle; he laid its bases, and set up its frames, and put in its poles, and raised up its pillars [LXX: *stylous*; MT: *'amud*]" (Exod. 40:18). Solomon commissioned two special pillars of bronze for the temple (1 Kgs. 7:15–22), by one of which the king of Judah later would customarily stand (2 Kgs. 11:14; 23:3). The Babylonians would later plunder these pillars (2 Kgs. 25:13–17; Jer. 52:17, 20). Pillars will be erected in the eschatological temple promised in Ezekiel (40:49; 42:6).[5] The New Testament Apocalypse also speaks of a pillar in the new temple: "He who conquers, I will make him a pillar in the temple of my God" (Rev. 3:12). C. K. Barrett suspects that Galatians 2:9 understands James, Peter (or Cephas), and John as "pillars of the new temple."[6]

The documentation for designating a human as a "pillar" on which people may be supported is sufficient (and is summarized by Barrett).[7] Helpful examples are found in the Dead Sea Scrolls: "At age twenty-five, he is eligible to take his place among the pillars [*yesodot*] of the holy congregation and to begin serving the congregation" (1QSa 1.12–13). "These are the pillars [*yesodot*] of the foundations of the assembly" (CD 14.17–18).[8] Richard Bauckham has argued that the leaders of the Jesus movement were called pillars as part of the "early church's understanding

Figure 3.1. Pillar, with impressive base and capital. From the Herodian period, excavated in Jerusalem. Photograph courtesy of Israelphotoarchiv©Alexander Schick bibelausstellung.de.

Literature Associated with James, the brother of Jesus

Letter of James (in the New Testament)
First Apocalypse of James (Nag Hammadi Codices V.3 = Codex Tchacos 10–32)
Second Apocalypse of James (Nag Hammadi Codices V.4)
Apocryphon of James (Nag Hammadi Codices I.2)
Ascents of James (in the New Testament Apocrypha)
The Protevangelium [Pre-Gospel] of James (in the New Testament Pseudepigrapha)

of itself as the eschatological temple," on analogy with the Qumran community, which also saw itself as a spiritual temple. In Christian tradition Peter is the rock on which Jesus will build his church (Matt. 16:18), Jesus himself is the foundation (1 Cor. 3:11) or cornerstone (Eph. 2:20; 1 Pet. 2:4, 6–7), and Christian believers are themselves the building blocks of a living temple (1 Pet. 2:5; Hermas, *Visions* 3; idem, *Similitudes* 9). Some of this imagery is itself based on the temple imagery found in the old Scriptures, especially in reference to the promised and awaited eschatological temple: stones and foundations (Isa. 54:11), cornerstone (Isa. 28:16; Ps. 118:22; both quoted in 1 Pet. 2:6–7), and pillars (Prov. 9:1).[9] In post–New Testament traditions James is himself called the "Rampart of the People" (apud Eusebius, *Hist. eccl.* 2.23.7), a title probably based on Isaiah 54:11–12 and likely also part of the imagery of the eschatological temple.

In some of the post–New Testament traditions, the reputation of James is such that he becomes the subject of a lively hagiography. James figures prominently in the second-century *Memoirs* by Hegesippus, in the second-century *Second Apocalypse of James*, in the *Gospel of Thomas* (logion 12), in the early third-century *Hypotyposeis* by Clement of Alexandria, and in the fourth-century *Ecclesiastical History* by Eusebius, who preserves and augments some of these traditions.[10] In these materials the piety of James and his association with the Jerusalem temple are underscored.

These traditions, some of which in their earliest forms are reflected in two of Paul's letters, testify to the great esteem with which James the brother of Jesus was held in the early church and perhaps also among some of the population of Jerusalem that did not otherwise identify with the Jesus movement. Although we can only speculate how James attained such a rank and reputation, the book of Acts does recount some highly significant moments in the life of the early church in which James plays a leading role.

James first appears in the book of Acts in the context of King Agrippa I's violence against the leaders of the church. In Acts 12:1–5 we have an account of these actions:

> About that time Herod the king laid violent hands upon some who belonged to the church. ²He killed James the brother of John with the sword; ³and when he saw that it pleased the Jews, he proceeded to arrest Peter also. This was during the days of Unleavened Bread. ⁴And when he had seized him, he put him in prison, and delivered him to four squads of soldiers to guard him, intending after the Passover to bring him out to the people. ⁵So Peter was kept in prison; but earnest prayer for him was made to God by the church.

Agrippa I was the son of Aristobulus IV and Bernice I and was the brother of Herodias (cf. Mark 6:15–28). Only the New Testament refers to Agrippa I as "Herod," a name that more or less functioned as a dynastic name since the time of Agrippa's famous grandfather Herod the Great. (Agrippa I is called Herod several more times in Acts 12:6, 11, 19–21.) We know that Agrippa's name was Julius Agrippa, and it is possible that his full name was Marcus Julius Agrippa, the name he gave his son, who would eventually succeed him as Agrippa II. Agrippa I acquired some territory in 37 CE, when that year his friend Gaius Caligula became the Roman emperor. When his uncle Antipas was deposed in 39 CE, Agrippa received his tetrarchy, which included Galilee, Peraea, and other territories. Upon the death of Caligula and the accession of Claudius in 41 CE, Agrippa was given the remainder of the territory that had been ruled by his grandfather Herod the Great and so officially became "king" of the Jews (Josephus, *Ant.* 19.295: "King Agrippa had been once bound in a chain for a small cause, but recovered his former dignity again . . . and was advanced to be a more illustrious king than he was before").[11]

In the passage cited from the book of Acts, we are not told specifically why Agrippa arrested some of the Christians. His motives will be considered later. For now it is enough to observe that Agrippa executed James son of Zebedee, the brother of John, and then, seeing that it pleased certain people, he proceeded to arrest Peter also. The church prays for Peter, who then enjoys a miraculous escape and safely reaches the house of a woman named Mary, the mother of John Mark (Acts 12:6–16), who later will accompany Paul on part of his first missionary journey. It is in the conclusion of this remarkable story that James the brother of Jesus is mentioned. After Peter describes his escape (12:17a), he says: "Tell this to James and to the brethren" (12:17b). The narrator then remarks abruptly and with little detail: "Then he departed and went to another place" (12:17c). From this cryptic remark it is assumed that Peter has quit Jerusalem and that James the brother of Jesus has assumed the leadership. Not long after leaving Jerusalem, Peter visits Antioch and eventually takes up residence in Rome.[12]

Peter's instructions, "Tell this to James and to the brethren," implies that James is "second in command," as it were. But it also implies that James was not expected to quit Jerusalem, as Peter and others found it necessary to do. Why is this? Judging by the advice that James will later give (in Acts 15) and by the tradition of his piety and devotion in the precincts of the Jerusalem temple, along with no evidence that James either condemned the temple priesthood or threatened the temple with its destruction (at least not until he was killed), we may infer that James's commitment to Jewish faith and practice was such that the religious and political authorities saw no reason to take action against him. The dynamics that later came into play, resulting in the killing of James, will be considered in the next chapter. For now it is only necessary to remark that the religious devotion of James was such that the temple authorities saw no reason to persecute this particular leader of the Jesus movement.

Figure 3.2. High Priest Inscription on limestone, found in Jerusalem, reading "son of the high priest" (*ben hakohen hagadol*). Photograph courtesy of Anders Runesson.

What we learn from Acts 12:17, which records Peter's abrupt words, "Tell this to James and to the brethren," is that James, in the absence of Peter, has become the leader of the Jesus movement. When the church grapples with the vexatious question of whether Gentiles who become believers must also become Jewish proselytes, they turn to James (and not to Peter or Paul) for guidance; thus we begin to appreciate the gravity of his leadership and the respect with which James is treated by the church.

Arguably the most important and divisive question faced by the church concerned the Gentiles, that is, to what extent, if any, they must conform to Jewish faith and practice in order to join the church. Was it necessary for Gentiles to become proselytes, to be circumcised, to observe the Sabbath, to eat kosher food, and to follow the rules of purity? Some in the church believed that it was necessary; others did not think so. This great question is debated in Acts 15. The debate begins as follows:

> But some men came down from Judea and were teaching the brethren, "Unless you are circumcised according to the custom of Moses, you cannot be saved." [2]And when Paul and Barnabas had no small dissension and debate with them, Paul and Barnabas and some of the others were appointed to go up to Jerusalem to the apostles and the elders about this question. [3]So, being sent on their way by the church, they passed through both Phoenicia and Samaria, reporting the conversion of the Gentiles, and they gave great joy to all the brethren. [4]When they came to Jerusalem, they were welcomed by the church and the apostles and the elders, and they declared all that God had done with them. [5]But some believers who belonged to the party of the Pharisees rose up, and said, "It is necessary to circumcise them, and to charge them to keep the law of Moses." (Acts 15:1–5)

The assertion of the Pharisees in Acts 15:5 means nothing less than that Gentiles who wish to join the Jesus movement, the church, must become Jewish proselytes.[13] This is not Paul's view, as we see in his letters and in the book of Acts, where his activities and teachings are narrated.

Many scholars, perhaps even most, believe that Paul's account of his visit to Jerusalem—where his understanding of the gospel was presented to the "pillars" James, Peter, and John—is in reference to the controversy and council described in Acts 15.[14] I concur with this interpretation. Accordingly, it will be helpful to present Paul's version of it, as we have in Galatians 2:1–10:

Then after fourteen years I went up again to Jerusalem with Barnabas, taking Titus along with me. [2]I went up by revelation; and I laid before them (but privately before those who were of repute) the gospel which I preach among the Gentiles, lest somehow I should be running or had run in vain. [3]But even Titus, who was with me, was not compelled to be circumcised, though he was a Greek. [4]But because of false brethren secretly brought in, who slipped in to spy out our freedom which we have in Christ Jesus, that they might bring us into bondage—[5]to them we did not yield submission even for a moment, that the truth of the gospel might be preserved for you. [6]And from those who were reputed to be something (what they were makes no difference to me; God shows no partiality)—those, I say, who were of repute added nothing to me; [7]but on the contrary, when they saw that I had been entrusted with the gospel to the uncircumcised, just as Peter had been entrusted with the gospel to the circumcised [8](for he who worked through Peter for the mission to the circumcised worked through me also for the Gentiles), [9]and when they perceived the grace that was given to me, James and Cephas and John, who were reputed to be pillars, gave to me and Barnabas the right hand of fellowship, that we should go to the Gentiles and they to the circumcised; [10]only they would have us remember the poor, which very thing I was eager to do.

Comparison of the accounts in Acts 15 and Galatians reveals minor discrepancies, to be sure, but the major points in these accounts cohere. In the context of Acts, Paul and Barnabas have returned from a successful missionary journey, in which a number of churches have been founded in Asia Minor (Acts 13–14). In no case did Paul require Gentile converts to be circumcised or become Jewish proselytes.[15] In some of his letters, the apostle even inveighs against such a requirement. In the narrative of Acts, Paul is sometimes overtaken by controversy. His preaching is contradicted, and he is sometimes driven from town and even pursued (cf. Acts 13:44–51; 14:4–6, 19; 17:5–9, 13–14; 18:6, 12–17; 19:8–9; 20:3). In one of his letters, Paul reports that on five occasions the Jews (presumably in the context of the synagogue) gave him thirty-nine lashes (2 Cor. 11:24; cf. Gal. 6:17, "I bear on my body the marks [*stigmata*] of Jesus").

Christian readers usually assume that Paul's Jewish critics oppose him because they reject the claim that Jesus has been resurrected and that he is Israel's Messiah. To some extent this assumption may well be true, but

Comparing Peter and Paul in the Book of Acts

Peter's Activity		Paul's Activity
3:1–10	Heals a lame man	14:8–10
3:11–26	Preaches a historical sermon	13:16–41
4:1–22	Brought before religious leaders	22:1–22
5:17–20	Miraculously released from prison	16:19–34
8:9–24	Encounters a magician	13:4–12
10:1–48	Evangelizes Gentiles	13:44–52
11:1–18	Prominent at a Jerusalem Council	15:1–35

it is also possible that Paul's preaching of justification apart from circumcision and embracing the law of Moses was a major part of the offense. Indeed, it may have been the apparent rejection of the law that raised doubts about the veracity of Paul's claims about Jesus (cf. Acts 21:20–21: "They are all zealous for the law, and they have been told about you that you are teaching all the Jews who are among the Gentiles to forsake Moses, telling them not to circumcise their children"). I suspect that if Paul had preached the gospel and had at the same time urged Gentiles to become Jewish proselytes (as some of the Pharisees in Acts 15 believed should be done), Paul and Barnabas would have encountered little opposition, perhaps none.

In any event, the church is deeply divided on this question. A difficult decision must be made. What is surprising is that the decision is not made by Peter, the principal spokesman of the original band of disciples, nor is it made by Paul, who in the narrative of Acts has emerged as a major figure. The decision is made by James, the brother of Jesus. To be sure, both Peter (Acts 15:7–11) and Paul (15:12) contribute to the debate, but it is James who settles the matter. James sides with Peter, articulates the position that the church will take, and then entrusts Paul, Barnabas, and a few others with the task of making this decision known outside the land of Israel, in the Diaspora, where Paul has been engaged in evangelism and missionary work. The letter that contains the decision reads as follows:

> The brethren, both the apostles and the elders, to the brethren who are of the Gentiles in Antioch and Syria and Cilicia, greeting. [24]Since we have heard that some persons from us have troubled you with words, unsettling your minds, although we gave them no instructions, [25]it has seemed good to us, having come to one accord, to

choose men and send them to you with our beloved Barnabas and Paul, [26]men who have risked their lives for the sake of our Lord Jesus Christ. [27]We have therefore sent Judas and Silas, who themselves will tell you the same things by word of mouth. [28]For it has seemed good to the Holy Spirit and to us to lay upon you no greater burden than these necessary things: [29]that you abstain from what has been sacrificed to idols and from blood and from what is strangled and from unchastity. If you keep yourselves from these, you will do well. Farewell. (Acts 15:23b–29)

Some interpreters believe that the council's decision contradicts Paul's teaching that believers have freedom in matters of food and drink. For example, Paul says, "Food will not commend us to God. We are no worse off if we do not eat, and no better off if we do" (1 Cor. 8:8). In the whole chapter (of 1 Cor. 8) Paul argues that because idols are nothing, eating meat sacrificed to idols is nothing. Of course, Paul urges the "strong" to be considerate of the "weak" who are offended by those who eat meat sacrificed to idols from knowing that idols are not gods. And later, Paul warns Gentile believers not to join pagans in sacrificing to demons (1 Cor. 10:20) and not to eat meat sacrificed to idols if this meat has been identified as such (10:28). So is Paul's position at odds with the letter issued by James and the Jerusalem Council?

Recent scholarship says no. Peder Borgen has argued that the letter is not a "decree," as it is often assumed. Rather, the letter is a catalog of vices, not too different from the vices that Paul himself articulates (as in Gal. 5:19–21). When converted, the Gentiles are to turn away from pagan vices, such as idolatry, sexual sin, and partaking of foods associated with these kinds of activities. The question addressed by the Jerusalem letter concerns the requirement of circumcision and acceptance of the law of Moses on the part of the Gentile converts. The letter directs these Gentile converts to avoid pagan practices.[16] But beyond these basic requirements, no other "burden" should be laid upon them (Acts 15:28; cf. v. 19: "we should not trouble those of the Gentiles who turn to God"). What Paul attacks in his Letter to the Galatians is the teaching of some fellow Jewish believers in Christ, called "Judaizers," that Gentiles must be circumcised. This requirement is flatly rejected by the Jerusalem Council, and Paul is authorized to relate this decision to the believers of Antioch (Acts 15:30–33).[17]

It is in this context that Paul's explanation in Galatians 2:1–3 should be understood:

I went up again to Jerusalem with Barnabas, taking Titus along with me. [2]I went up by revelation; and I laid before them (but privately before those who were of repute) the gospel which I preach among the Gentiles, lest somehow I should be running or had run in vain. [3]But even Titus, who was with me, was not compelled to be circumcised, though he was a Greek.

That is, Paul went up to Jerusalem to participate in the council described in Acts 15 and there he laid before the "pillars" of the early church his understanding of the gospel, namely, that Gentiles who respond in faith are not required to become Jewish proselytes. Paul notes in his support that Titus, an uncircumcised Gentile, was not required to be circumcised.

The apostle goes on to say in his letter: "When they saw that I had been entrusted with the gospel to the uncircumcised, just as Peter had been entrusted with the gospel to the circumcised, . . . and when they perceived the grace that was given to me, James and Cephas and John, who were reputed to be pillars, gave to me and Barnabas the right hand of fellowship, that we should go to the Gentiles and they to the circumcised" (Gal. 2:7, 9). Extending to Paul "the right hand of fellowship" means agreement with his understanding of the gospel as it pertained to Gentiles. The basic meaning of the word "fellowship" (*koinōnia*) has to do with things held in common and, in reference to ideas, things on which people agree (e.g., Josephus, *Ant.* 8.387: "Ahab gave him his hand, and made him come up to him into his chariot, and kissed him, and bid him be of good cheer"). The giving of the "right hand" in antiquity usually implied a pledge (e.g., Josephus, *J.W.* 6.318–20, 345, 356; LXX: 1 Macc. 6:58; 11:50).[18] Accordingly, giving Paul and Barnabas the "right hand of fellowship" implies a pledge that recognizes the validity of Paul's understanding of the gospel as applied to Gentiles and at the same time is a pledge to work in partnership with Paul.

The leadership of James in Jerusalem is seen again in the book of Acts when he directs Paul to purify himself and pay the expenses of four men who are under a Nazirite vow. Not only do we catch an important glimpse of James's continuing leadership and authority; we may also discover how it is that James was able to reside in Jerusalem while others, like Peter and the original apostles, found it necessary to relocate.

When Paul returned to Jerusalem in 58 CE, in time for the Feast of Pentecost, he visited James and "all the elders" (Acts 21:18). Paul related to them what he had experienced in his recent travels and missionary activities, to which James and his colleagues expressed joy (21:19–20a). But then James has this advice for Paul:

> You see, brother, how many thousands there are among the Jews of those who have believed; *they are all zealous for the law*, [21]and they have been told about you that *you teach all the Jews who are among the Gentiles to forsake Moses, telling them not to circumcise their children or observe the customs.* [22]What then is to be done? They will certainly hear that you have come. [23]Do therefore what we tell you. We have four men who are under a vow; [24]take these men and *purify yourself along with them and pay their expenses*, so that they may shave their heads. *Thus all will know that there is nothing in what they have been told about you but that you yourself live in observance of the law.* [25]But as for the Gentiles who have believed, we have sent a letter with our judgment that they should abstain from what has been sacrificed to idols and from blood and from what is strangled and from unchastity. (Acts 21:20b–25, emphasis added)

This passage is quite revealing of several important features. First, the apologetic interests are obvious. James tells Paul that "thousands" of Jews have believed the good news relating to Jesus and that these believing Jews remain (lit.) "zealots for the law" (v. 20b). The implication is clear: Belief in Jesus does not require abandonment of one's Jewish lifestyle. This statement is not so much for the benefit of Paul as for the benefit of the readers of Acts, especially those who are under the impression that conversion to faith in Jesus as Israel's Messiah requires apostasy from Jewish faith and lifestyle.

Second, in recounting James's advice to Paul, the evangelist has the opportunity to make explicit the accusation, of which many in the Jewish community believed Paul was guilty, that Paul teaches "all the Jews who are among the Gentiles to forsake Moses, telling them not to circumcise their children or observe the customs" (v. 21). Readers of the book of Acts know that this accusation is false. Nowhere in the narrative of Acts has Paul taught any such thing. Indeed, Paul has Timothy, a man whose mother is Jewish and whose father is Gentile, circumcised (Acts 16:3). And, of course, readers of Paul's Letters know that this accusation is not true. In fact, Paul commands those who are circumcised and have become followers of Jesus "not [to] seek to remove the marks of circumcision" (1 Cor. 7:18a), something that Jewish apostates did in the years leading up to the Maccabean Revolt (1 Macc. 1:15: "They removed the marks of circumcision, and abandoned the holy covenant"). Nevertheless, it is not difficult to imagine how Paul's teaching—that Gentile converts need not be circumcised (e.g., 1 Cor. 7:18b), that "in Christ" (the Messiah) "there is neither Jew nor Greek" (Gal. 3:28), that true circumcision is a matter of the heart and not the flesh (Rom. 2:25–29), that "neither circumcision nor uncircumcision counts for anything" (Gal. 6:15)—could lead some to conclude that Paul was guilty of the accusations leveled against him.

Third, James recommends that Paul participate in bringing to completion the vows of four Jewish men whose fidelity to the law is not in question. To do this Paul will purify himself "along with them and pay their expenses" (Acts 21:24). Though not stated, it is possible that the money Paul will use for the required sacrifices (cf. Num. 6:14–15)[19] comes from the collection he has received from Gentile converts as part of a show of support for Jewish believers and demonstration of the unity of the church. According to Paul, at the conclusion of the Jerusalem Council, narrated in Acts 15 and personally described by Paul in his letter to the Galatian churches, he says he has been asked to "remember the poor" (Gal. 2:10). Paul did so and collected money for the poor of Jerusalem. His most explicit teaching on the matter is found in one of his letters to the Christians of Corinth:

> Now concerning the contribution for the saints: as I directed the churches of Galatia, so you also are to do. [2]On the first day of every week, each of you is to put something aside and store it up, as he may prosper, so that contributions need not be made when I come. [3]And when I arrive, I will send those whom you accredit by letter to carry your gift to Jerusalem. (1 Cor. 16:1–3; cf. Acts 21:17; Rom. 15:25–28, 31)

Paul brought this gift with him to Jerusalem (as implied in Acts 24:17–18), though there is no mention of it when greets James and the elders (Acts 21:17–19). Later in Acts we have reference to this gift as well as Paul's purification: "Now after some years I came to bring to my nation alms and offerings. As I was doing this, they found me purified in the temple" (Acts 24:17–18). In any event, Paul's participation in and financial support of the four men's completion of their respective Nazirite vows demonstrates Paul's fidelity to and respect for the law of Moses.

Fourth, James tells Paul that by doing what has been suggested, "all will know that there is nothing in what they have been told about you but that you yourself live in observance of the law" (Acts 21:24). James then

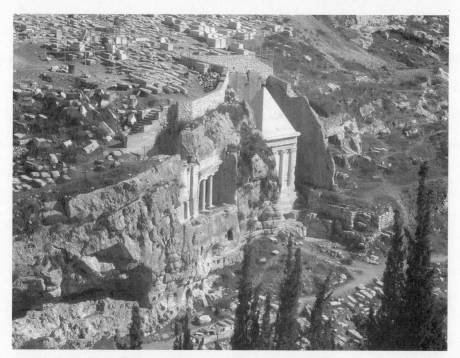

Figure 3.3. Kidron Valley. This valley runs between the Mount of Olives and the Temple Mount. According to legend, James the brother of Jesus was cast from the wall of the Temple Mount, clubbed to death, and buried somewhere in the Kidron Valley. Photograph courtesy of Ginny Evans.

goes on to recall the council's letter, in which a catalog of vices was composed (v. 25), perhaps to show that by assisting the men under the vow Paul demonstrates his compliance with the letter. The narrative in Acts goes on to say that Paul enters the temple precincts with the four men, who then fulfill their vows and present offerings.

The seriousness of the allegations against Paul is witnessed in Acts 21:27–36, where we are told that Paul was mobbed in the temple precincts, with accusers saying: "Men of Israel, help! This is the man who is teaching men everywhere against the people and the law and this place; moreover he also brought Greeks into the temple, and he has defiled this holy place" (v. 28). From this serious accusation we may infer that although James's strategy may have satisfied Jews who believed in Jesus and respected the authority of James, it did not satisfy everyone. Paul's reputation as a man who taught that circumcision was unnecessary for righteous standing before God evidently gave rise to the suspicion that Paul was even willing to bring an uncircumcised man into the area restricted to Israelite men. As well known, this restricted area was marked off by a fence, with posted signs warning of death for transgressors. One of these warnings, inscribed on stone and found early in the twentieth century, reads: "No one of another nation may enter within the fence and enclosure round the temple. Whoever is caught shall have himself to blame that his death ensues" (*CII* 1400; *OGIS* 598). These warning inscriptions are mentioned by Philo (*Legatio ad Gaium* 212) and Josephus (*J.W.* 5.193–94; *Ant.* 15.417).[20] James's hope that "all will know that there is nothing in what they have been told about you [Paul] but that you yourself live in observance of the law" (Acts 21:24) was not realized.

The author of the book of Acts has labored to show that Paul and James held to essentially the same view with respect to the crucial question of circumcision and law. Fair and careful reading of Paul's Letters suggests that the portrait in Acts is accurate, even if vague and incomplete in places. Nevertheless, one important point of comparison remains to be considered. Did Paul and James differ over the place of "works of law" in the life of the believer? It is time now to turn once again to the Letter of James.

Did James and Paul Differ over "Works"?

In his polemical and at times heated letter to the churches of Galatia, Paul emphatically gives expression to his view that no one can be justified by works of the law:

> We ourselves, who are Jews by birth and not Gentile sinners, [16]yet who know that a man is not justified by works of the law but through faith in Jesus Christ, even we have believed in Christ Jesus, in order to be justified by faith in Christ, and not by works of the law, because by works of the law shall no one be justified. (Gal. 2:15–16)

> Thus Abraham "believed God, and it was reckoned to him as righteousness." [7]So you see that it is men of faith who are the sons of Abraham. (3:6–7)

> Now it is evident that no man is justified before God by the law; for "He who through faith is righteous shall live"; [12]but the law does not rest on faith, for "He who does them shall live by them." (3:11–12)

One hardly needs to be a theologian or Bible scholar to hear what Paul is saying in these passages: "No one is justified by works of the law." For the most part, Paul bases his argument on the well-known passage in Genesis, where Abraham, in response to God's promise of land, seed, and blessing, "believed the LORD; and he reckoned it to him as righteousness" (Gen. 15:6). He also appeals to Habakkuk 2:4 (in Gal. 3:11). That the law requires "works" (or "doing") is seen in Leviticus 18:5, which Paul also quotes (in Gal. 3:12).

In a less polemical tone Paul restates his argument in his letter to the Christians in Rome. Here Paul has given careful thought to this interpretation of Scripture and how it sheds light on the question the law and justification. Paul declares:

> But now the righteousness of God has been manifested apart from law, although the law and the prophets bear witness to it, [22]the righteousness of God through faith in Jesus Christ for all who believe. For there is no distinction; [23]since all have sinned and fall short of the glory of God, [24]they are justified by his grace as a gift, through the redemption which is in Christ Jesus, [25]whom God put forward as an expiation by his blood, to be received by faith. . . . [28]For we hold that a man is justified by faith apart from works of law. (Rom. 3:21–28)

For Paul, salvation cannot be earned. If righteousness before God—and therefore salvation—could be earned, then to provide salvation there would have been no need for the Messiah, God's Son, to die on the cross. Rather, salvation is a gift of God, received through faith, not through works. This is seen in the great patriarch Abraham, who believed God's promise—understood to include the saving work of the Messiah—and was therefore reckoned righteous. Abraham's faith transformed him from a Gentile, as it were, to the father of the Jewish people. It was his faith, not his obedience to law or his later circumcision, that effected this transformation. So goes Paul's thinking.

For Martin Luther, the great German reformer of the sixteenth century, Paul's emphasis on God's grace and the demand for faith was just what was needed to challenge what he perceived to be an unhealthy and unbiblical emphasis on legalism and works in the church of his day. The only problem was that the Letter of James appeared to contradict Paul's teaching. Near the end of a major teaching section, James concludes: "You see that a man is justified by works and not by faith alone" (2:24).

No wonder, then, that Luther showed little regard for James, referring to it dismissively as a "strawy epistle" (German: *strohern Epistel*) and—in comparison to the works of Paul, Peter, and the Gospel of John, which "show thee Christ"—saw it as containing little of the gospel.[21]

The problem for Luther is that he did not interpret James correctly. James's references to "works" have nothing to do with "works of the law," which Paul saw as antithetical to gospel of grace, freely received through faith. Study of the whole of James 2 shows that the brother of Jesus offers an exposition of Jesus' principal teaching, his so-called Great Commandment, that one is to love God with all that one is and has, and one is to love one's neighbor as oneself (Mark 12:28–34; cf. Luke 10:25–28).

James speaks to the two commandments in reverse order, first treating the commandment to love one's neighbor (Lev. 19:18), and then treating the commandment to love God (Deut. 6:4–5). James's real concern is with the commandment to love one's neighbor. This concern exhibits itself not only in chapter 2, which will be considered in a moment, but elsewhere in his letter. We see it where he warns the rich who trust in their wealth (4:13; 5:1–3) and exploit the poor (5:4–6). We see it when he warns believers not to show favoritism to the rich, to the disadvantage or disrespect of the poor (1:9–10; 2:1–6). James also demands deeds and not just pious words. The faithful person should not be a "hearer that forgets but a doer that acts" (1:25). Accordingly, "religion that is pure and undefiled before God and the Father is this: to visit orphans and widows in their affliction" (1:27). It is in the light of these concerns that the exegetical and theological arguments of James 2 should be understood.

James 2 begins with an exhortation that the faithful not show favoritism to the rich and discourtesy to the poor (2:1–6). Instead, the faithful are to fulfill the "royal law," that is, the law that commands, "Love your neighbor as yourself" (2:8). But if God's people show partiality, they transgress this great law (2:9). It is as though they have broken all the laws of Moses (2:10–11).

It is in this context that James discusses true faith, the kind of faith that truly fulfills the royal law and so truly saves. A faith that has no works is not a faith that can save (2:14). James explains with a very practical example:

> If a brother or sister is ill-clad and in lack of daily food, [16]and one of you says to them, "Go in peace, be warmed and filled," without giving them the things needed for the body, what does it profit? [17]So faith by itself, if it has no works, is dead. (2:15–17)

James speaks of such works as an effective demonstration of the command to love one's neighbor and of the claim that one in fact does love one's neighbor. Mere words, such as "Go in peace, be warmed and filled," do not provide warmth or fill empty stomachs. If one claims to have faith and cannot or will not fulfill the royal law in any meaningful way, then it is right to regard such faith as dead.

James drives home this point by referring to the other commandment that is part of the Great Commandment that Jesus taught: "You believe that God is one" (2:19a). This alludes to Deuteronomy 6:4, "Hear, O Israel: The LORD our God is one LORD," which is then followed by the command to love God with all that one is and has (6:5). Mere belief that God is one is hardly evidence of fidelity to the royal law, for after all, "the demons believe [that God is one]—and shudder" (Jas. 2:19b). James offers a second example in his appeal to Abraham. While it is true that the patriarch "believed God, and it was reckoned to him as righteousness" (2:23; citing Gen. 15:6), Abraham demonstrated the reality of his faith by obeying God, even when God commanded him to offer up his son Isaac. Accordingly, Abraham is an example of a man "justified by works." James does not say that Abraham was justified by circumcision. He says he was justified by a faith that included active obedience.

In a later letter, written either by Paul himself or by one of Paul's students writing in his name, we find similar thinking, where grace and faith, on the one hand, go hand in hand with good works, on the other:

> For by grace you have been saved through faith; and this is not your own doing, it is the gift of God—[9]not because of works, lest any man should boast. [10]For we are his workmanship, created in Christ Jesus for good works, which God prepared beforehand, that we should walk in them. (Eph. 2:8–10)

Thus James and Paul agreed with respect to the essence of the gospel message. But their respective ministries were directed to two very different constituencies ethnically, culturally, and geographically. It is not a surprise that their language is not always easy to reconcile. It is these different ethnic and cultural settings, as well as differing purposes in writing, that go a long way in clarifying and perhaps even reconciling what James and Paul have to say about faith and works. We shall explore this important question further in the next chapter.

Chapter Four

Phinehan Zeal and Works of the Law

What Paul and James Are Really Saying

The discovery and eventual publication of Qumran scroll 4QMMT, in which appear the phrases "works of the law" and "It will be reckoned to you as righteousness," have thrown the debate over Paul's meaning of this language into a whole new light. The purpose of this chapter is to add to what was said in chapter 3, focusing on the figure of Phinehas. I make no claim to resolve any important aspect of the debate concerning Paul, but I do contend that proper understanding of works of law and being declared righteous, either for what one does or what one believes, must take into account the way Phinehas the zealous priest was appreciated among Jews and Christians in late antiquity.

The Zeal of Phinehas

Phinehas appears in Exodus 6:25, where he is identified as Aaron's grandson (cf. 1 Chr. 6:4, 50; 9:20; Ezra 7:5). He next appears in Numbers 25, in the episode where many Israelites join Moabites and Midianites in worshiping the god (or "Baal," presumably Chemosh; cf. Num. 21:29) of Peor while they are encamped on the plain within sight of Mount Peor (cf. Num. 23:28; 24:2; 31:16; Deut. 3:29; 4:3; Ps. 106:28). These activities include sexual promiscuity and feasting in honor of the god of Peor and resulted in a plague.[1] While Moses and others are weeping before the entrance of the tent of meeting, an Israelite man brings a Midianite woman into the camp. He does this in the very sight of the grieving Moses. The reader should infer that this man has no regard whatsoever for Moses or for Israel's sacred covenant with God.

Figure 4.1. The Negev Wilderness. Before entering the land of the Canaanites, Israel spent several decades in marginal-rainfall wilderness regions south (*negev*) of Hebron. Photograph courtesy of Ginny Evans.

When Phinehas sees this outrage, he takes a spear, kills both the man and the woman, and so brings the plague to an end. The reader learns why, when God tells Moses:

> Phinehas the son of Eleazar, son of Aaron the priest, has turned back my wrath from the people of Israel, in that he was jealous with my jealousy among them, so that I did not consume the people of Israel in my jealousy. [12]Therefore say, "Behold, I give to him my covenant of peace; [13]and it shall be to him, and to his descendants after him, the covenant of a perpetual priesthood, because he was jealous for his God, and made atonement for the people of Israel." (Num. 25:11–13)

What is translated "He was jealous with my jealousy" (Greek: *en tō zēlōsai mou ton zēlon*) could also be translated "He was zealous with my zeal." So also, "jealous for his God" (Greek: *ezēlōsen tō theō autou*) in verse 13 could be translated "zealous for his God."

On account of this episode, Phinehas is remembered for his zeal. God gives this priest a "covenant of peace" and his descendants a "covenant of a perpetual priesthood."

Phinehas reappears in the war with Midian (Num. 31:1–12). He joins the army and is entrusted with the holy vessels and the trumpets (v. 6). Israel routs the kings of Midian, taking spoils and captives (vv. 7–12). Again Phinehas appears in Joshua 22, in which he is sent as an emissary of sorts, to rebuke the tribes of Reuben, Gad, and Manasseh (vv. 13–20). When the leaders of these tribes convince the priest of their fidelity, Phinehas is pleased and is able to give the rest of Israel a favorable report (vv. 30–34). Phinehas is mentioned later, in Judges 20, when readers are reminded that he used to stand before the ark of the covenant and minister (vv. 27–28). In his recounting of the principal priests in Israel's early history, the Chronicler mentions Phinehas, saying "Phinehas the son of Eleazar was the ruler over them in time past; the LORD was with him" (1 Chr. 9:20).

Phinehas makes an appearance in the Psalter, in Psalm 106, a psalm of repentance that recalls and confesses the many instances of Israel's sin and rebellion, including the aforementioned apostasy at Peor:

> Then they attached themselves to the Baal of Peor,
>   and ate sacrifices offered to the dead;
> [29]they provoked the LORD to anger with their doings,
>   and a plague broke out among them.
> [30]Then Phinehas stood up and interposed,
>   and the plague was stayed.
> [31]And that has been reckoned to him as righteousness
>   from generation to generation for ever.
>   (Ps. 106:28–31)

The importance of the phrase "reckoned to him as righteousness" will be considered shortly.

The zeal of Phinehas, dramatically witnessed in the incident near Peor, resulted in an almost iconic status for this priest. One of the oldest testimonies is found in Sirach, who lauds Phinehas in his Praise for Famous Men (Sir. 44–51). In his praise of Phinehas, one hears echoes of Numbers 25 and Psalm 106:

> Phinehas the son of Eleazar is the third in glory,
>   for he was zealous in the fear of the Lord
>   [Greek: *en tō zēlōsai auton en phobo kyriou*],
> and stood fast, when the people turned away,
>   in the ready goodness of his soul, and made atonement for Israel.

²⁴Therefore a covenant of peace was established with him,
    that he should be leader of the sanctuary and of his people,
that he and his descendants should have
    the dignity of the priesthood for ever.

                                                    (Sir. 45:23–24)

Joshua ben Sira ("Jesus the son of Sirach") composed his work in Hebrew sometime around 180 BC. About fifty years later his grandson prefaced and translated it into Greek. Phinehas appears in exalted company indeed, preceded by Moses (vv. 1–5) and Aaron (vv. 6–22) and followed by David (vv. 25–26). The appearance of David is chronologically out of sequence, for Joshua the son of Nun, successor to Moses, will make his appearance in Sirach 46:1–12. Mention of David is brought forward, because he too was honored with a covenant. A covenant of peace and priesthood was established with Phinehas, and a covenant of kingship was established with David. The coupling of Phinehas with David, each blessed with a covenant, one priestly and the other kingly, is highly significant, testifying to the dyarchic nature of Israel's ordained leadership.

In 1 Maccabees the zealous actions of Mattathias, father of Judas Maccabeus and his brothers, are compared to the zeal and violence of Phinehas:

When Mattathias saw it, he burned with zeal [*ezēlōsen*] and his heart was stirred. He gave vent to righteous anger; he ran and killed him upon the altar. ²⁵At the same time he killed the king's officer who was forcing them to sacrifice, and he tore down the altar. ²⁶Thus he burned with zeal for the law [*ezēlōsen tō nomō*], as Phinehas did against Zimri the son of Salu. ²⁷Then Mattathias cried out in the city with a loud voice, saying: "Let every one who is zealous for the law and supports the covenant [*ho zēlōn tō nomō kai histōn diathēkēn*] come out with me!" (1 Macc. 2:24–27)

Phinehas is again mentioned by name in Mattathias's farewell to his sons, a farewell modeled after Jacob's farewell to his sons in Genesis 49, which gave rise to a genre that became very popular in the intertestamental and New Testament periods. Here is part of Mattathias's farewell:

Now, my children, show zeal for the law [*zēlōsate tō nomō*], and give your lives for the covenant of our fathers. ⁵¹Remember the deeds of the fathers [*ta erga tōn paterōn*], which they did in their generations; and receive great honor and an everlasting name. [52]Was not Abraham found faithful when tested [*en peirasmō heurethē pistos*], and it was reckoned to him as righteousness [*elogisthē autō eis dikaiosynēn*]? [53]Joseph in the time of his distress kept the commandment, and became lord of Egypt. [54]Phinehas our father, because he was deeply zealous [*en tō zelōsai zēlon*], received the covenant of everlasting priesthood. . . . [58]Elijah because of great zeal for the law [*en tō zēlōsai zēlon nomou*] was taken up into heaven. (1 Macc. 2:50–54, 58)

Zeal for the law is the theme that runs throughout this farewell testament. Once again we find Phinehas in illustrious company. The author of 1 Maccabees, a book composed sometime around 100 BCE, cites the examples of Abraham, Joseph, Joshua, Caleb, David, Elijah, Daniel, and the three faithful young men in Daniel 3 (1 Macc. 2:52–60). Mattathias is a priest (1 Macc. 2:1) and can find no better example of priestly zeal than that of Phinehas, grandson of Aaron. The allusion to the testing of Abraham and his faith being reckoned as righteousness will be taken up below.

Phinehas is mentioned in two writings from the first century CE. In the retelling of the martyrdom of the mother and her seven sons (4 Macc. 18:6–19; cf. 2 Macc. 7:22–29), the mother reminds her sons that their

---

The Hasmonean/Maccabean Leaders/Rulers

Mattathias (167–166 BCE)
Judas Maccabeus (166–160)
Jonathan Apphus (160–142)
Eleazar Abaran (d. 163)
Simon Thassi (142–134)
John Gaddi (d. 159)
John Hyrcanus, son of Simon (134–104)
Aristobulus, son of John Hyrcanus (104–103)
Alexander Jannaeus, son of John Hyrcanus (103–76)
Salome Alexandra, widow of Alexander Jannaeus (76–67)
Aristobulus II, son of Alexander Jannaeus (67–63)
Hyrcanus II, son of Alexander Jannaeus (63–40)
Antigonus II Mattathias, son of Aristobulus II (40–37 BCE)

father "told you of the zeal of Phinehas [*ton zēlōtēn Phinees*], and he taught you about Hananiah, Azariah, and Mishael [Dan. 1:19; 3:12–30] in the fire" (4 Macc. 18:12, alluding to 1 Macc. 2). Writing sometime later, the author of *Biblical Antiquities* describes Phinehas as the priest who "guards the commands of the Lord" (Pseudo-Philo, *Bib. Ant.* 28:1). We are told, moreover, that "truth goes forth from his mouth and a shining light from his heart" (28:3). Later in *Biblical Antiquities*, Phinehas, who lives beyond 120 years, is exalted in terms reminiscent of Elijah (48:1–3). Phinehas is also mentioned in a pseudepigraphal synagogue prayer, perhaps dating to the second century CE. Here the zealous priest is cited in a list of heroes of the faith (*Hel. Syn. Pr.* 8.4). The phrase that appears in the next line, "from iniquity into righteousness" (v. 5), may refer to Phinehas's achievement.

Finally, Phinehas appears by name in three fragmentary scrolls from Qumran. In one we find "Phinehas [father] of Abishua" (4Q243 frag. 28, line 2; cf. 1 Chr. 6:4). In another we read (with some reconstruction): "and Zadok shall serve as priest there, first from the sons of Phinehas and of Aaron, and with him he will be pleased in all the days of his life" (4Q522 frag. 9, 2.6–7). In the third we find the phrase "from the sons of Phinehas" (6Q13 frag. 1, line 4).

Mention should also be made of *Jubilees*, another intertestamental writing, in which the law prohibiting marriage with foreigners (cf. Gen. 34:7, 14) is emphasized. *Jubilees* retells the story of the Shechemites, who out of vengeance were slaughtered by Jacob's sons Simeon and Levi (34:25–26). In the Genesis narrative, Jacob expresses displeasure over his sons' treachery (34:30) and finds it necessary to relocate (35:1–3). But in *Jubilees*, Simeon and Levi are praised for their violent action: "And it was a righteousness for them and it was written down for them for righteousness" (30:17). The author of *Jubilees* goes on to say that those who violate the law that prohibits intermarriage will be "blotted out of the book of life and will be written in the book of those who will be destroyed" (30:22). At the conclusion of the section, the action of Simeon and Levi is again praised; the author claims that when the sons of Jacob killed the Shechemites, God "wrote for them a book in heaven that they did righteousness and uprightness and vengeance against the sinners and it was written down for a blessing" (30:23). There is little doubt that this remarkable revision of the Genesis story has been inspired by Scripture's praise for the zeal of Phinehas.

In sum, we have four major texts in which the zeal of Phinehas is underscored. In Numbers 25 we hear of the priest's zeal, a promised

Figure 4.2. Qumran Cave 4. Its entrance is at the center of the photo. Cave 4 held around 600 documents, about two-thirds of the texts found at or near Qumran. Photograph courtesy of Israelphotoarchiv©Alexander Schick bibelausstellung.de.

covenant of peace, and an eternal priesthood. In Psalm 106 we hear of his zeal, his action being reckoned to him as righteousness, and "from generation to generation," which may allude to the promise of perpetual priesthood. In Sirach 45 we hear of zeal, the covenant of peace, and an eternal priesthood. And in 1 Maccabees 2 we read of zeal and everlasting priesthood. In 1 Maccabees 2 we also are reminded of Abraham's faith being reckoned as righteousness (cf. Gen. 15:6).

4QMMT and "Works of the Law"

This brings us to one more text, in which the name Phinehas does not appear, yet a text that probably does allude to the zealous action of the famous priest. As his halakic letter draws to a close, the author of 4QMMT (4Q394–99) exhorts his readers to embrace his teaching regarding "some of the works of the law" (*miqsat ma'asey hatorah*), about which he had written. If they follow his teaching, "it will be reckoned to [them] as righteousness." The relevant portion of the text reads as follows:

> Now, we have written to you [3](C27) some of the works of the Law [Torah], those which we determined would be beneficial for you and your people, because we have seen that [4](C28) you possess insight and knowledge of the Law. Understand all these things and beseech Him to set [5](C29) your counsel straight and so keep you away from evil thoughts and the counsel of Belial. [6](C30) Then you shall rejoice at the end time when you find the essence of our words to be true. [7](C31) And it will be reckoned to you as righteousness, in that you have done what is right and good before Him, to your own benefit [8](C32) and to that of Israel. (4Q398 frags. 14–17, 2.2b–8 = 4Q399 1.10–2.5 [= C26b–C32])[2]

Only two passages in the Hebrew Bible link the verb "reckon" (*hashab*) and the noun "righteousness" (*tsedaqah*). They are Genesis 15:6 and Psalm 106:31:

> And he believed the LORD;
>   and he reckoned it to him as righteousness.
>   (Gen. 15:6)

> And that has been reckoned to him as righteousness
>   from generation to generation for ever.
>   (Ps. 106:31)

The verb "he reckoned" (*wayaheshbeah*) in Genesis 15:6 is a Qal, while in Psalm 106:31, "has been reckoned" (*watehasheb*) is a Niphal, the same form that appears in 4QMMT.[3] Yet more than simply the grammar suggests that the author of 4QMMT has in mind Psalm 106 and the zealous priest Phinehas. The priestly orientation of 4QMMT and of the Qumran sect itself also encourages us to think that we have an allusion to Psalm 106 and not Genesis 15. Perhaps even more important is the observation that

Figure 4.3. Fragments of 4QMMT. Six fragmentary copies of a letter discussing "works of the law" were recovered from Qumran's Cave 4. The letter is called MMT, from *miqsat ma'esey hatorah*, "Some of the Works of the Law," and sheds light on Paul's discussion of "works of law" and justification through faith. Photograph courtesy of Israelphotoarchiv©Alexander Schick bibelausstellung de.

the author of 4QMMT is sharply opposed to intermarriage with non-Jews. Recall that this was part of Israel's apostasy near Peor that prompted Phinehas to take violent action.[4] For these reasons I think it is probable that 4QMMT has alluded to the famous zealous priest, not to the great patriarch Abraham (see fig. 4.3).

In any case, the point that the author of 4QMMT is making seems clear enough. He has enumerated some two dozen legal rulings, about half of which are bans on various foods and practices. "These are some of our pronouncements concerning the law of God," begins 4QMMT, "concerning works of the law that we have determined, . . . and all of them concern defiling mixtures and the purity of the sanctuary" (4Q394 frags. 3–7, 1.4–6, with restorations). When at the end of his letter the author refers to "works of the law," we know what he is talking about. They are not works of compassion or acts of kindness. They are works designed to maintain purity, especially in reference to the sanctuary. In doing these works, readers of the letter will benefit and "will rejoice at the end time," which probably refers to future judgment.

Martin Abegg Jr., James Dunn, and others believe that in 4QMMT we finally have a true parallel to the position that Paul opposes with such heat in Galatians 2 and 3.[5] It will be sufficient to cite one verse:

> We ourselves, . . . [16]who know that a [person] is not justified [*dikaioutai*] by works of the law [*ex ergōn nomou*] but through faith in Jesus Christ, even we have believed in Christ Jesus, in order to be justified [*dikaiōthōmen*] through faith in Christ, and not by works of the law [*ex ergōn nomou*], because by works of the law [*ex ergōn nomou*] shall no one be justified [*dikaiōthēsetai*]. (Gal. 2:15–16)

The phrase "works of law" occurs in Paul several times (cf. Rom. 3:20, 28; Gal. 3:2, 5, 10). Moreover, his "works of law" (*erga nomou*) and "justified" (*dikaioun*) language echoes the language we find in the two passages of Old Testament Scripture already mentioned. However, whereas Paul explicitly draws on Genesis 15:6, the author of 4QMMT draws on Psalm 106:31. The difference is that Paul focuses on faith, the faith of Abraham (cf. Rom. 4:3, 9, 22; Gal. 3:6), while the author of 4QMMT focuses on obedience to the law, as exemplified by the zealous Phinehas, who safeguarded the purity of Israel's cultus.

What Paul is challenging so passionately in Galatians and then again with somewhat reduced emotions in Romans is an understanding of the law that requires the performance of certain "works of the law," such as eating kosher food and avoiding impurity, in order to maintain one's place in the covenant. Paul is especially opposed to works of the law that encourage holding Gentiles at arm's length.[6] Some of the works of the law articulated in 4QMMT do just that. The example states: "No one should eat from the Gentile grain nor bring it into the sanctuary" (4Q394 frags. 3–7, 1.6–8). Other examples articulate bans against Gentile offerings and Jews with blemishes. Attempts to establish righteousness such as these are what Paul so vigorously opposes. Recall the apostle's anger at Peter for withdrawing from Gentile Christians when "certain people came from James" (Gal. 2:11–14). Peter and Barnabas, Paul charges, "were not acting consistently with the truth of the gospel" (2:14 NRSV). Indeed, their refusal to eat with Gentiles fails to follow the example of Jesus himself, who ate with sinners, whose food at least on some occasions, we should assume, would not have met with the approval of many scribes and Pharisees.

Paul and James on "Works of the Law"

The difficulty interpreters have in relating Paul's application of Genesis 15 to the application we find in James 2 is that the debate itself, of which both Paul and James are reflecting but small parts, is not appreciated in its entirety. I have examined the Phinehan tradition because I think it provides the thread that ties together most of the elements making up this larger discussion. We need to pull as many of these elements together as we can, if we are to make sense of the smaller parts we find in Paul and James. Perhaps we will discover that James and Paul can be reconciled after all.

Several of these key components appear in 1 Maccabees 2. The narrator asserts that the violent action of Mattathias, in which he killed both a foreigner and an Israelite who were engaged in pagan sacrifice, is comparable to the action of Phinehas. Indeed it is, for Phinehas killed an Israelite and a Midianite, who were engaged in foreign worship. Accordingly, the narrator can say that Mattathias "burned with zeal for the law, as Phinehas did" (1 Macc. 2:26). On his deathbed, Mattathias once again refers to the zeal of Phinehas (vv. 50, 54), but he also refers to Abraham, who was "found faithful when tested," and "it was reckoned to him as righteousness" (v. 52). The testing to which the author of 1 Maccabees refers is the binding of Isaac (Gen. 22:15–18). The reference to having it reckoned as righteousness refers, of course, to Genesis 15:6, but understood in the light of Genesis 22. In other words, Abraham's faithfulness, as seen in his willingness to sacrifice his son Isaac, is what was "reckoned as righteousness." The faith, or faithfulness, of which 15:6 speaks is qualified by the act of obedience narrated in Genesis 22. True faith results in righteous deeds.[7]

James makes a similar point. He begins the discussion by asking if faith that does not result in works can save (2:14). He illustrates the point by showing that greetings and platitudes, but with no good actions, do not fulfill the commandment to love one's neighbor as one's self (vv. 15–16). Accordingly, a faith that has no works is dead (v. 17). James then mounts a scriptural argument that is very similar to the thinking underlying 1 Maccabees 2. Abraham was "justified by works, when he offered his son Isaac upon the altar" (Jas. 2:21). His willingness to offer Isaac means that his faith was more than a mere belief, but a readiness to obey God, to put one's faith into action, as it were. Because Abraham's "faith was active along with his works, and [his] faith was completed by works" (v. 22), the earlier Scripture, "Abraham believed God, and it was reckoned to him as

Herodian Rulers

Antipater I the Idumean, captain of Idumea under Alexander Jannaeus (103–76 BCE)

Antipater II, son of Antipater I—for some years procurator of Judea under the Romans

Herod (the Great), son of Antipater II—"King of the Jews" (37–4 BCE)

Alexander, son of Herod (executed 7 BCE)

Aristobulus, son of Herod (executed 7 BCE)

Antipater, son of Herod (executed 4 BCE)

Herod Archelaus, son of Herod and Malthace the Samaritan—ethnarch ("ruler of the people") of Samaria and Judea (4 BCE–6 CE)

Herod Antipas, son of Herod and Malthace the Samaritan—tetrarch ("ruler of one quarter") of Galilee and Peraea (4 BCE–39 CE)

Philip, son of Herod and Mariamne II—tetrarch of Gaulanitis (4 BCE–34 CE)

Agrippa I, son of Aristobulus and Bernice, tetrarch of Galilee (39–40 CE), later "king of the Jews" (41–44 CE)

Herod of Chalcis, son of Aristobulus and Bernice, tetrarch of Chalcis (d. 48 CE)

Agrippa II, son of Agrippa I (ca. 49–93 CE)

righteousness" (v. 23, citing Gen. 15:6), was fulfilled. Accordingly, James can say that a human "is justified by works and not by faith alone" (2:24). For James and the author of 1 Maccabees, deeds demonstrate real faith. Accordingly, deeds must accompany faith.[8]

It is also important to recognize the allusions to dominical teaching in the letter of James. I have in mind primarily the treatment of the Double Commandment in the James 2, to which I shall turn shortly, but there are some important antecedents. James exhorts his readers to accept trials and testing with joy and to let it have its "perfect work [*ergon teleion*]" (1:3–4 KJV). He urges his readers to become "doers of the word [*poiētai logou*], and not hearers only" (1:22). He speaks of the "perfect law [*nomon teleion*]" (1:25a). He urges his readers not to be forgetful hearers but to be "a doer of work" (*poiētēs ergou*), who "shall be blessed" (1:25b).

The spirit of this teaching, as well as some of the vocabulary, brings to mind the teaching of Jesus, especially as we find it assembled in the Sermon on the Mount. According to Jesus, the person who "does and teaches [*poiēsē kai didaxē*] [the commandments] shall be called great in the kingdom of heaven" (Matt. 5:19). The righteousness (*dikaiosynē*) of the disciples must exceed that of the scribes and Pharisees. How this can be accomplished is spelled out in the five antitheses that follow (5:21–47). At the conclusion of the antitheses, Jesus sums up his teaching: "You, therefore, must be perfect [*teleioi*], as your heavenly Father is perfect [*teleios*]" (5:48).[9] Perfection cannot be achieved without doing the commandments, as Jesus has taught. The conclusion of the Sermon on the Mount drives home this point (emphasis added):

> Not every one who says to me, "Lord, Lord," shall enter the kingdom of heaven, but he who *does* the will of my Father who is in heaven. (7:21)

> Every one then who hears these words [*tous logous*] of mine and *does* them will be like a wise man who built his house upon the rock. (7:24)

> And every one who hears these words of mine and *does not do* them will be like a foolish man who built his house upon the sand." (7:26)

Elsewhere in Jesus' sayings in Matthew, we find similar teaching (emphasis added):

> For whoever *does* the will of my Father in heaven is my brother, and sister, and mother. (12:50)

> Which of the two *did* the will of his father? (21:31)

> *Do and observe* whatever they tell you, but not what they do;
>   for they preach, but do not do. (23:3 AT)

> They *do* all their deeds to be seen by others. (23:5 NRSV)

We may well hear echoes of this teaching in James's exhortations to be "doers of the word" and a "doer of work," works that exemplify the "perfect work," "perfect law," and the "royal law."

Verse 27 sums up the point of the first chapter of James: "Religion that is pure and undefiled before God and the Father is this: to visit orphans and widows in their affliction, and to keep oneself unstained from the world."

This brings us to James 2. The second chapter is chiefly concerned to explicate the second commandment of the famous Great (or Double) Commandment (Mark 12:28–34; Luke 10:25–29), whereby one is to love God with all that one is and all that one has (Deut. 6:4–5) and to love one's neighbor as one's self (Lev. 19:18). The partiality described in James 2:1–13 fails to fulfill the second commandment, which is quoted in James 2:8. Although the remainder of the chapter (vv. 14–26) defines genuine faith, the focus remains on what it means to fulfill the second commandment. To fulfill "the royal law" (Jas. 2:8) is to fulfill Leviticus 19:18, a commandment that lay behind much of what Jesus taught, either explicitly or implicitly.[10]

Failure to fulfill the second commandment has implications for the first commandment, to which allusion is made in 2:19: "You believe that God is one; you do well. Even the demons believe—and shudder." The mere belief, or faith, that God is one hardly fulfills the obligations to love one's neighbor or, harking back to James 1:27, hardly fulfills the command to "visit orphans and widows in their affliction."

To support his argument, James appeals to the example of Abraham, who was "justified by [his] works [*ex ergōn edikaiōthē*], when he offered his son Isaac upon the altar" (2:21). His willingness to obey God demonstrated that his faith was genuine. His "work" in Genesis 22 fulfilled the statement of Scripture in Genesis 15:6 (Jas. 2:23). I suspect that James had in mind Abraham's example of faith early on. We may hear an allusion to it in 1:3, where James declares that "the testing of your faith produces steadfastness," which in turn will lead to perfection (1:4).

At this point the argument of James parallels some of the argument in 1 Maccabees 2 very closely. In both books the claim is made that Abraham's faith in God was witnessed in his willingness to offer up his son. It was this faith that was reckoned to him as righteousness. The overlap in the scriptural appeal of 1 Maccabees and James helps us understand more clearly the differences in the respective arguments of James and Paul.

Paul is not countering James or 1 Maccabees, where Abraham's faith is defined in terms of obedience. Instead, Paul is countering a theology similar to what we see in 4QMMT, which assumes that works of law, including those concerned with separating the pure the from the impure, save a person. What Paul faced in the churches of Galatia was the teaching that "works of the law"—such as circumcision, kashruth, and

Sabbath observance—were necessary if converts (esp. Gentile converts) were to mature and grow in righteousness. This parallels the thinking in 4QMMT, in which a person could secure righteous standing in the covenant by practicing certain works of the law. Paul and the author of 4QMMT are squarely at odds.

However, the works of 4QMMT are not the "works" to which James makes reference. The "works" that demonstrate the reality of faith are not circumcision, kashruth, and Sabbath observance, but fulfillment of "the royal law" (Jas. 2:8), as he dubs it, the law of loving one's neighbor as oneself, the very commandment that Jesus enjoined (Mark 12:28–34; Luke 10:25–28) and his early movement attempted to fulfill in its care for widows and orphans and the poor (cf. Acts 2:44–45; 4:32–37; 6:1; Rom. 15:26; Gal. 2:10; 1 Tim. 5:3, 16). James does not have in mind the zealous works of Phinehas, which are appealed to explicitly in 1 Maccabees 2 and alluded to in 4QMMT. He has in mind genuine faith that proves itself in righteous works, especially with regard to love for one's neighbor.

Paul and his disciples know this well, as we see in Ephesians 2:8–10:

> For by grace you have been saved through faith; and this is not your own doing, it is the gift of God—[9]not because of works, lest any man should boast. [10]For we are his workmanship, created in Christ Jesus for good works, which God prepared beforehand, that we should walk in them.

Whatever one's view of the authorship of Ephesians, this passage sums up the Pauline perspective. By God's grace human beings are saved through faith and not through their works. Salvation is God's gift; it is not something earned by righteous deeds. But genuine faith demonstrates itself in good works, such as love for one another (Rom. 12:10; 13:8; Gal. 5:13; 1 Thess. 3:12; 4:9). Christians are "created in Messiah Jesus for good works, which God prepared beforehand, that we should walk in them." With this assertion James would be in hearty agreement.

The example of Phinehan zeal and the interpretive tradition that grew up alongside it clarify an important facet of the discussion of faith, works of law, and having one's faith or deeds accounted as righteousness, a discussion that developed at least two centuries before the emergence of the Christian movement. James, Paul, and other writers presuppose this larger discussion, each embracing and/or qualifying or denying parts of it. James and Paul both appeal to the faith of Abraham and to God's reckoning of that faith as righteousness, but the point each is trying to make is very different.

Paul's declaration that "a person is justified not by works of the law but through faith" (Gal. 2:16 NRSV; cf. Rom. 3:20; 4:2) squarely opposes the thinking expressed in 4QMMT. James's conclusion that "a person is justified by works and not by faith alone" (2:24 NRSV; cf. 2:21, 25) is not a rebuttal of Pauline teaching or even in reference to Paul. It is instead a challenge directed against those whose faith fails to take practical form, especially in reference to the neighbor in need. In other words, a faith that fails to comply with Jesus' teaching to love God and love neighbor as oneself is no faith at all. With this assertion Paul would be in hearty agreement.

Chapter Five

Jerusalem Communities in Conflict

In a recent study, Eyal Regev traces the history of conflict between Jerusalem's priestly aristocracy and the leaders of the Jesus movement.[1] Regev observes that in most of the deadly or near-deadly encounters between the ruling priests and leaders of the Jesus movement, the sanctity and/or security of the temple is at issue. His insightful study very helpfully lays the groundwork on which the present chapter hopes to build further.[2]

In what follows we shall consider the stories relating to Jesus of Nazareth, the twelve apostles, Stephen the deacon-evangelist, James son of Zebedee, Peter, Paul, James the brother of Jesus, and Jesus son of Ananias. In most cases temple controversy is quite apparent. In other cases it is conjectured but probable. In the case of the last man mentioned, in which temple controversy is obvious, I will suggest that Jesus ben Ananias also belonged to the Jesus movement. I will also suggest that the principal priestly family at odds with the Jesus movement was the family of Annas.

Jesus of Nazareth and the Family of Annas

Down through the centuries, Christian interpreters and theologians have not always correctly analyzed Jesus' conflict with the aristocratic priesthood of Jerusalem. Some interpreters have quite erroneously claimed that Jesus was critical of Judaism or the Jewish people. Nothing could be further from the truth. Jesus embraced Torah, recited the Shema with approval (Deut. 6:4–5), along with its corollary, the command to love one's neighbor as oneself (Lev. 19:18). Jesus assumed the validity of Jerusalem's temple and presupposed the past election and future redemption

94

of Israel. Indeed, when Jesus sent his disciples to proclaim the message of the kingdom of God, he commanded them, "Go nowhere among the Gentiles, . . . but go rather to the lost sheep of the house of Israel" (Matt. 10:5–6), thus setting a pattern later followed by his movement, as we see in Paul's words about the gospel: "to the Jew first and also to the Greek" (Rom. 1:16).

When Jesus entered Jerusalem the week before Passover (we think in the year 30 CE), his disciples hailed him with the familiar words from Psalm 118: "Hosanna! Blessed is he who comes in the name of the Lord! Blessed is the kingdom of our father David that is coming! Hosanna in the highest!" (Mark 11:9–10; cf. Ps. 118:25–26). The appearance of the name "David" in this citation of Psalm 118 reflects acquaintance with the Jewish interpretive tendencies present in the Aramaic tradition that in time will emerge as the Targum (cf. esp. *Tg. Pss.* 118:26, 28),[3] as well as in rabbinic interpretation of Psalm 118 (cf. *Midr. Pss.* 118.17 [on Ps. 118:19]).[4]

The reception itself, complete with riding the colt, the spreading of clothing and leafy branches, and the joyous procession into the city and up to the temple precincts (Mark 11:4–10), reflects a long tradition of the Jewish people greeting dignitaries and heroes.[5] This entrance and reception suggest that Jesus was highly popular. His popularity is also attested in various remarks that the ruling priests are unable or reluctant to take action against Jesus because they "feared the multitude" (Mark 11:18; 12:12; cf. 14:2).

What set Jesus on a collision course with the ruling priests was his provocative action in the temple precincts, traditionally called the "cleansing of the temple" (Mark 11:15–18). Once again, Christian interpretation usually fails to understand the significance of Jesus' actions. His interference with the buying and selling of sacrificial animals and the money changing that accompanied this commerce had nothing to do with opposing long-standing customs of sacrifice (as commanded in the Torah!), nor did it have anything to do with a supposed preference for internal religious commitment in contrast to external religious practice.[6]

Jesus' citation of Isaiah 56:7 and his allusion to Jeremiah 7:11 make it clear that in his view the temple leadership has failed to live up to its God-ordained task and that it therefore faces the certainty of judgment. Let me explain. Isaiah 56:3–8 is an oracle that looks forward to the time when the Jerusalem temple, atop God's holy mountain, will be the religious capital of the world, the place where all people, including Gentiles, will be welcome.[7] Their gifts will be welcome, and their prayers will be heard.

Figure 5.1. Temple. This reconstruction depicts the Temple Mount, with the holy sanctuary on its center. Photograph courtesy of Israelphotoarchiv©Alexander Schick bibelausstellung.de.

Accordingly, the temple will be known as the "house of prayer for all peoples" (56:7), the very phrase that Jesus quotes (Mark 11:17a). Isaiah's great oracle is itself based on Solomon's prayer of dedication of the temple (1 Kgs. 8:41–43). The legendary king prays that when foreigners (Gentiles) hear of the Lord and come to the temple of Jerusalem, seeking the Lord, their prayers will be heard, and they will know that the temple Solomon has built is truly the Lord's.

But Jesus declares that the temple has in fact not lived up to this great legacy. The hopes of Solomon and the prophecy of Isaiah have not been fulfilled. They have not been fulfilled because of the corrupt and oppressive leadership of the ruling priests, who have made the temple, in the words of Jeremiah the prophet, a "den of robbers" (Mark 11:17b; cf. Jer. 7:11). Lest anyone think this is a distinctively Christian view, perhaps not really the view of Jesus himself, it should be recognized that there is a well-attested and widespread tradition, seen in a number of Jewish sources, including rabbinic literature, that complains of corruption and oppression in the final decades of the Second Temple.[8]

Jesus' appeal to Jeremiah 7, a passage in which the great prophet criticizes the ruling priests of his day and warns of coming judgment and destruction of the very temple that Solomon built, would have been highly offensive to the priestly leadership. Jesus' prophetic threat was clearly directed against the aristocratic priesthood, not against the people and the lower-ranking priests, whom the people—including Jesus

Jerusalem Temple Warning

A nineteen-inch-high limestone fragment contains a warning to Gentiles to stay out of the area that is restricted to Jews. This fragment was found in 1935 outside the wall around Jerusalem's Old City. A complete version of the same inscription (found in 1871) is in the Archaeological Museum in Istanbul. The Greek inscription reads:

Let no Gentile enter within the partition and barrier surrounding the
  Temple;
whosoever is caught shall be responsible for his subsequent death.

This is probably the warning described by Josephus: "Upon [the partition wall of the Temple Court] stood pillars, at equal distances from one another, declaring the law of purity, some in Greek, and some in Latin letters, that 'no foreigner should go within the sanctuary'" (*J.W.* 5.193–94).

himself—respected.[9] Indeed, the cursing of the fruitless fig tree did not symbolize the coming end of the Jewish people (as, regrettably, some Christian interpreters have thought) but the end of the corrupt temple establishment (Mark 11:12–14, 20–22). The insertion of the story of the temple action into the fig tree story makes this clear. So does the parable of the vineyard (Mark 12:1–12), where Jesus alters and retells the vineyard parable of Isaiah 5:1–7, in order to shift blame away from the Jewish people to the caretakers of the vineyard: the ruling priests. The ruling priests rightly recognize that Jesus has told the parable "against them" (Mark 12:12).[10] They desire to arrest Jesus but cannot do so on account of the crowds that support Jesus.

Jesus' popular support makes it necessary for the ruling priests to arrest Jesus at night and at a time when he is not surrounded by large numbers of people who appreciate his teaching and his criticisms of the temple establishment. When Jesus is taken into custody, he is accused of threatening to destroy the temple (Mark 14:58). Although the Markan evangelist regards the allegation as false (14:59), it is quite probable that Jesus said something like this (cf. John 2:19). After all, Jesus was remembered to have predicted the destruction of the temple (Mark 13:2

"There will not be left here one stone upon another, that will not be thrown down"). If this prophecy were accompanied by a promise that someday God would raise up a new temple, perhaps as part of a new Jerusalem, something anticipated in several scrolls from Qumran (1Q32; 2Q24; 4Q554–55; 5Q15; 11Q18), it would not be difficult to imagine how such an accusation arose.

Jesus is seized and accused by the ruling priests and their colleagues and supporters (Mark 14:43–65 and parallels). The high priest Caiaphas is mentioned by name (twice in Matt. 26:3, 57; five times in John 11:49; 18:13, 14, 24, 28); his father-in-law, Annas, is mentioned twice (John 18:13, 24; cf. Luke 3:2; Acts 4:6). As already noted, Jesus is accused of threatening to destroy the temple. However, Jesus admits that he is the Messiah, the Son of God, who will be seated at God's right hand and will come with the clouds of heaven (Mark 14:61–62); this is an unmistakable allusion to Psalm 110:1 and Daniel 7:13–14. The first passage bids the king to sit at God's right hand while God makes the king's enemies a "footstool" for his feet. The second passage speaks of the human being ("one like a son of man") who receives from God (the "Ancient of Days") "dominion and glory and kingdom." However, this authority is granted in the context of a heavenly court that has been convened to enter judgment against Israel's enemies (cf. Dan. 7:9–10: "Thrones were placed and one that was ancient of days took his seat. . . . The court sat in judgment"). The implications of Jesus' reply to the high priest are quite clear: The next time Jesus and Caiaphas meet, the former will sit in judgment on the latter. It is hardly surprising that the high priest regards such a reply as blasphemous and worthy of death, for Jesus has spoken against a high priest, which is forbidden by the law (cf. Exod. 22:28; Acts 23:2–5); and in claiming messianic kingship, he is guilty of sedition, for which he will be condemned by Roman authority.

In the writings of Josephus we have an independent account of the juridical process that overtook Jesus. In a much-discussed passage, which is probably authentic but glossed by later Christian scribes, Josephus has this to say about Jesus of Nazareth:

> Now, there was about this time Jesus, a wise man, *if it be lawful to call him a man*, for he was a doer of wonderful works—a teacher of such men as receive the truth with pleasure. He drew over to him both many of the Jews, and many of the Gentiles. *He was [the] Christ*; [64]and when Pilate, at the suggestion of the principal men among us, had condemned him to the cross, those that loved him at the first did

not forsake him, *for he appeared to them alive again the third day, as the divine prophets had foretold these and ten thousand other wonderful things concerning him*; and the tribe of Christians, so named from him, are not extinct at this day. (*Ant.* 18.63–64, emphasis added)

The words placed in italics are the Christian glosses, which take the passage in directions that are meaningful to Christians.[11] But stripped of the glosses, the passage coheres closely with the broad outline provided by the New Testament Gospels. Jesus is described as teacher and wonderworker; and he is condemned by Pilate to the cross, at the suggestion of the "principal men" (by which Josephus means the ruling priests).[12] All that is missing in this terse account is the reason why the principal men of the Jewish people encouraged the Roman governor to eliminate Jesus. The New Testament Gospels supply us with the reason and, as we shall see in the balance of this chapter, we shall encounter this reason several more times in the thirty-five years or so following the death of Jesus.

The Apostles and the Family of Annas

Josephus remarks that although Jesus was condemned to the cross, "those that loved him at the first did not forsake him; and the tribe of Christians, so named from him, are not extinct at this day." The tribe of Christians were not extinct in the year 93, when Josephus published the first edition of his *Antiquities*, because the Jesus movement was convinced that its master had been resurrected.

This conviction prompted the disciples and apostles of Jesus to continue preaching the message of the kingdom of God and the resurrection of his Son (Acts 2–3). It is not surprising that the very high-priestly authorities who have opposed and condemned Jesus take umbrage at this preaching. While Peter and the apostles are speaking in the temple precincts (Acts 3:12–26), "the priests and the captain of the temple and the Sadducees came upon them, . . . arrested them[,] and put them in custody" (Acts 4:1–3).

The next day the Jewish "rulers and elders and scribes were gathered together in Jerusalem, with Annas the high priest and Caiaphas and John and Alexander, and all who were of the high-priestly family" (Acts 4:5–6). Peter and the apostles are brought before these leaders and ordered to cease proclaiming Jesus. But Peter and his colleagues refuse, asserting that they must obey God (4:19; cf. 5:29). The evangelist ends the story

Figure 5.2. Mansion. These excavated remains of a mansion in Jerusalem are thought to have belonged to a high-priestly family. Photograph courtesy of Ginny Evans.

with these words: "And when they had further threatened them, they let them go, finding no way to punish them, because of the people; for all men praised God for" the healing of the lame man (4:21; cf. 3:1–10). What we see here closely parallels the situation with Jesus. Annas, his son-in-law Caiaphas, and other members of the aristocratic priesthood oppose Peter and the apostles, but they find it difficult to move against them because of popular support.

Sometime later "the high priest rose up and all who were with him, that is, the party of the Sadducees, and filled with jealousy they arrested the apostles and put them in the common prison" (Acts 5:17–18). However, the apostles enjoy a miraculous escape, much to the annoyance of the high priest, the Sanhedrin, the captain of the temple, and the ruling priests (5:25). The apostles are again brought before the priestly rulers and are again warned not to continue speaking of Jesus (5:27–28). Regev rightly remarks that the real concern is not the miracle supposedly performed by Peter (3:1–10) or even the fact that the apostles believe God has raised up Jesus. Rather, what is at issue is desecration of the temple.[13] Regev is correct so far as he goes. But what is it about Peter's preaching that desecrates the temple? It is the implicit accusation that the ruling priests are complicit in murder (Acts 4:10). Accordingly, the ruling priests accuse Peter and the apostles of intending "to bring this man's blood upon us" (5:28b).

Such an accusation must be taken very seriously. The accusation is implicit from the very beginning of the post-Easter preaching, when on the Day of Pentecost Peter tells the Jerusalem crowd, "This Jesus . . . you crucified and killed by the hands of lawless men" (Acts 2:23; cf. 2:36). The "lawless men" refer to the Romans, but the statement "you crucified" refers primarily to the ruling priests and to those in the crowd who supported them by calling for the release of Barabbas and the crucifixion of Jesus (Mark 15:6–15). We see the accusation again in the sermon on the steps before the Beautiful Gate, when Peter reminds the crowd, astonished at the miraculous healing of the lame man, "You denied the Holy and Righteous One, and asked for a murderer to be granted to you, and killed the Author of life, whom God raised from the dead" (Acts 3:14–15). Peter partially excuses them, stating, "You acted in ignorance, as did also your rulers" (3:17). Nevertheless, the mere hint that the high priest and his colleagues are guilty of murder can be interpreted as a violation of Exodus 22:28 ("You shall not revile God, nor curse a ruler of your people"; and again cf. Acts 23:2–5), and as such it could be seen as a threat against the temple.

It is impossible to ascertain how Peter and his colleagues escape long imprisonment and perhaps execution. After all, the author of Acts tells us that it was the "party of the Sadducees" who arrested Peter and the apostles (5:17–18), and Josephus himself tells us that the Sadducees were the harshest of the religious parties and most "rigid in judging offenders" (*Ant.* 20.199). In any case, they remain at liberty, at least for a time.

Stephen and the Family of Annas

In the first year or so of the life of the Jesus movement, that is, in the first year of the movement after the execution of its founder and the widespread conviction that God had raised him up, the new community found it necessary to appoint deacons, or servants, to assist in the distribution of goods and funds to the poor of Jerusalem and Judea. One of these deacons is Stephen, who in short order begins to preach the Christian gospel. He becomes embroiled in a dispute with various Diaspora Jews, which coheres with his appointment as a servant to "Hellenists," Greek-speaking Jews, who are from the Diaspora (cf. Acts 6:1).[14]

Those who dispute with Stephen accuse him, saying, "We have heard him speak blasphemous words against Moses and God" (6:11). From the author's point of view, the accusation is not true. This is made clear when we are told that "false witnesses" say of Stephen: "This man never ceases to speak words against this holy place and the law; for we have heard him say that this Jesus of Nazareth will destroy this place, and will change the customs which Moses delivered to us" (6:13–14).[15]

The accusations leveled against Stephen remind us of some of the accusations against Jesus. First, Stephen is accused of speaking blasphemous words, even as Jesus was (cf. Mark 14:64, "You have heard his blasphemy"). Second, he is accused of not ceasing to "speak words against this holy place" and then is explicitly compared to Jesus, who also was accused of threatening to destroy the temple (cf. Mark 14:58), as already noted. The high priest, who is Caiaphas and remains in office until the end of 36 CE,[16] asks Stephen if the accusations are true. Stephen provides no direct answer but instead gives a long speech summarizing some of Israel's history. The conclusion of his speech, however, does provide an implicit answer to the high priest's question:

> So it was until the days of David, [46]who found favor in the sight of God and asked leave to find a habitation for the God of Jacob. [47]But it was Solomon who built a house for him. [48]Yet the Most High does not dwell in houses made with hands; as the prophet says, [49]"Heaven is my throne, and earth my footstool. What house will you build for me, says the Lord, or what is the place of my rest? [50]Did not my hand make all these things?" (Acts 7:45b–50)

The assertion that God "does not dwell in houses made with hands" takes us back to the accusation originally leveled against Jesus: "We heard him say, 'I will destroy this temple that is made with hands, and in three days I will build another, not made with hands'" (Mark 14:58). Stephen's assertion and quotation of Isaiah 66:1–2 ("What is the house which you would build for me? . . .") at the very least imply that the Jerusalem temple is obsolete. It may also hint at its eventual destruction, even as Jesus himself had predicted (Mark 13:1–2). From the high-priestly point of view, Stephen completes his outrageous blasphemy by saying, "Behold, I see the heavens opened, and the Son of man standing at the right hand of God" (Acts 7:56), thereby implying that the high priest no longer mediates between humanity and God; instead, the risen Jesus (aka the "Son of man") does so. The ruling priests and those with them, including Saul of Tarsus, interpret Stephen's words as capital blasphemy and stone him.[17]

Stephen the deacon becomes the second member of the Jesus movement to die at the hands of or at the instigation of the high-priestly family of Annas. He will not be the last.

James Son of Zebedee and the Family of Annas

Following the martyrdom of Stephen, the author of the book of Acts states, "On that day a great persecution arose against the church in Jerusalem; and they were all scattered throughout the region of Judea and Samaria, except the apostles" (8:1). The general persecution is mentioned again, to explain the establishment of the Jesus movement in Antioch, where the disciples for the first time are called "Christians" (Acts 11:19–26). The narrative of Acts returns to Judea, where with little explanation or preparation we are told that "Herod the king [Agrippa I] laid violent hands[18] upon some who belonged to the church. He killed James the brother of John with the sword" (Acts 12:1–2). This James is the son of Zebedee and brother of John, two of Jesus' closest disciples.

Regev reasonably omits discussion of the death of James son of Zebedee because there is nothing said of controversy with the temple. He says that "when Agrippa I executed James, . . . he was not concerned with such cultic or religious issues."[19] Regev, moreover, calls our attention to Daniel Schwartz's suggestion that Agrippa's purpose was to avoid political disturbances.[20] This is a plausible suggestion. Regev and Schwartz may well be correct; to some extent they must be. However, we notice that the author of Acts supplies no reason at all—at least no obvious reason—for Agrippa I's action against James son of Zebedee.[21] Nothing is said of political disturbances. What would the reader of Acts assume? All of the previous actions taken against Jesus and his following have been at the instigation of the ruling priests: Jesus of Nazareth, Peter and the apostles, and Stephen. Although it is true that in the book of Acts the temple is not mentioned and no high priest is named, readers may have assumed that Agrippa I probably acts in concert with the ruling priests.

There is more to my suggestion than merely guessing at what readers of Acts would have assumed. We need to ask about the political and religious situation at the time of Agrippa I's execution of James. Theophilus son of Annas was appointed high priest in 37 CE, the year when Agrippa was given the tetrarchies of Philip and Lysanius. Agrippa, who took his Jewish faith seriously, in all probability would have become acquainted with Theophilus and his family and may well have come under their influence. In early 41 CE Agrippa is given the whole of the kingdom and

Inscriptions Relating to High-Priestly Families

Joseph, son of Caiaphas (ossuary, Jerusalem)

Miriam, daughter of Yeshua son of Caiaphas
priests of Ma'aziah from Beth 'Imri (ossuary, Jerusalem)

Yehohanah, daughter of Yehohanan
son of Theophilus the high priest (ossuary, Jerusalem)

Ananias the high priest, 'Aqavia his son (ostracon, Masada)

[of] the son of Qatros (stone weight, "Burnt House," Jerusalem)

Boethos
Shim'on, of (the family of) Boethos (ossuary, Jerusalem)

officially becomes "king of the Jews," like his grandfather Herod. Later that year Theophilus is removed from office and replaced by Simon Cantheras, son of Boethus.

In the final year of Theophilus's administration, Agrippa and Petronius the Roman legate of Syria narrowly escaped a Jewish rebellion over Caligula's desire to have his image erected in Jerusalem. Petronius temporized and wrote the emperor, asking him to reconsider; the emperor died, and the new emperor, Claudius, rescinded the reckless order. But even so, young fools in Dora (north of Mount Carmel) set up the image of the emperor in a synagogue and precipitated a fresh crisis (Josephus, *Ant.* 19.300). Both Petronius and Agrippa intervened and again prevented what could have become a riot. It is in the aftermath of these chaotic events (still in the year 41 CE) that Agrippa removed Simon Cantheras from the high priesthood and bestowed the office upon Matthias son of Annas (cf. *Ant.* 19.312–16), whose brother-in-law Caiaphas had been involved in the deaths of Jesus and Stephen and the imprisonment and flogging of Peter and other apostles.

I find it more than a coincidence that shortly after the appointment of another son of Annas, another member of the Jesus movement is killed. And it is not hard to see why. In the aftermath of the near desecration of the temple and the actual desecration of a synagogue, sensitivities regarding the sanctity of the temple would have been greatly increased. And once again, the rumors—perhaps not entirely unfounded—that members of the Jesus movement believed the temple was doomed or obsolete could have incited the new high priest Matthias, a member of a family that has been in deadly competition and conflict with the Jesus family and movement for more than ten years, to incite his political ally and benefactor Agrippa I to launch a pogrom.

There is an old tradition in the Mishnah that remembers Agrippa I's receiving a scroll of Deuteronomy from the high priest, reading it, and being praised by the sages and assured that he is indeed a brother, that he is Jewish (*m. Sotah* 7:8). The account is legendary, to be sure, but it is nevertheless hard to explain if it were not based on a generally favorable memory of Herod's grandson. It may also hint at a cordial relationship between Agrippa and his high-priestly appointment Matthias. In my opinion Agrippa's actions against James son of Zebedee, as well as against Peter, were planned and religious, not simply capricious.[22]

Peter and the Family of Annas

After mentioning the death of James, the author of Acts goes on to narrate the arrest and imprisonment of Peter:

> When he saw that it pleased the Jews, he proceeded to arrest Peter also. This was during the days of Unleavened Bread. [4]And when he had seized him, he put him in prison, and delivered him to four squads of soldiers to guard him, intending after the Passover to bring him out to the people. [5]So Peter was kept in prison; but earnest prayer for him was made to God by the church. (12:3b–5)

As in his escape from prison earlier in Acts (cf. 5:17–20), Peter once again enjoys a miraculous escape (12:6–11). To the mind of the author of Acts, these escapes are indeed miraculous, by agency of angels. Other readers, however, may wonder if the escapes of Peter and his colleagues are being facilitated by human sympathizers, for the leaders of the Jesus movement are popular and held in high esteem (2:47; 3:9; 4:21; 5:13). Their popularity should occasion no surprise, for the aristocratic priesthood is viewed with misgivings by many Jews, and the Jesus community is seen as a reforming movement, freely distributing money and goods to those in need (2:44–47; 4:32–37; 6:1) and healing the sick (3:1–9; 5:14–16).

As in the case of James, whose death was discussed above, I am suggesting that the arrest and imprisonment of Peter was part of the same pogrom initiated by Agrippa I against the Jesus movement in the aftermath of the near desecration of the temple (see above) and with the encouragement of the newly appointed high priest Matthias, son of Annas. There is one additional hint in the Peter story, however. The story of Peter's escape is remembered as one of being rescued "from the hand of Herod [Agrippa I] and from all . . . the Jewish people" (Acts 12:11). The "Jewish people" (lit., "people of the Jews") probably alludes to the Jewish leadership (as in 22:30; 25:2, 15), not to the numerous commoners, many of whom remain, for the most part, sympathetic to the leadership of the Jesus movement. In other words, the author of Acts is claiming that Agrippa did not act on his own volition but was encouraged by "Jews," including perhaps the newly installed high priest and his family and colleagues.

Paul and the Temple

There is no evidence that Paul encountered the family of Annas, but he did encounter Ananias son of Nedebaeus[23] and was charged with attempts to desecrate or in some way injure the temple. I can hardly improve on Regev's succinct and accurate assessment of Paul's conflict with the temple authorities.[24]

Paul enters the temple and is seized when some shout, "Men of Israel, help! This is the man who is teaching men everywhere against the people and the law and this place; moreover he also brought Greeks into the temple, and he has defiled this holy place" (Acts 21:28). Paul was then "dragged . . . out of the temple, and at once the gates were shut" (21:30). His life is spared only by arrival of Roman troops and, perhaps, by his Roman citizenship (21:30–36; 22:25–29). Paul is later accused of attempting to "profane the temple" (24:6). Ananias the high priest becomes involved in bringing charges against Paul (24:1). In fact, when Paul is initially brought before Ananias and is given a chance to speak, the high priest has Paul struck on the mouth (23:1–5). When Paul speaks in his own defense, he swears that he did not dispute with anyone or stir up a crowd, "either in the temple or in the synagogue" (24:12). Defending himself before his fellow Jews, Paul says that when he returned to Jerusalem, he spent time praying in the temple (22:17). Before the Roman procurator Festus (60–62 CE), Paul solemnly testifies: "Neither against the law of the Jews, nor against the temple, nor against Caesar have I offended at all" (25:8).

From all of this, Regev rightly sees Luke as taking pains to show that Paul is loyal to the temple and that the charges brought against him are false. Regardless of one's assessment of the charges and of Paul's defense, what is clear is that temple controversy lies behind the attack on Paul and that this attack involves the high priest himself, to one degree or

Figure 5.3. Temple Stones. Excavators left some stones as they found them alongside the southern end of the Western Wall of the Temple Mount. Some of the stones pictured may have come from the sanctuary itself. Photograph courtesy of Israelphotoarchiv©Alexander Schick bibelausstellung.de.

another.[25] In all probability what spares Paul death or some form of harsh punishment is his Roman citizenship and his appeal to Caesar.

James Brother of Jesus and the Family of Annas

The book of Acts concludes with Paul in Rome, under house arrest and awaiting trial (28:16). The year is probably 61 CE. Thus the narrative of the book of Acts ends before the death of James, the brother of Jesus.

Accordingly, there is no report in the book of Acts regarding the fate of James. Thanks to Josephus, we do have a report, but only because the fate of a high priest, as it happens, was tied to the fate of James.

Josephus tells his Roman readers of the family of Annas (also spelled Ananus) and how fortunate this priestly dynasty was. Along the way he tells of the execution of James:

> Now the report goes, that this elder Ananus proved a most fortunate man; for he had five sons, who had all performed the office of a high priest to God, and he had himself enjoyed that dignity a long time formerly, which had never happened to any other of our high priests: [199]but this younger Ananus, who, as we have told you already, took the high priesthood, was a bold man in his temper, and very insolent; he was also of the sect of the Sadducees, who are very rigid in judging offenders, above all the rest of the Jews, as we have already observed; [200]when, therefore, Ananus was of this disposition, he thought he had now a proper opportunity [to exercise his authority]. Festus was now dead, and Albinus was but upon the road; so he assembled the sanhedrin of judges, and brought before them the brother of Jesus, who was called Christ, whose name was James, and some others; and when he had formed an accusation against them as breakers of the law, he delivered them to be stoned; [201]but as for those who seemed the most equitable of the citizens, and such as were the most uneasy at the breach of the laws, they disliked what was done; they also sent to the king [Agrippa II], desiring him to send to Ananus that he should act so no more, for that what he had already done was not to be justified; [202]nay, some of them went also to meet Albinus, as he was upon his journey from Alexandria, and informed him that it was not lawful for Ananus to assemble a sanhedrin without his consent;—[203]whereupon Albinus complied with what they said, and wrote in anger to Ananus, and threatened that he would bring him to punishment for what he had done; on which king Agrippa took the high priesthood from him, when he had ruled but three months, and made Jesus, the son of Damneus, high priest. (*Ant.* 20.198–203)[26]

Because we know the dates of the death of Festus (in office 60–62 CE) and of his replacement with Albinus (in office 62–64), we know that James was executed in the year 62, when he was probably in his late 50s or early

60s. For thirty years or so James was able to navigate the troubled waters of Jerusalem politics. Even when other leaders of the Jesus movement found it necessary to flee, James was able to remain in Jerusalem and give leadership to the Jesus movement.

Comparison of the executions of Jesus in 30 CE and his brother James in 62 is quite interesting. Jesus had been accused of blasphemy and pretending to royal authority, while James later was accused of being a lawbreaker. Both were condemned by high priests—high priests who were related by marriage. Jesus was handed over to the Roman governor, who complied with the wishes of the ruling priests, while James was executed without the approval of the Roman authority. We may presume that neither Festus nor Albinus would have approved. In the case of Jesus, Pilate saw warrant in execution, for a serious political charge could be made (i.e., "king of the Jews"). In the case of James, however, evidently no such compelling case could be made. If it could have been, one would have thought that Annas (or Ananus) would not have acted so rashly. Evidently he realized that apart from a grave charge against James, the type of charge that would be taken seriously by Rome, execution was doubtful. We should remember that Roman governors had no interest in meddling in purely religious matters. One thinks of the position adopted by the proconsul Gallio, at least as it is depicted in Acts: "If it were a matter of crime or serious villainy, I would be justified in accepting the complaint of you Jews; but since it is a matter of questions about words and names and your own law, see to it yourselves; I refuse to be a judge of these things" (Acts 18:14–15b NRSV; 18:15c RSV). There is no reason to believe that under ordinary circumstances the policies of Pilate in the time of Jesus or of either Festus or Albinus in the time of James would have been significantly different.

The important point thus far is that two Galilean brothers—Jesus and James—were put to death either indirectly or directly by two high-priestly brothers-in-law—Caiaphas and Annas. In the case of Jesus, we know that a demonstration and series of criticisms were leveled in the temple precincts, to which ruling priests reacted angrily (Mark 11–12). In the case of James, we are told that he was accused of breaking the law. Can the critical points of antagonism between brothers Jesus and James, on the one hand, and brothers-in-law Caiaphas and Annas (or Ananus), on the other, be brought into sharper relief? I believe we can understand the underlying causes of this antagonism more clearly if we highlight and scrutinize temple traditions linked to both Jesus and James.

In the New Testament Gospels, Psalm 118 is associated with Jesus' entry into the city of Jerusalem. We see this in the cries of the excited crowds: "Hosanna! Blessed is he who comes in the name of the Lord! Blessed is the kingdom of our father David that is coming! Hosanna in the highest!" (Mark 11:9–10). We also see it in the conclusion of the parable of the Vineyard, where Jesus asks the elders and ruling priests: "Have you not read this scripture: 'The very stone which the builders rejected has become the head of the corner; this was the Lord's doing, and it is marvelous in our eyes'?" (12:10–11). The "builders" refer to the religious leaders, in this context the ruling priests (as also in Acts 4:11 and in the Aramaic paraphrase of Psalm 118). In the interpretive Aramaic paraphrase, the rejected stone is none other than the lad David, initially passed over by Samuel the priest (1 Sam. 16:1–10).

In Christian tradition, James the brother of Jesus is also associated with Psalm 118. During his lifetime he was called a "pillar" (Gal. 2:9), perhaps as part of an eschatological vision in which the apostles and the church were seen as comprising a new temple (as argued in chap. 3 above). The metaphors of building and temple applied to James are recalled in later Christian writings.

As has been mentioned, James was known as the "Rampart of the People" and the "Righteous" (Eusebius, *Hist. eccl.* 2.1.2; 2.23.7, 12). Although the term translated "Rampart" remains mysterious, it is widely believed to have something to do with the temple. In my view we have an allusion to Psalm 118: "Open to me the gates of righteousness, that I may enter through them. . . . This is the gate of the Lord; the righteous shall enter through it" (vv. 19–20). The "righteous" who enters the temple of the Lord very likely is what lies behind James's sobriquet "James the Righteous" or "Just" (Greek: *ho dikaios*). Opening the gates and "gate of the Lord" may well allude either to James or to his brother Jesus. These elements come together in a legendary account provided by Hegesippus and preserved in Eusebius:

> So the scribes and Pharisees . . . made James stand on the battlement of the Temple, and they cried out to him and said, "Oh, Righteous [One], to whom we all owe obedience, since the people are straying after Jesus who was crucified, tell us who is the gate of Jesus?" [13]And he answered with a loud voice, "Why do you ask me concerning the Son of man? He is sitting in heaven on the right hand of the great power, and he will come on the clouds of heaven." [14]And many were

convinced and glorified because of the testimony of James and said, "Hosanna to the son of David." And they went up and threw down the Just. . . . (*Hist. eccl.* 2.23.12–14, 16)

Who is the gate of Jesus? The "gate of Jesus" seems to be James. Those who pass through this gate will enter the temple of the Lord, that is, will become part of the Jesus movement. James the Righteous has already entered the temple, just as Psalm 118:19 says, "This is the gate of the Lord; the righteous shall enter through it." This interpretation of the Hegesippus tradition receives support from another second-century source, whose material is also quite embellished: James is told, "Through you those who wish to enter will open the good door, . . . and they follow you and enter" (*2 Apocalypse of James* 55; in Codex V from Nag Hammadi). The Hegesippus tradition concludes with an allusion to Psalm 118:25–26 and its paraphrase in Mark 11:9–10. When combined, the traditions of Hegesippus and the *Second Apocalypse of James* suggest that James was attacked by temple authorities for leading the people astray, that is, for leading them away from the authorities and their understanding of temple practice and worship, and toward the understanding of Jesus and his movement.[27]

Although certainty cannot be obtained, it seems clear enough that the family of Annas viewed brothers Jesus and James as in some sense rivals to their authority, perhaps as competitors for the allegiance of the people.[28] Regev makes a very interesting comment when he concludes that the "actual attitude towards the temple displayed by Peter, Paul, and James was not very different from that of their fellow Jews."[29] I agree. What distinguished the leaders of the Jesus movement from the leaders of the Jerusalem temple was the conviction held by the former that Jesus was indeed Israel's Messiah and that those who had rejected and killed him, the temple leaders, faced judgment. We see this in Jesus' messianic affirmation in the presence of the high priest Caiaphas, in the preaching of Peter and the Twelve, as well as in the preaching of Stephen and Paul. We also see it in James if we have correctly understood the second-century traditions that have been reviewed.

Jesus Son of Ananias and the Family of Annas

In Jesus ben Ananias we may have one more Christian opposed by the family of Annas. Let us take another look at this man's interesting story:

Four years before the war . . . there came to the feast, at which is the custom of all Jews to erect tabernacles to God, one Jesus son of Ananias, an untrained peasant, who, standing in the temple, suddenly began to cry out, "A voice from the east, a voice from the west, a voice from the four winds, a voice against Jerusalem and the sanctuary, a voice against the bridegroom and the bride, a voice against all the people." . . . Some of the leading citizens, angered at this evil speech, arrested the man and whipped him with many blows. But he, not speaking anything in his own behalf or in private to those who struck him, continued his cries as before. Thereupon, the rulers . . . brought him to the Roman governor. There, though flayed to the bone with scourges, he neither begged for mercy nor wept. . . . When Albinus the governor asked him who and whence he was and why he uttered these cries, he gave no answer to these things. . . . Albinus pronounced him a maniac and released him. . . . He cried out especially at the feasts. . . . While shouting from the wall, "Woe once more to the city and to the people and to the sanctuary . . . ," a stone . . . struck and killed him. (Josephus, *J.W.* 6.300–309)[30]

Josephus provides this account as one more omen of Jerusalem's approaching fate. The many parallels between Jesus of Nazareth and Jesus ben Ananias, especially as they pertain to the juridical process that overtook each, are quite interesting and have been explored elsewhere.[31] Here I raise a question: Was this peasant prophet a member of the Jesus movement?

The words of the prophecy, "A voice from the east, a voice from the west, a voice from the four winds, a voice against Jerusalem and the sanctuary, a voice against the bridegroom and the bride, a voice against all the people," are based on Jeremiah 7 (the Temple Sermon), which contains criticism of the temple authorities in the sixth century BCE and predicts destruction of the temple. Specifically, Jesus ben Ananias has alluded to verse 34, the last verse of Jeremiah 7: "I will make to cease from the cities of Judah and from the streets of Jerusalem the voice of mirth and the voice of gladness, the voice of the bridegroom and the voice of the bride; for the land shall become a waste." The phrase "voice of the bridegroom and the voice of the bride" is clearly echoed in the prophecy of Jesus ben Ananias. His adaptation is also quite clear, adding phrases such as "a voice against Jerusalem and the sanctuary" and "a voice against all the people."[32]

Figure 5.4. Siege Stones. A number of siege stones have been found at Masada and within the walls of the Old City of Jerusalem. These stones were flung by Roman catapults. Josephus tells us that Jesus ben Ananias, who for several years had prophesied the coming destruction of Jerusalem and the temple, was killed by one of these stones. Photograph courtesy of Israelphotoarchiv©Alexander Schick bibelausstellung.de.

The angry response from the "leading citizens" and "rulers," which surely include ruling priests, is hardly surprising. Jeremiah was nearly killed for his original prophecy. Jesus of Nazareth, who also quoted from Jeremiah 7, was killed, and Jesus ben Ananias was nearly killed for employing the same language in and around the temple precincts.

I suggest that we explore the possibility that Jesus ben Ananias was a member of the Jesus movement for the following reasons: First, ben Ananias taught and prophesied in the temple precincts, as did Jesus of Nazareth. Second, ben Ananias appealed specifically to Jeremiah 7, as did Jesus of Nazareth. Third, ben Ananias spoke of the temple's destruction, as did Jesus of Nazareth. Fourth, ben Ananias was violently opposed by the ruling priests. There may even be a fifth reason, perhaps the most important one, for thinking Jesus ben Ananias belonged to the Jesus movement.

The priests who opposed ben Ananias and called for his death undoubtedly included members of the family of Annas. Although Annas son of Annas had been deposed shortly after the arrival of Albinus (in 62 CE) and shortly before the preaching of Jesus ben Ananias, he would have remained an influential figure. Moreover, his nephew Matthias, son of Theophilus and grandson of Annas, ascended to the office in 65 CE. He too would have taken a malevolent interest in Jesus ben Ananias.

What motivated ben Ananias to take up his prophecy of woe? Given the number of parallels with Jesus of Nazareth and given the possibility that the peasant prophet was a follower of Jesus of Nazareth, the martyrdom of James brother of Jesus may have been what prompted ben Ananias to begin his ministry.

The scenario, though admittedly conjectural, is quite plausible. In 62 CE the Roman procurator Festus dies. Before his replacement can arrive, Annas son of Annas seizes the opportunity to round up James and a few others, probably also Christians, and have them executed for breaking the law, probably with respect to the temple. This action arouses Jesus ben Ananias, who after Agrippa II removes Annas from office and the new procurator has arrived, begins uttering prophecies based on Jeremiah 7, even as Jesus of Nazareth had more than thirty years earlier. Jesus ben Ananias suffers violent opposition, but because of the presence of the procurator the ruling priests are unable to take action against him the way they had against James, the brother of Jesus.

Ben Ananias is seized and taken to the procurator, very likely with the intention of having him executed. Albinus whips and interrogates ben Ananias but releases him as harmless. (Did a sympathetic crowd clamor for his release?) Albinus leaves office in 64 and is replaced by Gesius Florus, and in 65 Matthias is given the high priesthood. In 66 the war overtakes both of these men, and in late 69 the Roman army, under the command of Titus son of Vespasian, the new Roman emperor, surrounds and besieges Jerusalem. Sometime in the spring or early summer of 70, Jesus ben Ananias is killed by a siege stone, about seven years after his gloomy prophetic activities commenced.

Although Josephus does not tell us, it may be that the death of Jesus ben Ananias was a concluding footnote to the leadership of James, who for more than thirty years was well known in the city of Jerusalem and in the precincts of the temple, well known for his piety and well known for his competition and rivalry with the aristocratic priesthood, especially as it was embodied in the family of Annas. The death of ben Ananias is also a concluding footnote to the first generation. For the deaths of Jesus of Nazareth and Jesus ben Ananias, two men who had spoken oracles inspired by Jeremiah 7 against the temple establishment, bracket the forty-year history of the church in Jerusalem.

In chapter 6, I shall review some major developments in the life of the Jesus movement during the years following the capture of Jerusalem and the destruction of the city's famous temple. This movement is increasingly known as the church and its followers as Christians. The controversies that emerged in the first forty years adumbrate controversies still to come.

Chapter Six

The Church between Paul, James, and Ignatius

It is widely acknowledged that the tragic events of the great Jewish rebellion in 66–70 CE significantly impacted the Jesus movement. Although the roots of the split between this movement—what in time would be known as the church—and Jewish faith and practice not oriented toward Jesus predated the destruction of Jerusalem and the temple, it was the destruction of the Jewish center of worship that played a major part in driving a wedge between Jews who believed in Jesus and Jews who did not.[1] The criticisms, accusations, and polemic generated by various Jewish groups and individuals and directed against one another changed in the aftermath of 70 CE. "Christians" and "Jews" increasingly came to be understood as two separate groups, and ethnicity came to play a decisive role.[2] The process was gradual and did not develop at the same speed in the many and diverse regions that made up the Roman Empire. In wings of the Christian church, polemic turned ugly and—informed by poor interpretation of Scripture and distorted theology—hostility toward Judaism began to emerge. Thus the older intramural polemic and criticism that existed among Jewish groups, which debated the relevance and significance of Jesus of Nazareth, in time among some Gentile Christians gave way to anti-Semitism.[3]

We can see some of this development in Christian literature produced between 70 CE and the Bar Kokhba revolt of 132–35. In what follows I shall look at the Gospels of Matthew and John. In the former we discern the ongoing struggle between Jewish disciples who believe in Jesus and Jewish teachers who do not. The Matthean circle hopes to convince the unconvinced that Jesus is truly the Son of David and Savior of the people of Israel. In the Gospel of John we find a community of disciples who

116

have been ejected from the synagogue and whose polemical language is quite sharp and categorical. I shall also look at the collections of letters produced by the author and compiler of the book of Revelation and by Ignatius, who wrote a few years later while on his way to martyrdom. This chapter will conclude with a few comments on the difficulties of Jewish believers in Jesus during the Bar Kokhba rebellion.

Jews and Christians in the Gospel of Matthew

In the last twenty years or so, a number of important studies have appeared that have attempted to place the Gospel of Matthew more fully into a Jewish context. One scholar has concluded that the Matthean community was in essence a sect within Judaism whose home was Galilee (and not Antioch).[4] Another believes that the evangelist was himself a Jewish teacher competing for the minds of the Jewish people in the aftermath of the calamity of 70.[5] A third interpreter agrees in large measure with these studies, describing the Matthean community as a group of Jews who believe in Jesus.[6]

In my view there is significant truth in these competing yet overlapping views. The Matthean evangelist addressed a synagogue and Jewish leadership that had rejected Jesus as Israel's Messiah and on occasion had persecuted those who believed in him. The evangelist was concerned to demonstrate that Jesus and his movement fulfill Jewish expectations and hopes and do not undermine the authoritative place of Torah.[7] In short, the Matthean evangelist hopes to convince enough skeptics so that his band of Jesus disciples can remain in the synagogue. Let us review some sayings that seem to support this interpretation.

The well-known Sermon on the Mount begins with a series of Beatitudes, nine or perhaps ten in number. The Beatitudes conclude with words of consolation:

> Blessed are you when men revile you and persecute you and utter all kinds of evil against you falsely on my account. [12]Rejoice and be glad, for your reward is great in heaven, for so men persecuted the prophets who were before you. (Matt. 5:11–12)

Two important points need to be made here. First, the utterances against Matthew's people are false (and this would also imply that the persecutions are unjust and undeserved). What is being said against the disciples of Jesus is simply not true. What is being said? The context of Matthew 5 suggests that the disciples of Jesus are being accused of breaking the law of Moses. This is why the Matthean Jesus says so emphatically, "Think not that I have come to abolish the law and the prophets; I have come not to abolish them but to fulfill them" (Matt. 5:17). It is probable that the opponents of Matthew's community have accused them of abolishing the law and, probably, have claimed that this is what their great rabbi Jesus taught them to do. Because they have abolished the law, so goes the argument, they have abandoned righteousness. Far from it, Matthew says. Jesus came to fulfill the law, and he taught his disciples that their righteousness must "exceed that of the scribes and Pharisees" (5:20).

The second important point is seen in the comparison with the prophets. The disciples of Jesus should rejoice in their persecution because people persecuted the prophets of long ago. Their persecution places them in good company. But more than that: Comparison with the prophets, who normally were persecuted by their own people, suggests that the reviling and persecuting envisioned here in the final beatitude is at the hands of fellow Jews. The comparison strongly implies that the evangelist sees himself and his circle of disciples as being persecuted *by their own people*—not by outsiders. The persecution of Matthew and his disciples is a persecution *within* the family, so to speak.

Jesus' warnings of severe discipline are consistent with the beatitude just considered. He tells his disciples:

> Behold, I send you out as sheep in the midst of wolves; so be wise as serpents and innocent as doves. [17]Beware of men; for they will deliver you up to councils, and flog you in their synagogues, [18]and you will be dragged before governors and kings for my sake, to bear testimony before them and the Gentiles. (Matt. 10:16–18)

This passage is drawn from the "source" (*Quelle* = Q) of Jesus' teaching on which the author of the Gospel of Luke also drew (cf. Luke 21:12–13). Matthew's editing of the material noticeably enhances its Judaic perspective. The image of sheep threatened by wolves is found in Scripture and is understood as the Jewish people suffering at the hands of either negligent or oppressive Jewish leadership or Gentile oppressors (Ezek. 34:8–15; *1 Enoch* 89:12–76). In either case, the self-identification as sheep suggests that Matthew and his disciples understand themselves as Jews. In Matthew 10:17 they are warned of being brought before "councils" (or "sanhedrins") and of being flogged in synagogues (Acts 5:40; 22:19; 2 Cor. 11:25: "Three times I have been beaten with rods"). Again, the implication is that Matthew envisions his disciples as being punished *as Jews by Jews*. Even in Matthew 10:18, where the Matthean Jesus warns his disciples that they will be "dragged before governors and kings . . . and the Gentiles," Jewish readers would think of a number of righteous Jews who stood before Gentile kings and tyrants and suffered. The disciples of Matthew's Jesus community clearly identify with the Jewish people who have been oppressed.

The Matthean Jesus goes on to warn his disciples:

> Brother will deliver up brother to death, and the father his child, and children will rise against parents and have them put to death; [22]and you will be hated by all for my name's sake. But he who endures to the end will be saved. (Matt. 10:21–22)

Here we have an especially interesting tradition. The saying alludes to Micah 7:6: "For the son treats the father with contempt, the daughter rises up against her mother, the daughter-in-law against her mother-in-law; a man's enemies are the men of his own house." In the context of Matthew the prophecy is cited in reference to the dark days of struggle that lie ahead, during times when faith is tested, times before the second advent of the Messiah (cf. Matt. 10:23). We should compare the allusion to Micah 7:6 in Matthew 10:21–22 to what we find in the Mishnah:

> With the footprints of the Messiah: presumption increases, and the vine gives its fruit and wine at great cost. And the government turns to heresy. And there is no reproof. Dearth increases. The gathering place will be for prostitution. And Galilee will be laid waste. And the Gablan will be made desolate. And the men of the frontier will go about from town to town, and none will take pity on them. And the wisdom of scribes will putrefy. And those who fear sin will be rejected. And the truth will be locked away. Children will shame elders, and elders will stand up before children. For "the son dishonors the father and the daughter rises up against her mother, the daughter-in-law against her mother-in-law; a man's enemies are the men of his own house" [Mic. 7:6]. The face of the generation in the face of a dog. A son is not ashamed before his father. Upon whom shall we depend? Upon our Father in heaven. (*m. Sotah* 9:15)

What we find in Matthew 10, as well as in related materials in the eschatological discourse in Matthew 24, is a perspective that approximates

Figure 6.1. Temple Inscription. During excavations in the vicinity of the southwest corner of the Temple Mount, an inscription was found that reads, "To the place of trumpeting . . . " Photograph courtesy of Ginny Evans.

some of the elements here in the Mishnah (*m. Sotah* 9:9–15), a curious digression that follows discussion of the rite of the heifer (9:1–8). Woe after woe is described, following the deaths of one notable rabbi after another. The nadir is reached as the advent of the Messiah approaches. Matthew 10 represents an early expression of what we find in the later and fuller form in the Mishnah.[8]

We also find in Matthew very positive affirmations of the temple system itself. One passage clearly presupposes the validity of the temple's altar:

> So if you are offering your gift at the altar, and there remember that your brother has something against you, [24]leave your gift there before the altar and go; first be reconciled to your brother, and then come and offer your gift. (Matt. 5:23–24)

Not only does this teaching presuppose the validity of the temple and altar; it also is entirely in step with rabbinic teaching, as we see in the

Mishnah: "The Day of Atonement atones for a person's transgression against God, but it does not atone for his transgressions against his fellow until he appeases him" (*m. Yoma* 8:9).

Another teaching presupposes the validity and sanctity of the altar. What we have here is a sharp criticism directed against "scribes and Pharisees" (Matt. 23:13):

> And you say, "If any one swears by the altar, it is nothing; but if any one swears by the gift that is on the altar, he is bound by his oath." [19]You blind men! For which is greater, the gift or the altar that makes the gift sacred? [20]So he who swears by the altar, swears by it and by everything on it. (Matt. 23:18–20)

Jesus' teaching in this passage is consistent with the law of Moses: "Seven days you shall make atonement for the altar, and consecrate it, and the altar shall be most holy; whatever touches the altar shall become holy" (Exod. 29:37; cf. 40:10). The same thinking is also reflected in rabbinic teaching: "The altar makes holy whatever is prescribed as its due" (*m. Zevah.* 9:1). The debate over swearing by the altar was also of great interest to the rabbis (e.g., *b. Pesah.* 118b; *Lam. Rab.* 2:10 §14).

The sanctity of the temple and altar is presupposed in another saying, in which Jesus accuses his opponents of complicity in shedding the blood of the righteous:

> I send you prophets and wise men and scribes, some of whom you will kill and crucify, and some you will scourge in your synagogues and persecute from town to town, [35]that upon you may come all the righteous blood shed on earth, from the blood of innocent Abel to the blood of Zechariah the son of Barachiah, whom you murdered between the sanctuary and the altar. (Matt. 23:34–35)

The identification of this "Zechariah the son of Barachiah" is uncertain. Perhaps he is "Zechariah the son of Jehoiada the priest," who was murdered in the house of the Lord (2 Chr. 24:20–21; cf. Luke 11:51).[9] Perhaps he is the prophet "Zechariah the son of Berechiah, son of Iddo" (Zech. 1:1); but we know nothing of the manner of his death. Perhaps he is Zechariah the son of Bareis (or Baruch in some manuscripts), who was murdered in the temple precincts during the great revolt (Josephus, *J.W.* 4.335–43: they "fell upon Zechariah in the middle of the temple and slew him"). If the latter (and perhaps in a typological sense, more than one

Zechariah was in mind),[10] then the defilement of the temple is in view, as we see in Josephus, who complains of the zealots who disregarded the sanctity of the temple by committing murder in its very precincts (*J.W.* 4.150, 313, 355–65; 5.14–19; 6.126–27). Indeed, says Josephus, it was necessary for God to purge the temple with fire (*J.W.* 6.110). If so, then part of Jesus' complaint is that in their misguided zeal, some religious leaders have not only committed murder; they have also defiled the very sacred precincts that they claim to honor.

There is another important feature that should be mentioned. Matthew speaks of a divided people of Israel. In Matthew we have parables that speak of good and bad, of those included and those excluded. But one of the most interesting is a saying in which Jesus says, "Many will come from east and west and sit at table with Abraham, Isaac, and Jacob in the kingdom of heaven, while the sons of the kingdom will be thrown into the outer darkness" (Matt. 8:11–12; cf. Luke 13:28–29). By "sons of the kingdom," the Matthean Jesus means fellow Jews who have not repented and embraced the good news of God's rule. Elsewhere in Matthew the epithet "sons of the kingdom" refers to those who have repented (Matt. 13:38). Accordingly, for Matthew the Jewish people, by virtue of their descent from Abraham, are "sons of the kingdom." By promise and birthright the kingdom of God is their inheritance. Yet Israel is divided; some of its sons are right before God; others are not.

Jews and Christians in the Gospel of John

In comparison with the Gospel of Matthew, the nature of the polemic in the Gospel of John has changed quite significantly. In Matthew the debate is taking place in the context of the synagogue. In John the believers in Jesus have been thrust out of the synagogue. The "whitewashed sepulchres" of Matthew's polemic (cf. 23:27) have become "sons of your father the devil" in John's polemic (cf. 8:44). Nevertheless, the Johannine evangelist still believes it is important to mount a defense of the messianic identity of Jesus in terms of themes and fulfillment of the Scriptures of Israel. The evangelist's perspective remains very Jewish, even if the evangelist and his circle of disciples are no longer associating with the synagogue.[11]

The clearest evidence of the evangelist's estrangement from the synagogue is seen in three explicit references to this expulsion. The first occurs in the context of the healing of the man born blind. The parents of the blind man, who is now healed, are reluctant to talk about their son and his healing, because the religious rulers (aka "Jews" or "Judeans")[12] have "agreed that if any one should confess him [Jesus] to be Christ [the Messiah], he was to be put out of the synagogue" (John 9:22). Literally, the one who confesses Jesus is to "become out-synagogued" (*aposynagōgos genētai*). The second reference is found in the evangelist's summary, at

Ancient Jewish Writers on Jesus

On the ministry of Jesus

Jesus had five disciples: Matthai, Nakai, Nezer, Buni, and Todah. (*b. Sanh.* 107b)

Jesus practiced magic and led Israel astray. (*b. Sanh.* 43a)

On the teaching of Jesus

He [a judge] said to them, "I looked at the end of the book, in which it is written, '*I am not come to take away the Law of Moses and I am not come to add to the Law of Moses*' [cf. Matt. 5:17], and it is written, 'Where there is a son, a daughter does not inherit.'" She said to him, "*Let your light shine forth as a lamp*" [cf. Matt. 5:16]. R. Gamaliel said to her, "The ass came and kicked the lamp over." (*b. Shabb.* 116b)

On the crucifixion of Jesus

On the eve of Passover they hanged Jesus the Nazarene. And a herald went out, in front of him, for forty days, saying: "He is going to be stoned, because he practiced sorcery and enticed and led Israel astray. Let anyone who knows anything in his favor come and plead on his behalf." But, not having found anything in his favor, they hanged him on the eve of Passover. (*b. Sanh.* 43a)

On the resurrection of Jesus

He then went and raised Jesus by incantation. (*b. Git.* 57a, manuscript M)

On healing in the name of Jesus

It once happened that ben Dama, the son of R. Ishmael's sister, was bitten by a serpent; and Jacob, a native of Kefar Sekaniah, came to him in the name of Jesus ben Pantera. But R. Ishmael did not permit him. (*t. Hul.* 2.22)

the midpoint of his narrative in chapter 12, where it is acknowledged that some of the authorities believed in Jesus, "but for fear of the Pharisees they did not confess it, lest they should be put out of the synagogue" (12:42). The third reference is found in the context of Jesus' farewell discourse (John 14–16), where he warns his disciples that their enemies "will put you out of the synagogues; indeed, the hour is coming when whoever kills you will think he is offering service to God" (16:2).

Most interpreters of the Gospel of John understand these passages as in some ways mirroring the experiences of the Johannine community sometime in the 80s and 90s CE. Confession of Jesus as Messiah has resulted in and continues to result in expulsion from the synagogue. Although some in the synagogue believe in Jesus, including some who could be identified as authorities or rulers, they are reluctant to let that be known (John 12:42) lest they be expelled from the synagogue. When one remembers that the Jewish religion was legal in the Roman Empire, which meant exemptions from certain requirements that Jews found unacceptable, one can understand why members of a synagogue would want to retain that membership. The third passage, in which there is reference to "offering service to God" (16:2), suggests that the identification of believers in Jesus and their expulsion from the synagogue may have been tied in some way to synagogue worship. Since this clause "offering service to God" is about killing Jesus believers (16:2b) rather than just expelling them from the synagogue (16:2a), we may have here another example of extreme Phinehan zeal (cf. Acts 9:1).

This link was explored years ago by J. Louis Martyn. Martyn examined the possibility that the references to expulsion from the synagogue in the Gospel of John are linked in some way to the revision of the Amidah, the Standing Prayer, or Eighteen Benedictions, that may have taken place in the 80s CE, not long before the Gospel of John was published.[13] I refer to the revision of the twelfth benediction, evidently so as to identify and remove Christians from synagogues, dating to the time of Gamaliel II (80–115 CE). According to the story, which is found in the Talmud, the twelfth benediction was revised by one Samuel the Small (cf. *b. Ber.* 28b–29a; *y. Ber.* 8a). If one did not pronounce the benediction audibly and clearly, it was assumed that one was a Christian (on the reasonable assumption that one did not want to utter a curse against oneself). Whoever did not recite the twelfth benediction audibly and clearly was ejected from the synagogue. An early medieval form of this benediction reads this way (with italicized words indicating the later expansion):

Figure 6.2. Nazareth Synagogue. The reconstructed synagogue at the Nazareth Village. It was from a synagogue like this that Jesus was driven out (Luke 4:16–30). Years later many Jewish Christians were ejected from synagogues for confessing their faith in Jesus as Israel's Messiah (as in John 9:22). Photograph courtesy of Israelphotoarchiv©Alexander Schick bibelausstellung.de.

> For apostates let there be no hope, and the dominion of arrogance do speedily root out. *Let the Nazarenes [Christians] and Minim [heretics] be destroyed in a moment, and let them be blotted out of the book of life and not be inscribed with the righteous.* Blessed are you, O Lord, who humble the arrogant!

This is called the Palestinian version. It is also found in Saadia Gaon (cf. *Siddur* 18).[14] The last part of the expansion ("Let them be blotted out . . .") is drawn verbatim from Psalm 69:28.

The threat of being blotted out of the book of life is ancient, reaching back to Israel's oldest Scriptures. One thinks of Moses' plea on behalf of Israel, which had sinned grievously in the matter of the golden calf. Moses begs God: "If you will forgive their sin—but if not, I pray, blot me out of your book which you have written" (Exod. 32:32 NKJV). The converse, that is, the hope of being written in God's book, is expressed elsewhere (Mal. 3:16; Ps. 139:16). The concept of a book of life, in which are inscribed the names of the righteous, or from which one's name may be erased, is found in postbiblical Jewish literature (*Jubilees* 30:22; 36:10; *1 Enoch* 108:3; *Joseph and Aseneth* 15:3; 4Q223 frag. 2, 2.54; *Testament of Benjamin* 11:4; Philo, *Who Is the Heir?* 20) and Christian literature (Paul in Phil. 4:3; also Rev. 3:5; 20:12; Irenaeus, *Against Heresies* 5.28.2; 5.35.2).

A few New Testament scholars have raised questions about aspects of Martyn's thesis,[15] but a number of major Johannine scholars have accepted it, or at least its essential components.[16] What supports Martyn's interpretation is the observation that at other points the author of the Gospel of John has devised an apologetic that clearly has a skeptical synagogue in view.

John's scriptural apologetic is designed to show that Jesus, in his experience of rejection and suffering, has fulfilled prophecy; thus the argument is intended to convince the synagogue that the crucifixion and death of Jesus do not disqualify him as Messiah and God's Son.[17] In his suffering and death, Scripture is fulfilled; and in the failure of many Jews to believe in Jesus, despite the impressive signs (John 12:37–41; cf. Deut. 29:2–4), we see the story of stubborn, unbelieving Israel once again unfolding.

Such an apologetic was necessary because Jewish skeptics were rightly and understandably demanding proof from Scripture that the promised Messiah was to die such a shameful death. In his *Dialogue with Trypho*, Justin Martyr is asked that very question. Trypho the Jew invites the Christian to provide proof from the Scriptures:

> "Lead us on, then," [Trypho] said, "*by the Scriptures*, that we may also be persuaded by you; for we know that he should suffer and be led as a sheep. But prove to us whether he must also be crucified and die such disgraceful and dishonorable death, cursed by the Law. For we cannot bring ourselves even to consider this." (*Dialogue with Typho* 90.1, emphasis added; cf. 89.1: "We are in doubt about whether the Messiah should be so shamefully crucified.")[18]

I believe that the evangelist John has attempted to do this very thing, in his formal quotations of Scripture, especially beginning at John 12:37–41, and in his theme of signs, which in various ways parallel the signs and events that Israel experienced during the nation's sojourn in the wilderness. The evangelist has written these signs and has cited these fulfillments of Scripture so that readers and hearers "may believe that Jesus is the Christ [the Messiah], the Son of God," and that in believing they "may have life in his name" (John 20:30–31).

Indeed, the promise in the book of Revelation (a writing in some way related to the Johannine community) that those who confess the name of Jesus will not have their names blotted out of the book of life (Rev. 3:5; cf. 20:12) may well be a direct response to the threat we see in the revised twelfth benediction of the Amidah. There are additional features of interest in the book of Revelation, to which I now turn.

Jews and Christians in the Letters of Revelation

One of the distinctive features of the New Testament book of Revelation is the inclusion of seven edited letters in chapters 2–3. A further distinction is that these letters have, in a sense, been dictated by the risen Jesus to his servant John, who for a time has been exiled on the island of Patmos in the northeastern Mediterranean Sea. What is of interest here is the strongly Judaic character of the seven letters. I shall highlight some of the most obvious features.[19]

First Letter: To the Church of Ephesus (Rev. 2:1–7)

The risen Jesus criticizes the church of Ephesus because it has lost its first love (v. 4). If it does not repent and once again do the works it did at first, its lampstand will be removed (v. 5). Those in this church who hear the word of Christ and conquer will be granted "to eat of the tree of life, which is in the paradise of God" (v. 7). In the warning and the promise we observe obvious Jewish traditions. The "lampstand" is the menorah, the seven-branched candelabrum, perhaps the best-known Jewish religious symbol in late antiquity (see fig. 6.3). If the church at Ephesus does not repent, its menorah will be removed, and its removal means a loss of Jewish identity as much as its loss of Christian witness in the city. The threat of the menorah's removal may have brought to mind the seizure of the great menorah that once stood in Jerusalem's temple. Following the capture of the city and the fiery destruction of the temple, it was removed and taken to Rome. By the time of the writing of the book of Revelation, the Arch of Titus, which still depicts the menorah and other trophies taken from the temple, had been completed.

The letter to Ephesus goes on to say that those who repent will "eat of the tree of life, which is in the paradise of God." Here the allusion is to the famous garden of Eden, in which was the tree of life, whose fruit was denied to fallen Adam and Eve (Gen. 2:9; 3:22, 24). The hope of regaining paradise, as well as the tree of life, is deeply rooted in Jewish eschatology

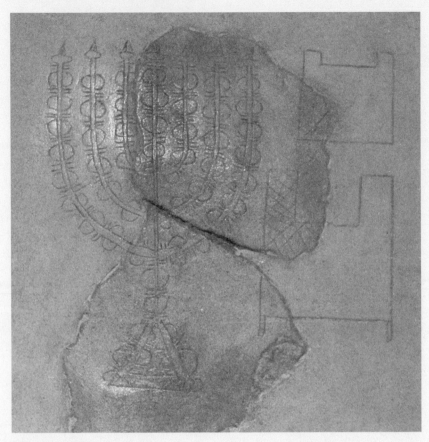

Figure 6.3. Menorah. A depiction of the seven-branched Menorah, incised on stone, found in Jerusalem. In the book of Revelation the exalted Jesus is portrayed as standing beside "seven golden lampstands" (Rev. 1:12–13) and addressing seven churches in Asia Minor (chaps. 2–3). Photograph courtesy of Israelphotoarchiv©Alexander Schick bibelausstellung.de.

(cf. Ezek. 47:12; *1 Enoch* 25:5; 32:3; *3 Enoch* 23:18; *T. Levi* 18:11; *Psalms of Solomon* 14:3; *Apocalypse of Moses* 28:4; 4Q385a frag. 17a–e, 2.3).

Second Letter: To the Church of Smyrna (Rev. 2:8–11)

The risen Jesus in the letter to the church of Smyrna is identified as "the first and the last" (v. 8). This is the very language used of God in Isaiah 44:6 ("I am the first and I am the last; besides me there is no god") and 48:12 ("I am He, I am the first, and I am the last").

The polemic in this letter is sharp and angry: "I know your tribulation . . . and the slander [lit., blasphemy] by those who say they are Jews and are not, but are a synagogue of Satan" (v. 9). In this outburst, modern readers are tempted to hear an example of Christian anti-Semitism, but this misses the mark widely. It is a reflection of intramural Jewish dispute. What is implied is that the church of Jesus is the true synagogue, the true gathering of the righteous. Those who *oppose* (which is the basic meaning of the word *satan*) the gospel make up a gathering, "a synagogue of Satan." The "ten days" of tribulation may allude to Daniel 1:12 ("Test your servants for ten days").

Those who are faithful in the face of persecution will be given "the crown of life" (v. 10) and will "not be hurt by the second death" (v. 11). The metaphor "crown of life" and close approximations have their roots in early Judaism (cf. Jas. 1:12, "crown of life"; *T. Levi* 8:2, "crown of righteousness"; *T. Benj.* 4:1, "crown of glory"; *T. Job* 4:10, "receiving the crown"; LXX: Jer. 13:18 and Lam. 2:15, "crown of glory"). The expression "second death" appears to have developed in the Aramaic-speaking synagogue, as we see in the Aramaic paraphrases of Scripture, or Targumim (e.g., *Tg. Onq.*, Deut. 33:6, "May Reuben . . . not die a second death"; *Tg. Isa.* 22:14; *Tg. Jer.* 51:39, 57).

Third Letter: To the Church of Pergamum (Rev. 2:12–17)

The city of Pergamum has the dubious distinction of being the place where "Satan's throne" is located. The reference is to a pagan temple (though scholars debate this point), but the manner of speaking appears to be Jewish. Righteous Job requests: "I beg you, if this really is the place of Satan, by whom humans are deceived, give me authority, that going I might cleanse this place" (*T. Job* 3:6; cf. 4:4). The description "Satan's throne" intensifies the language. Satan does not merely dwell in Pergamum: this is the place where he is enthroned and rules.

The major complaint is that members of the Pergamum church "hold the teaching of Balaam" and the "teaching of the Nicolaitans" (vv. 14–15). In Jewish Scripture (Num. 22:5–8; and passim) and lore (4Q339 frag. 1, lines 1–2; *b. Ber.* 7a; *b. Sanh.* 106a), as well as in Jewish Christian teaching (Jude 11; 2 Pet. 2:15–16), Balaam rises to the level of an all-time villain who sought to destroy the Jewish people. To hold to his teaching would be to embrace the worst teaching imaginable. Those who hold to it had better repent, lest the risen Christ come "against them with the sword of my mouth" (v. 16). The sword that issues forth from the mouth recalls Isaiah 11:4 ("He shall smite the earth with the rod of his mouth, and with the breath of his lips he shall slay the wicked") and 49:2 ("He made my mouth like a sharp sword"). The former is particularly apropos, for in late antiquity Isaiah 11 had come to be interpreted as a messianic prophecy.

The one who rejects the false teachings will receive "some of the hidden manna" (v. 17). Manna, of course (from the Hebrew, lit., "What is it?"), is the famous food that God provided the Israelites during their wilderness sojourn (Exod. 16:4–36). In Jewish interpretation this food took on all sorts of interesting properties and associations. In some tradition it is the heavenly bread that will be provided in the age to come (*2 Bar.* 29:8; *Exod. Rab.* 25:3 [on Exod. 16:4]), for it will convey eternal life (*Joseph and Aseneth* 16:14: "Everyone who eats of it will not die for ever").

Fourth Letter: To the Church of Thyatira (Rev. 2:18–29)

In the letter to the church of Thyatira, the risen Christ, the Son of God, is said to have "eyes like a flame of fire" and "feet . . . like burnished bronze" (v. 18). This description recalls the vision of Christ in 1:14–15 and appears to allude to the angel in Daniel 10:6 ("his face like the appearance of lightning, his eyes like flaming torches, his arms and legs like the gleam of burnished bronze").

The congregation of Thyatira is admonished for tolerating "the woman Jezebel, who calls herself a prophetess, and she teaches and leads astray" (v. 20 AT). Jezebel was the infamous Phoenician princess who married Israel's King Ahab (1 Kgs. 16:29–31), promoted the worship of Baal (16:31; Josephus, *Ant.* 8.317), murdered many of Israel's prophets who had remained faithful to Yahweh (1 Kgs. 18:4, 13; Josephus, *Ant.* 8.330, 334), and goaded her husband into murdering Naboth so that he might take possession of the man's vineyard (1 Kgs. 21:5–16). In fulfillment of the word of a prophet, the evil woman was herself murdered, and dogs ate her corpse (2 Kgs. 9:30–37). It is no surprise that Jezebel was vilified in later Jewish traditions (e.g., *Tg. 2 Kgs.* 9:22, where we read of "the idols of Jezebel"; in *2 Bar.* 62:3 we hear of the "curse of Jezebel" in reference to Israel's tragic legacy of idolatry).

He who overcomes the temptations and evil teaching of the false prophetess Jezebel will be given "power over the nations" (Rev. 2:26), and "he shall rule them with a rod of iron, as when earthen pots are broken in pieces" (v. 27). These words unmistakably allude to Psalm 2:8–9, the psalm that celebrates the victory the Lord's Messiah has over the nations:

he "shall break them with a rod of iron, and dash them in pieces like a potter's vessel."

Fifth Letter: To the Church of Sardis (Rev. 3:1–6)

The risen Christ assures the faithful believers of Sardis that they will be clad in "white garments" (3:5a). Given the eschatological context of the book of Revelation, it is likely that "white" is best understood in the light of Daniel, who says the righteous will "purify themselves, and make themselves white" (12:10; cf. 11:35, where the death of righteous will "refine and cleanse them and make them white, until the time of the end"), perhaps even as the Ancient of Days is himself clad "white as snow" (7:9; cf. Eccl. 9:8; 1QM 7.10). The faithful may be assured that their names will not be blotted out of the "book of life" (v. 5b). The "book of life" recalls biblical and Jewish traditions (see discussion above).

Figure 6.4. Sardis. The ruins of the synagogue at Sardis in Asia Minor (Turkey). One of the letters of Revelation was sent to the church of Sardis (Rev. 3:1–6). Photograph courtesy of Ginny Evans.

Sixth Letter: To the Church of Philadelphia (Rev. 3:7–13)

In the letter to the church of Philadelphia, the risen Jesus describes himself as "the holy one, the true one" (3:7). God is described the same way in 6:10 ("O Sovereign Lord, holy and true, how long . . . ?"). The language of both passages probably echoes Isaiah 49:7, where God is described as "the LORD, who is faithful, the Holy One of Israel." What is translated as "faithful" (Hebrew: *ne'eman*) can also mean "true" (and a number of times is translated in the Greek version with *alēthinos*, also used in Revelation 3:7 and 6:10 (and 3:14; see discussion of 3:14–22 below).

The risen Jesus is he who "has the key of David, who opens and no one shall shut, who shuts and no one opens" (v. 7). Here we have a clear allusion to Isaiah 22:22 ("I will place on his shoulder the key of the house of David; he shall open, and none shall shut; and he shall shut, and none shall open").

In the letter are also references to the "temple of my God," "city of my God," and the "New Jerusalem" (Rev. 3:12). This imagery recalls Ezekiel's vision of the new Jerusalem (esp. Ezek. 48), an imagery that has been thrown into a new light thanks to the discovery of the *New Jerusalem* texts at Qumran (1Q32; 2Q24; 4Q554; 5Q15; 11Q18). The Christians of the book of Revelation share the Jewish hope for Israel's redemption and a new Jerusalem.

Seventh Letter: To the Church of Laodicea (Rev. 3:14–22)

In the letter to the church of Laodicea, the risen Jesus describes himself as "the Amen, the faithful and true witness, the beginning of God's creation" (v. 14). The word "amen" (*amēn* in both Hebrew and Greek) occurs more than two dozen times in the Old Testament. It is even more frequent in the Targums. The words "faithful and true" (*pistos kai alēthinos*) are part of the meaning of "amen" (see the comment above on 3:7). The description "beginning of God's creation" immediately recalls Genesis 1:1, as well as personified Wisdom, who was in God's presence before the "beginning of the earth" (Prov. 8:22–23).

Given the Judaic orientation of much of the polemic in the letters to the seven churches, we should assume that the people who make up these Christian congregations are mostly Jewish. Their opponents are not gnostics or Hellenizers: they are Jewish skeptics and members of synagogues, who reject the claims that Christian Jews make about Jesus.

The Jewish identity of the community for whom the seer wrote his revelation is also seen in the numbering of the righteous: "I looked, and lo, on Mount Zion stood the Lamb, and with him a hundred and forty-four thousand who had his name and his Father's name written on their foreheads" (Rev. 14:1). They are the "redeemed from the earth" who "sing a new song" before the throne of God (14:3; cf. Isa. 42:10; Pss. 40:3; 98:1). This is the believing remnant, a remnant envisioned in unmistakably Jewish terms, consisting of twelve thousand from each of the twelve tribes of Israel. With the appearance of the number twelve, we return to the twelve symbolism seen explicitly in Jesus (Mark 3:14) and implicitly in John the Baptist (Matt. 3:9; Luke 3:8). Thus, from the beginning of the Christian story to its visionary conclusion runs the anticipation of the restoration of Israel.

As the Jesus movement enters the second century, its transformation accelerates, from Jewish membership in and alongside synagogues to an increasingly Gentile membership whose visible locus is the house church. But the Judaic heritage does not vanish; it continues to exhibit itself in interesting and important ways.

Jews and Christians in the Letters of Ignatius

The conservers of the work of Ignatius have given us another collection of seven letters (ca. 110 CE), which, like the letters in Revelation 2–3, reflect the Jewish roots of the Jesus movement, even eighty years or so after the death of its Jewish founder.[20] On his way to martyrdom in Rome, Ignatius wrote his letters, six to churches and one to Polycarp, the bishop of the church at Smyrna. We have no reliable report, but tradition assumes that Ignatius did actually suffer martyrdom in the capital city of the empire.

Ignatius quotes or alludes to Jewish Scripture several times. As we might expect, he shows familiarity with the newer literature of the Jesus movement, many times quoting or alluding to the Gospel of Matthew and several of Paul's Letters. As in Paul's Letters, Ignatius frequently uses the word "church" (*ekklēsia*), in all some thirty-eight times. However, on one occasion he refers to Christian gatherings as "synagogues": "Let meetings [*synagōgai*] be held more frequently; seek out everyone by name" (*To Polycarp* 4.2). The hard-and-fast distinction in church/synagogue terminology has not yet formed. We see this ambiguity in the Shepherd of Hermas, who speaks of a Christian gathering as "an assembly (or synagogue, lit., *synagōgē*) of righteous people" (43.9, 13, 14, in *Mandate* 11).

Like Paul, Ignatius too sees Jews and Gentiles united in the church, affirming that Jesus was "nailed in the flesh for us under Pontius Pilate and Herod the tetrarch . . . in order that he might raise a banner for the ages through his resurrection for his saints and faithful people, whether among Jews or among Gentiles, in the one body of his church" (*To the Smyrnaeans* 1.2). But not all of the churches to which Ignatius wrote were united. In one case, perhaps in two cases, the church was divided, and at the heart of the division were quarrels with the synagogue.

The Church of Philadelphia

The Jewish elements of the letter to the church of Philadelphia in the book of Revelation (3:7–13) were reviewed above. According to this older letter, part of the problem faced by the church stemmed from "those of the synagogue of Satan who say they are Jews and are not, but lie" (v. 9). In his newer letter, Ignatius exhorts the Christians of Philadelphia to be united and to avoid dissension (*To the Philadelphians* 8.1–2a). Apparently he has heard of dissension in this church:

> For I heard some people say, "If I do not find it in the archives, I do not believe it in the gospel." And when I said to them, "It is written," they answered me, "That is precisely the question." But for me, the "archives" are Jesus Christ, the unalterable archives are his cross and death and his resurrection and the faith that comes through him; by these things I want, through your prayers, to be justified. (8:2bc)

The reference to "archives" (*archeia*) has puzzled interpreters. Most think it is in reference to the older Jewish Scriptures.[21] There is also question about the meaning of "in the gospel" (*en tō euangeliō*). The great patristics scholar J. B. Lightfoot suggested the sense is "I do not believe it (because it appears) in the Gospel,"[22] that is, in one of the written Gospels (probably Matthew). In other words, some in the church of Philadelphia are not satisfied with the testimony of the Christian writings, but insist that the teaching in question must also be found in the older Scriptures. "The church was being challenged to prove its case from the Old Testament."[23] If this is correct, then the dynamics of the debate are similar to what we have seen in Trypho's objections. Those who insist on finding teaching or proof in the older Scriptures are probably related to those who "expound Judaism," mentioned earlier in the letter (6.1).

Ignatius even mentions uncircumcised men who teach Judaism (6.1). It is possible that the synagogue was attempting to lure Jewish Christians back to the synagogue.[24] To counter these efforts, Ignatius later asserts:

"The priests, too, were good, but the high priest, entrusted with the Holy of Holies, is better; he alone has been entrusted with the hidden things of God, for he himself is the door of the Father, through which Abraham and Isaac and Jacob and the prophets and the apostles and the church enter in" (9.1). That is, the priests of the old dispensation, who ministered to the people and served in the temple, were admittedly good yet limited. But Jesus, the "high priest for ever" (cf. Heb. 4:14–15; 5:1–10; 6:20; 7:26; 8:1–6; 9:11–28), is better, having become the door that provides access to God, through whom the patriarchs themselves pass.

In what way, if any, those who teach Judaism or at least insist on scriptural proofs that will satisfy the Jewish point of view are related to the "synagogue of Satan" is unclear.[25] But what seems clear is that in the time of Ignatius, there was still a lively interaction between church and synagogue in the city of Philadelphia.

The Church of Magnesia

There are two passages in Ignatius's letter to the church of Magnesia that call for brief comment. They are not especially polemical, but they do engage the synagogue in one way or another:

> Do not be deceived by heterodoxies or antiquated myths, since they are worthless. For if we continue to live in accordance with Judaism, we admit that we have not received grace. [2]For the most godly prophets lived in accordance with Christ Jesus. This is why they were persecuted. (*To the Magnesians* 8.1–2a)

> If, then, those who had lived according to ancient practices came to the newness of hope, no longer keeping the Sabbath but living in accordance with the Lord's day, on which our life also arose through him and his death (which some deny), the mystery through which we came to believe, and because of which we patiently endure, in order that we may be found to be disciples of Jesus Christ, our only teacher, [2]how can we possibly live without him, whom even the prophets, who were his disciples in the Spirit, were expecting as their teacher? This is why the one for whom they rightly waited raised them from the dead when he came. (9.1–2)

Exactly what "heterodoxies or antiquated myths" Ignatius has in mind is difficult to say. I am not convinced that docetism is in view[26] (as it certainly is in *To the Smyrnaeans* 5.2, "not confessing that he was clothed in flesh"). The language is rhetorical and pejorative. The point that Ignatius is making is seen in the second sentence: "For if we continue to live in accordance with Judaism, we admit that we have not received grace" (*Magn.* 8.1b). This is an unmistakable allusion to Paul's polemic in his letter to the churches of Galatia (cf. Gal. 5:2, 4). To return to Judaism, Ignatius reasons, is to abandon the grace of God made available in Jesus Christ. What Ignatius says next is most interesting: "For the most godly prophets lived in accordance with Christ Jesus. This is why they were persecuted" (*Magn.* 8.2). Ignatius is suggesting that the persecution the prophets suffered at the hands of Jewish leaders is evidence that they did not live in accordance with Judaism but with the teaching of Jesus. His argument may in fact be indebted to Jesus' concluding beatitudes: "Blessed are you when men revile you and persecute you. . . . Rejoice and be glad, for your reward is great in heaven, for so men persecuted the prophets who were before you" (Matt. 5:11–12).

The second paragraph continues the argument. If Jews who once lived "in ancient practices" (*en palaiois pragmasin*) came to the newness hope, "no longer keeping the Sabbath but living according to the Lord's day,"[27] "how can we possibly live without him?" (*Magn.* 9.1–2). That is, how can we abandon the new faith and return to the old? How can we live without him, whom the prophets of old were expecting as their teacher? A third paragraph, which I have not quoted (*Magn.* 10), concludes the argument with exhortations: "Let us learn to live in accordance with Christianity. For whoever is called by any other name than this one does not belong to God" (10.1). Indeed, Ignatius urges his readers to "throw out, therefore, the bad yeast, which has become stale and sour, and reach for the new yeast, which is Jesus Christ" (10.2). He concludes in very uncompromising language: "It is utterly absurd to profess Jesus Christ and to practice Judaism" (10.3).[28] This implies that there were some Jews (and proselytes too?) who did practice Judaism even though they were Christians.

Comparison of the seven letters of Revelation with the seven letters of Ignatius is instructive. In both we find sharp polemic. Indeed, the harshest polemic is in the letters of the book of Revelation, with its references to the "synagogue of Satan" (3:9) and "those who say that they are Jews but are not" (2:9). But in the letters of Revelation there is still something of an intramural struggle, a deep sense of being part of the Jewish people, of being part of Israel. That dimension, however, has receded in the letters of Ignatius. In Ignatius, to be Jewish is in some sense antithetical to being

Christian. Of course, he does not refer to ethnicity: he refers to religious practice. For example, to observe the Sabbath, instead of Sunday (the Lord's day), is wrong. The tolerance we see in the apostle Paul, for whom days, food, and customs were not important, for whom living as a Jew or as a Gentile (so long as this did not include immorality or idolatry) was acceptable, is not in evidence in Ignatius. The gulf between confessing Jew and confessing Christian has grown much wider. In the years ahead it will grow wider still.

Jews and Christians under Simon ben Kosiba

With the destruction of the temple and most of the city of Jerusalem in 70 CE, the rule of the high priest and his aristocratic colleagues came to an end. The benchmark for establishing Jewish identity and religious practice was now in the hands of the sages, who in time became known as rabbis, and in the hands of synagogues, where Jews gathered to read Scripture, pray, sing, and socialize. But there would be one last political force centered in Judea, not far from Jerusalem, that would have a major impact on the Jewish people and on their increasingly estranged brothers and sisters who maintained that the crucified and resurrected Jesus was Israel's Messiah. I refer, of course, to the well-known Simon ben Kosiba, better known by his sobriquet Bar Kokhba, "Son of the Star."

In a well-known passage Rabbi Aqiba is said to have recognized Simon ben Kosiba as "the Messiah" (*y. Ta'an.* 4.5 = *Lam. Rab.* 2.2 §4).[29] I agree with Peter Schäfer, who cautiously suggests that Aqiba may very well have recognized Simon as Messiah.[30] The sobriquet "Son of the Star" is an obvious allusion to Numbers 24:17, a prophecy that foretold the coming of the Messiah: "A star shall come forth out of Jacob, and a scepter shall rise out of Israel." In all of the versions of the Targum (*Onqelos, Neofiti, Fragmentary, Pseudo-Jonathan*), the Aramaic paraphrase of Scripture, the "star" is understood as the Messiah.

If the famous Rabbi Aqiba hailed Simon ben Kosiba as the Son of a Star, the Messiah, and a great number of Jews rallied to him, to fight for Israel's independence from Rome (132–35 CE),[31] what were the implications for Christians, if any? Apparently the implications were serious.

According to Justin Martyr, in his *First Apology*:

> [The prophetic books] are also in the possession of all Jews throughout the world; but they, though they read, do not understand what is said, but count us foes and enemies; and, like yourselves,

they kill and punish us whenever they have the power, as you can well believe. For in the Jewish war which lately raged, Barchochebas [Bar Kokhba], the leader of the revolt of the Jews, gave orders that Christians alone should be led to cruel punishments, unless they should deny Jesus the Christ and blaspheme. (31.5–6).

Church historian Eusebius is familiar with Justin's account and repeats some of it:

The same writer, speaking of the Jewish war which took place at that time, adds the following: "For in the late Jewish war Barchochebas, the leader of the Jewish rebellion, commanded that Christians alone should be visited with terrible punishments unless they would deny and blaspheme Jesus Christ." (*Hist. eccl.* 4.8.4)

Elsewhere Eusebius expands upon Simon ben Kosiba's villainy:

The leader of the Jews at this time was a man by the name of Barchocheba, which means "star," who possessed the character of a robber and a murderer, but nevertheless, relying upon his name, boasted to them, as if they were slaves, that he possessed wonderful powers; and he pretended that he was a star that had come down to them out of heaven to bring them light in the midst of their misfortunes. (*Hist. eccl.* 4.6.2)

And in his *Chronicle*, Eusebius has yet more to say:

Cochebas, prince of the Jewish sect, killed the Christians with all kinds of persecutions, (when) they refused to help him against the Roman troops. (*Hadrian Year 17*; cf. PG 19.558)

The Jesus movement is no longer violently opposed by the aristocratic priesthood of the temple, for after 70 CE that priesthood no longer existed; but it is opposed by the authority that has taken its place, in the person of the charismatic leader Simon ben Kosiba, "Son of a Star," or Bar Kokhba.

References to persecution of Jews who confess Jesus of Nazareth as Messiah supports the view that Bar Kokhba had himself made messianic claims. According to Justin Martyr, Christians "alone" were tortured and executed if they did not renounce Jesus as Messiah. Presumably this

Figure 6.5. Bar Kokhba Village. A village in southern Judea destroyed during the Bar Kokhba revolt against Rome (132–35 CE). Photograph courtesy of Ginny Evans.

renunciation was required because Bar Kokhba *alone* was recognized as Israel's Messiah, not the Jesus of Christian beliefs. So far as we know, Christians were the only sect among second-century Jews to hold fiercely to a particular person (other than Bar Kokhba) as Israel's "Messiah." Eusebius's claim that Christians were persecuted if they refused to aid Bar Kokhba coheres with Justin's statement. (It also is in agreement with some of the Bar Kokhba letters that threaten punishment and order certain persons to be arrested and placed in custody.[32]) Christians' refusal to support the revolt was probably due not only to pacifism, but also to their refusal to recognize both Bar Kokhba's messianic identity and the goals of the revolt itself.

The Bar Kokhba rebellion/revolt and its disastrous consequences left a lasting mark on Jews and Christians, on synagogue and church. The gulf thus continued to widen between Jews with proselytes who believed in Jesus on one hand, and on the other hand Jews with proselytes who did not believe in Jesus. The estrangement of synagogue and church is in evidence in Ignatius. After Bar Kokhba this estrangement became

Greco-Roman Writers on the Christian Movement

Cornelius Tacitus (ca. 56–ca. 118 CE) was proconsul of Asia (112–13 CE), friend of Pliny the Younger, and author of *Annals* and the *Histories*. Only portions of these works are extant. In *Annals* 15.44 he provides a passing reference to Jesus:

> Therefore, to squelch the rumor [that the burning of Rome had taken place by order], Nero supplied (as culprits) and punished in the most extraordinary fashion those hated for their vice, whom the crowd called "Christians." Christus, the author of their name, had suffered the death penalty during the reign of Tiberius, by sentence of the procurator [*sic*] Pontius Pilate. The pernicious superstition was checked for a time, only to break out once more, not merely in Judea, the origin of the evil, but in the capital itself, where all things horrible and shameful collect and are practiced.

In his fifth volume of *De vita Caesarum* (ca. 120), the Roman historian Suetonius refers to the expulsion of the Jews from Rome in 49 CE during the reign of Claudius (*Divus Claudius* 25.4; cf. Acts 18:2). In his description he refers to one "Chrestus":

> [Claudius] expelled the Jews from Rome who, instigated by Chrestus [*sic*], continuously caused unrest.

Pliny the Younger (or Gaius Plinius Caecilius Secundus, ca. 61–ca. 113), who in 111–13 CE was the governor of Bithynia in Asia Minor, wrote to Emperor Trajan for advice on how to deal with Christians. The passage that is of interest is found in his *Epistles* 10.96:

> They [the Christians] assured me that the sum total of their error consisted in the fact that they regularly assembled on a certain day before daybreak. They recited a hymn antiphonally to Christus as to a god and bound themselves with an oath not to commit any crime, but to abstain from theft, robbery, adultery, breach of faith, and embezzlement of property entrusted to them. After this it was their custom to separate, and then to come together again to partake of a meal, but an ordinary and innocent one.

a divorce. Tragically the animosity continued to grow until it became hatred.

As a result of the tumultuous events of the first and second centuries, a church emerged that stood outside and over against Israel. This is not what Jesus envisioned. But this does not mean that Jesus did not foresee or attempt to found a church, a community of disciples who embraced his teaching and proclaimed it to others. The problem is not Jesus' "founding and setting in motion an organized society intended to endure for ages to come," as Géza Vermès has recently described it.[33] After all, Jesus averred that the very gates of hell will not prevail against his *qahal*, his assembly, his church (Matt. 16:18). The *qahal* of Jesus, his *ekklēsia*, would endure, but the corrupt and violent aristocratic priesthood would not.

What Jesus longed for, echoed in various ways by Paul and other leaders of the church, was for all humans—Israel and the nations—to embrace the rule of God and in time to see the very cosmos itself liberated from sin and imperfection. This is what Jesus inaugurated with his proclamation of God's rule. Time and eternity will tell how successful his program was.

Root Causes of the Jewish-Christian Rift

From Jesus to Justin

In recent years the factors involved in the separation of Christianity from Judaism have stimulated much discussion and are themselves a by-product of a healthy Jewish-Christian dialogue that has been under way for some time. Review of these factors helps explain why Judaism and Christianity have moved so far apart, even though both religions sprang from common roots, and in part helps explain the origin of anti-Semitism. Critical study of these religions' common roots and the causes of their separation is important, and its continuation should be encouraged.

In recent years Christian and Jewish separation has often been referred to in terms of the "partings of the ways."[1] This more or less neutral language may, however, mask aspects of the bitterly opposed perspectives of early Jews and Christians themselves.[2] But our concern in this book has to do with the root causes of the Jewish-Christian rift. Several factors could be reviewed. One that immediately comes to mind is Christianity's aggressive Gentile mission and lenient requirements for entry into the church. Christian evangelization of Gentiles was out of step with Jewish proselytism. Jewish proselytes were instructed to take on the yoke of the Torah (*m. ʾAbot* 3:5), which involved scrupulous observation of Sabbath and food laws. But early Christian proselytism seemed, in the eyes of its Jewish critics, bent on removing the yoke of the Torah. The Christian councils depicted in Acts 11 and 15 exemplify the nature of the problems brought on by early Christianity's aggressive Gentile mission. Pauline polemic against the "Judaizers" (as esp. seen in the Letter to the Galatians) offers firsthand evidence of how divisive this issue was.

Another serious point of disagreement between Christians and non-Christian Jews concerned the divinity of Jesus.[3] The tendency of the

Greco-Roman church to deify Jesus in the absolute sense—that is, to intensify Johannine and Pauline Christology in terms of Jesus as God (in contrast to Ebionite Christology, which accepted Jesus as Israel's Messiah and fulfillment of prophetic Scripture, but refused to ascribe divinity to him)—only made Christianity all the more unacceptable to Jews. The divinization of Jesus stood in tension with strict Jewish monotheism and in its most extreme form of presentation, appeared to be a direct violation of the first commandment (Exod. 20:3; Deut. 5:7).

Both of these factors—liberal inclusion of Gentiles and the deification of Jesus—only created a context for further estrangement. Failure to observe Jewish food laws, laws of purity, and Sabbath observance forced complete separation between Gentile Christians and Jews, whether the latter were sympathetic to the Christian faith or not. Jewish membership in the early church began to decline, while Gentile membership increased geometrically. The ethnic shift began to efface the Jewish character of the church, which in turn discouraged entry of Jewish converts. The preferred version of the Scriptures of the early church, which within a generation of its founding was primarily Greek speaking, was the Septuagint, the Greek Old Testament, not the Hebrew and its Aramaic interpretation, preferred by the synagogue.[4] Thus the choice of Bible version itself drove Gentile and Jewish believers further apart.

Jewish nationalist interests also played an important part in the growing rift between church and synagogue. A major catalyst that led to the partings of the ways was the destruction of Jerusalem and the Herodian Temple in 70 CE and the later Bar Kokhba defeat (135), which resulted in the loss of Jerusalem as a Jewish city and the loss of Israel as a state. Prior to the destruction of Jerusalem, the temple remained important to Christian Jews. We see this in the book of Acts especially (2:46; 3:1; 5:20, 42; 21:26; 22:17). The destruction of the temple proved to be a significant loss of common ground shared by Gentile and Jewish Christians.

The Bar Kokhba war also intensified hostilities between Christian Jews and non-Christian Jews. According to patristic sources, Christians were persecuted by Simon ben Kosiba, who evidently had been dubbed "Bar Kokhba" (Aramaic for "Son of a Star"). Justin Martyr, a contemporary of Simon's, relates that the Jews "count us foes and enemies; and, like yourselves, they kill and punish us whenever they have the power, as you can well believe. For in the Jewish war which lately raged, Bar Kokhba, the leader of the revolt of the Jews, gave orders that Christians alone should be led away to cruel punishments, unless they should deny

[that] Jesus [is] the Christ and blaspheme" (*1 Apology* 31.5–6). Eusebius, possibly dependent on Justin, similarly states that "Kokhba, prince of the Jewish sect, killed the Christians with all kinds of persecutions, when they refused to help him against the Roman troops" (*Hadrian Year 17*). Why did the Christians refuse to support Simon's bid for freedom? The most probable reason is because Simon was regarded as the Messiah, as both Jewish and Christian sources relate (Eusebius, *Hist. eccl.* 4.6.1–4; *y. Ta'an.* 4.5; *b. Sanh.* 93b). Therefore, Christian allegiance to Jesus as the Messiah contradicted Simon's claims and undermined his authority. Christians "alone" were dealt with severely, because among the Jews they alone regarded someone else as Israel's Messiah.

The Jewish hope of rebuilding the temple created tensions of its own. William Horbury draws our attention to *Barnabas* 16.1–4, a polemical passage that expresses criticism of the Jews for placing their confidence in the temple and, after it had been destroyed, hoping to rebuild it.[5] Horbury thinks that the author of *Barnabas* was alluding to the Jewish hope to rebuild the temple, perhaps at some time near the end of the Flavian dynasty. The author of *Barnabas*, as well as other Christians, may have feared a Jewish resurgence that would have undermined Christianity. In fact, such a resurgence was in some sense under way, and many Christian Jews were abandoning Christian teaching in order to remain loyal to the synagogue. Pressure to do so was greatly increased by the introduction of the *birkat haminim* (lit., "the blessing [or cursing] of the heretics"). We may reasonably surmise that Jews willing to utter this "benediction" tended to abandon Christianity, while Jews or proselytes unwilling to utter it were put out of the synagogue.

The Jewish wars for liberation from Roman control and the hopes for rebuilding the temple tended to pit Gentile Christians against Jewish Christians. For Jewish Christians, this proved to be especially difficult, often forcing them to chose between their faith in Jesus on the one hand, and loyalty to their nation and people on the other.

All of the factors thus far surveyed are secondary to what I believe was the root cause behind the Jewish-Christian rift. The fundamental sticking points for many Jewish people were the simple facts that Jesus had been put to death and the kingdom of God had failed to materialize. Both of these points apparently nullified any messianic claim. The very definition of the messianic task, as it was understood in Judaism in late antiquity, envisioned the restoration of Israel and a long, prosperous reign of Israel's anointed king, the Messiah. Jesus' death and with it the fading of hope for the appearance of the kingdom of God (which had been the essence of Jesus' proclamation) surely proved (to Judaism) that he was not the Messiah after all. Even the proclamation of the resurrection, as marvelous as it was and as significant as it may have been for questions about the afterlife, could not overcome the simple facts that Jesus never began his reign over Israel and that Israel remained under Roman subjugation.

Jewish messianic expectation in late antiquity was diverse, to be sure, but it had important common ingredients. Among these was the anticipation of victory and tangible benefits. A heavenly reign of the Messiah, with no appreciable alteration of conditions on earth for Israel, did not correspond to Jewish messianic expectation that, so far as I can determine, was ever held by anyone. Even among Jesus' own disciples there are indications of popular messianic expectation. Toward the end of his ministry, Jesus' talk of death, no matter how qualified in terms of scriptural fulfillment, even atoning significance, led to the defection of even his closest followers. We should not be surprised that those who had not known Jesus and who had not had the opportunity to be impressed by his teaching and works of power would react with skepticism to assertions of Jesus' messiahship in the face of the facts surrounding his death.

The nature of Jewish messianic expectation is clarified in important ways by the actions of men who by all accounts attempted to fulfill this expectation in daring bids to win Israel's freedom and end Roman domination. Although scholars dispute the point,[6] I think it is probable that at least two or three of these men regarded themselves as in some sense Israel's Messiah and deliverer.

If some of these Jewish liberation movements of the first century had messianic overtones, and I believe that some of them did,[7] it is clear that there were Jews who hoped for a violent overthrow of Roman authority in Israel. Seen against these hopes, Jesus' crucifixion at the hands of the Romans, tinged with the mockery of the *titulus* that proclaimed him "The King of the Jews" (Matt. 27:37; Mark 15:26; Luke 23:38; John 19:19–22), could hardly have been viewed by the synagogue in any other light than as evidence of Jesus' utter failure. The crucifixion of Jesus, from a Jewish perspective, would have been taken as political defeat and prophetic failure. For Jesus not only offered himself as Israel's anointed deliverer, acting as prophet he also proclaimed the advent of the kingdom of God. The kingdom did not appear, and its proclaimer was executed.

Jesus' apparent defeat at the hands of the Romans, along with his rejection by the religious authorities of Jerusalem, would have made Christian proclamation of Jesus' messiahship in the context of the synagogue seem to be ludicrous. An apologetic that would have any hope of persuading Jews that Jesus really was Israel's Messiah would have to explain both the religious rejection and the apparent political defeat. This apologetic, moreover, would need to be scripturally grounded if it were to make any significant headway against the objections of the synagogue's teachers of Scripture. Although due allowance must be made for its obvious apologetic slant, the question with which Justin Martyr credits Trypho the Jew very likely approximates the misgivings many Jews would have entertained when hearing Christian claims:

> Then Trypho remarked, "Be assured that all our nation awaits the Messiah; and we admit that all the Scriptures which you have quoted refer to him. Moreover, I also admit that the name of Jesus by which the son of Nun was called, has inclined me very strongly to adopt this view. But we are in doubt about whether the Messiah should be so shamefully crucified. For whoever is crucified is said in the Law to be accursed, so that I am very skeptical on this point. It is quite clear, to be sure, that the Scriptures announce that the Messiah had to suffer; but we wish to learn if you can prove it to us whether by suffering he was cursed." (*Dialogue with Trypho* 89.1)

> "Lead us on, then," [Trypho] said, "*by the Scriptures*, that we may also be persuaded by you; for we know that he should suffer and be led as a sheep. But prove to us whether he must also be crucified and die such a disgraceful and dishonorable death, cursed by the Law. For we cannot bring ourselves even to consider this." (90.1, emphasis added)

When Trypho says, "The Scriptures announce that the Messiah had to suffer," or "We know that he should suffer and be led as a sheep," he is alluding to Isaiah 53: "He was oppressed, and he was afflicted, yet he opened not his mouth; like a lamb that is led to the slaughter, and like a sheep that before its shearers is dumb, so he opened not his mouth" (v. 7). Trypho's admission that the Messiah was expected to suffer may very well be genuine, for traditions of a period of woe preceding the coming of the Messiah are attested in Jewish sources (such as in *m. Sotah* 9:15) and are probably based on the general prophetic pattern of punishment preceding restoration. One should also review Daniel 7, where a terrific struggle is envisioned to take place before the people of God finally prevail over the forces of evil.

Targum Isaiah attests messianic interpretation of the famous song of the Suffering Servant. However, discomfort with the idea of suffering is also attested in the Targum. The Suffering Servant of Isaiah 53 is turned into a triumphant victor. His grave is not assigned with the wicked (as in v. 9); on the contrary, he assigns the wicked to their graves!

But suffering as prelude to victory did not envision death, and certainly not a shameful death on a Roman cross. In a Jewish context, even claims of resurrection would do little to mitigate the evident failure of Jesus' bid to be Israel's Messiah. Of course, Jews were not alone in mocking the Christian proclamation that the crucified Galilean was none other than Israel's King and God's Messiah. According to Origen, Celsus regarded the notion as absurd, that someone betrayed, abandoned, captured, and executed could be regarded as God and Savior. The whole notion is preposterous (Origen, *Contra Celsum* 2.9, 35, 68; 6.10, 34, 36).[8] To make any headway at all, especially in a Jewish context, a Christian apologetic would have to explain the circumstances of the passion and would have to show how the passion was in keeping with scriptural expectation.

Ultimately, however, Christian apologetic that was well-grounded in Scripture failed to persuade a significant number of Jews. Despite rather sophisticated attempts by Paul and the Matthean and Johannine evangelists, Jewish misgivings arising from Jesus' apparent defeat and unmitigated shameful defeat, a death that may actually attest God's curse (cf. Deut. 21:23: "A hanged man is accursed by God")—these doubts were left unsatisfied. It is not for nothing that Paul tackles this very point head-on in Galatians, a letter in which his teaching and authority have been undermined by "Judaizers" (Gal. 3:10–14). The apostle must show that the curse endured by Christ while hanging on the cross substitutes for the curse that attaches itself to any person who fails to observe all that is written in the law (cf. Deut. 27:26). Paul's midrashic exegesis ultimately arises from the difficulty that the crucifixion posed for the Christian proclamation of Jesus as Israel's Messiah.

We may conclude that the primary objection to Christian claims that the crucified Jesus of Nazareth is in fact Israel's Messiah was the fact of his death, and a shameful one at that. From a Jewish perspective, this objection was fatal. The only possible way to answer was in terms that a Jewish person would appreciate, and that was appeal to Jewish Scripture. If it could be shown in Scripture that the Messiah was to suffer, then perhaps Jesus could be accepted as Israel's Messiah after all. But this stratagem ultimately persuaded very few Jews (though it did some, as attested by Ebionite Christianity).[9] It failed because the promised kingdom did not materialize, and neither did Jesus return, as his followers expected.

As messianism faded in importance for Judaism, a fading probably resulting from the catastrophic wars against Rome,[10] the Christian message that Jesus was the Messiah became increasingly irrelevant. Early on, it mattered and was hotly disputed; later on, it mattered much less and so was ignored. After Christianity swept the Roman Empire, the polemic between Christians and Jews took on a new complexion, becoming increasingly bitter and ugly. Christian polemic was open and explicit, while for obvious reasons Jewish polemic tended to be allusive, often buried in obscure talmudic and midrashic passages inaccessible to Christians. With the eventual disappearance of Ebionite Christianity, the rift between Judaism and Christianity had become wide.

Notes

Introduction

1. ON IDENTIFICATION OF THE "AMBIGUOUS ORACLE" WITH NUM. 24:17: See Martin Hengel, *The Zealots: Investigations into the Jewish Freedom Movement in the Period from Herod I until 70 A.D.*, trans. D. Smith (Edinburgh: T&T Clark, 1989), 239–40, 384 n. 17. For more on Num. 24:17 and the star in Matthew, see Tobias Nicklas, "Balaam and the Star of the Magi," in *The Prestige of the Prophet Balaam in Judaism, Early Christianity and Islam*, ed. Geurt Hendrik van Kooten and J. van Ruiten, TBN 11 (Leiden: E. J. Brill, 2008), 233–46.

2. ON MESSIANIC PROPHECIES: A number of Old Testament texts were appealed to as messianic prophecies. These esp. included Gen. 49:8–12 and Isa. 11:1–10, as well as Num. 24:17. For learned discussion of this important topic, see John J. Collins, *The Scepter and the Star: The Messiahs of the Dead Sea Scrolls and Other Ancient Literature*, ABRL (New York: Doubleday, 1995); Gerbern S. Oegema, *The Anointed and His People: Messianic Expectations from the Maccabees to Bar Kochba*, JSPSup 27 (Sheffield: Sheffield Academic Press, 1998).

3. ON THE PROPHECY OF JOSEPHUS: Josephus tells his readers that he said the following to Vespasian: "You will be Caesar, Vespasian, you will be emperor, you and your son here. . . . I ask to be punished by stricter custody, if I have dared to trifle with the words of God" (*J.W.* 3.401–2). We are told that Vespasian made inquiry and learned that Josephus indeed did have a reputation of being a "veracious prophet in other matters" (6.405). When Josephus spoke of "the words of God," he may well have had in mind various scriptural prophecies, including Num. 24:17, and not special revelations given to him (see *J.W.* 3.352, where Josephus refers to the "the prophecies in the sacred books").

4. FOR LATIN TEXT, ENGLISH TRANSLATION, AND NOTES: See Clifford F. Moore, *Tacitus: The Histories*, LCL (London: Heinemann; Cambridge, MA: Harvard University Press, 1931), 196–99; Menaham Stern, *Greek and Latin Authors on Jews and Judaism*, 3 vols. (Jerusalem: The Israel Academy of Sciences and Humanities, 1974, 1980, 1984), 2:23, 31, 60–62. On the omen of the opening of the temple door, see K. J. McKay, "Door Magic and the Epiphany Hymn," *CQ* 17 (1967): 184–94.

5. For Latin text, English translation, and notes: See John Carew Rolfe, *Suetonius*, vol. 2, LCL (London: Heinemann; Cambridge, MA: Harvard University Press, 1914; rev., 1997), 272–73, 276–77; Stern, *Greek and Latin Authors on Jews and Judaism*, 2:119–21.

6. On widespread knowledge of the Jewish prophecy of a coming world leader: See Stern, *Greek and Latin Authors*, 2:61–62.

7. For discussion of texts that may contain genuine prophecies of the destruction or replacement of the Herodian Temple: See Jostein Ådna, *Jesu Stellung zum Tempel: Die Tempelaktion und das Tempelwort als Ausdruck seiner messianischen Sendung*, WUNT 2/119 (Tübingen: Mohr Siebeck, 2000), 25–89.

8. For discussion of the anticipated new temple in *1 Enoch* 90 and 91: See George W. E. Nickelsburg, *1 Enoch 1: A Commentary on the Book of 1 Enoch, Chapters 1–36; 81–108*, Hermeneia (Minneapolis: Fortress Press, 2001), 404–5, 449; Martha Himmelfarb, "Temple and Priests in the Book of the Watchers, the Animal Apocalypse, and the Apocalypse of Weeks," in *The Early Enoch Literature*, ed. Gabriele Boccaccini and John J. Collins, JSJSup 121 (Leiden: E. J. Brill, 2007), 219–35, esp. 230–31; Loren T. Stuckenbruck, *1 Enoch 91–108*, CEJL (Berlin: Walter de Gruyter, 2007), 138–39.

9. On the eschatological temple prophesied by Tobit: The author of Tobit has been influenced by Isa. 66:7–16 and Hag. 2:9. To these prophets and perhaps to others (e.g., Ezek. 40–48; Zech. 14:11–17) he alludes when he says, "just as the prophets said of it." For discussion of Tob. 14:5, see Frank Zimmermann, *The Book of Tobit: An English Translation with Introduction and Commentary*, Dropsie College Edition: JAL (New York: Harper & Brothers, 1958), 25–27, 120; Joseph A. Fitzmyer, *Tobit*, CEJL (Berlin: Walter de Gruyter, 2003), 330. It is not likely that the author of Tobit was speaking of the Herodian Temple (ca. 20 BCE), which was grander than the original Second Temple. *Pace* Carey A. Moore, *Tobit*, AB 40A (New York: Doubleday, 1996), 291. Zimmermann and others have argued that Tobit 14 was appended after the destruction of the Herodian Temple in 70 CE, but portions of this chapter have been found in the Tobit scrolls from Qumran (e.g., 4Q196 frag. 18; 4Q198 frag. 2; 4Q200 frag. 7), all of which date to the first century BCE. Fitzmyer (*Tobit*, 52) agrees with a number of scholars who date the book of Tobit to 225–175 BCE.

10. That the prophecy of *T. Levi* 15 is genuine: See R. H. Charles, *The Testaments of the Twelve Patriarchs* (London: A&C Black, 1908), 58: "I take these verses as a *bona fide* prediction." The patriarch's "prophecies" are old, perhaps dating to the second century BCE. Predictive elements in 15:1–2; 16:1; and 17:1–11 overlap with apocalyptic features in the book of Daniel, which was composed sometime in the 160s BCE. See Howard Clark Kee, "Testaments of the Twelve Patriarchs," in *The Old Testament Pseudepigrapha*, ed. James H. Charlesworth, 2 vols., ABRL (New York: Doubleday, 1983–85), 1:775–828, here 793.

11. On the prediction of the temple's destruction in *Testament of Judah*: Kee ("Testaments of the Twelve Patriarchs," 800 n. 23a) admits to uncertainty with respect to *T. Judah* 23:3, saying that the prediction is either a post-70 interpolation or a genuine prophecy based on Dan. 9:26.

12. On the interpretation of the commentary on Nahum: See Greg L. Doudna, *4Q Pesher Nahum: A Critical Edition*, JSPSup 35, CIS 8 (London and New York: Sheffield Academic Press, 2001), 318–61, esp. 335–36. Doudna rightly argues that the subject of "it will be trampled" is the city of Jerusalem, mentioned in line 2.

13. ON THE DATE OF THE *LIVES OF THE PROPHETS*: See Charles Cutler Torrey (*The Lives of the Prophets*, SBLMS 1 [Philadelphia: SBL, 1946], 11), who concluded that "the probability is very strong . . . that the work was composed and given out before the year 80." Douglas R. A. Hare ("The Lives of the Prophets," in *The Old Testament Pseudepigrapha*, 2:381 n. 11) agrees, dating much of the material before 70 CE.

14. FOR TRANSLATION: See Hare, "Lives of the Prophets," 2:393–94.

15. ON THE PROPHECY OF *LIVES OF THE PROPHETS*: See Hare, "Lives of the Prophets," 2:381 n. 11.

16. FOR ARGUMENTS THAT JESUS DID PREDICT THE TEMPLE'S DESTRUCTION: See Ed Parish Sanders, *Jesus and Judaism* (London: SCM Press, 1985), 71–76.

17. FOR DISCUSSION OF THE EVIDENCE OF ABUSE AND CORRUPTION IN THE HERODIAN TEMPLE OF THE FIRST CENTURY CE: See Craig A. Evans, "Jesus' Action in the Temple and Evidence of Corruption in the First-Century Temple," in *Society of Biblical Literature 1989 Seminar Papers*, ed. David J. Lull, SBLSP 28 (Atlanta: Scholars Press, 1989), 522–39; idem, "Jesus' Action in the Temple: Cleansing or Portent of Destruction?," *CBQ* 51 (1989): 237–70, esp. 248–64.

Chapter 1: Did Jesus Intend to Found a Church?

1. ON JESUS AS FOUNDER OF THE CHURCH: Several scholars have claimed that Paul was the founder of the Christian church. See William Wrede, *Paul* (London: Green, 1907), 179; Géza Vermès, *Jesus and the World of Judaism* (London: SCM Press, 1983; Philadelphia: Fortress, 1984), 56–57; idem, *The Religion of Jesus the Jew* (London: SCM Press; Minneapolis: Fortress, 1993), 212; idem, *The Authentic Gospel of Jesus* (London: Penguin Books, 2003), 370; Paula Fredriksen, *From Jesus to Christ: The Origins of the New Testament Images of Jesus* (New Haven: Yale University Press, 1988); Maurice Casey, *From Jewish Prophet to Gentile God: The Origins and Development of New Testament Christology* (Louisville, KY: Westminster John Knox Press, 1991). In *Religion of Jesus*, Vermès concludes that Jesus "could not have entertained the idea of the founding and setting in motion an organized society intended to endure for ages to come" (214–15). This statement can be challenged on different levels. See Nicholas Thomas Wright, *What Saint Paul Really Said: Was Paul of Tarsus the Real Founder of Christianity?* (Grand Rapids: Eerdmans, 1997); David Wenham, *Paul: Follower of Jesus or Founder of Christianity?* (Grand Rapids: Eerdmans, 1995); idem, *Paul and Jesus: The True Story* (Grand Rapids: Eerdmans, 2002).

2. ON THE ORIGIN OF MATT. 16:17–19: For arguments that Matt. 16:13–19 represents Matthean composition, see Robert H. Gundry, *Matthew: A Commentary on His Literary and Theological Art* (Grand Rapids: Wm. B. Eerdmans Publishing Co., 1982), 330–36. For arguments that Matt. 16:17–19 probably derives from early, pre-Matthean tradition, see Dale C. Allison Jr. and W. D. Davies, *A Critical and Exegetical Commentary on the Gospel according to Saint Matthew*, vol. II, *Commentary on Matthew VIII–XVIII*, ICC (Edinburgh: T&T Clark, 1991), 602–15. Allison and Davies prudently conclude that Matt. 16:17–19 "*may* preserve the original conclusion to the incident at Caesarea Philippi, and the text *may* give us an important glimpse into the life of Jesus" (615, with their emphasis).

3. ON PAUL AND THE QUMRAN SCROLLS: See Joseph A. Fitzmyer, "Paul and the Dead Sea Scrolls," in *The Dead Sea Scrolls after Fifty Years: A Comprehensive Assessment*, ed. Peter W. Flint and James C. VanderKam, 2 vols. (Leiden: E. J. Brill, 1998–99), 2:599–621.

4. On the symbolism of the Twelve: Some interpreters wanted to find ever-deeper meaning behind the number twelve. Hecataeus of Abdera (ca. 300 BCE) suggested that God divided Israel into twelve tribes, "since this is regarded as the most perfect number and corresponds to the number of months that make up a year" (*Aegyptiaca* [*On the Egyptians*], according to Diodorus Siculus, *Bibliotheca historica* 40.3.3). Hecataeus may have been inspired by Plato, who two generations earlier spoke of the necessity of every city setting aside "twelve portions of land" (Plato, *Laws* 5.745B). Hecataeus himself is echoed in Philo, the turn-of-the-era Jew who lived in Alexandria. Philo probes the significance of twelve (tribes, sons, priestly vestment stones, sacred loaves, and the like), commenting that "twelve is the perfect number, of which the circle of the zodiac in the heaven is a witness, . . . for he accomplishes his circle in twelve months" (*On Flight and Finding* 183–85).

5. For further discussion of the twelve typology in Jesus: See John P. Meier, "The Circle of the Twelve: Did It Exist during Jesus' Public Ministry?," *JBL* 116 (1997): 635–72; Scot McKnight, "Jesus and the Twelve," *BBR* 11 (2001): 203–31; Craig A. Evans, "The Baptism of John in a Typological Context," in *Dimensions of Baptism: Biblical and Theological Studies*, ed. Anthony R. Cross and Stanley E. Porter, JSNTSup 234 (Sheffield: Sheffield Academic Press, 2002), 45–71.

6. On the meaning of "pillars": See Craig S. Keener, "The Pillars and the Right Hand of Fellowship in Galatians 2:9," *JGRChJ* 7 (2010): 51–58.

Chapter 2: From Kingdom of God to Church of Christ

1. On Jesus and his use of Isaiah: See Bruce D. Chilton, *A Galilean Rabbi and His Bible: Jesus' Use of the Interpreted Scripture of His Time*, GNS 8 (Wilmington, DE: Michael Glazier, 1984); Craig A. Evans, "The Scriptures of Jesus and His Earliest Followers," in *The Canon Debate*, ed. Lee M. McDonald and James A. Sanders (Peabody, MA: Hendrickson Publishers, 2002), 185–95. For a helpful tabulation of Jesus' use of Scripture, see Richard Thomas France, *Jesus and the Old Testament: His Application of Old Testament Passages to Himself and His Mission* (London: Tyndale Press, 1971), 259–63. For an assessment of Jesus' use of Scripture in comparison with rabbinic usage and the Aramaic tradition, see Bruce D. Chilton and Craig A. Evans, "Jesus and Israel's Scriptures," in *Studying the Historical Jesus: Evaluations of the State of Current Research*, ed. Bruce D. Chilton and Craig A. Evans, NTTS 19 (Leiden: Brill, 1994), 281–335.

2. Translations of the Aramaic are from Bruce D. Chilton, *The Isaiah Targum*, ArBib 11 (Wilmington, DE: Michael Glazier, 1987), 49, 62, 77, 102.

3. On God as king in the Old Testament and related literature: See Rudolf Schnackenburg, *Gottes Herrschaft und Reich: Eine biblische-theologische Studie* (Freiburg im Breisgau: Herder Verlag, 1959); Martin Buber, *Kingship of God* (New York: Harper & Row, 1967). For the role of Old Testament literature in Jesus' proclamation of the kingdom of God, see George R. Beasley-Murray, *Jesus and the Kingdom of God* (Grand Rapids: Eerdmans, 1986), 3–51; Bruce D. Chilton, "The Kingdom of God in Recent Discussion," in Chilton and Evans, *Studying the Historical Jesus*, 255–80, esp. 273–80.

4. On Zechariah's relationship to the Shema: See the discussion in David L. Petersen, *Zechariah 9–14 and Malachi*, OTL (Louisville, KY: Westminster John Knox

Press, 1995), 148–49. It has been suggested that Zech. 14:9 could be commentary on Deut. 6:4. See Ralph L. Smith, *Micah–Malachi*, WBC 32 (Dallas: Word Books, 1984), 288–89.

5. TRANSLATION OF THE ARAMAIC IS FROM Samson H. Levey, *The Targum of Ezekiel*, ArBib 13 (Wilmington, DE: Michael Glazier, 1987), 32.

6. ON EZEKIEL 7 AND JUDGMENT: See Walther Eichrodt, *Ezekiel*, OTL (London: SCM Press; Philadelphia: Westminster Press, 1970), 97–103, esp. 102; Walther Zimmerli, *Ezekiel 1*, Hermeneia (Philadelphia: Fortress Press, 1979), 206–8; William H. Brownlee, *Ezekiel 1–19*, WBC 28 (Dallas: Word Books, 1986), 108–15.

7. TRANSLATIONS OF THE ARAMAIC OBADIAH, ZECHARIAH, AND MICAH ARE FROM Kevin J. Cathcart and Robert P. Gordon, *The Targum of the Minor Prophets*, ArBib 14 (Wilmington, DE: Michael Glazier, 1989), 102, 120, 224.

8. TRANSLATIONS OF THE ARAMAIC ARE FROM Chilton, *The Isaiah Targum*, 26–27. For discussion of repentance, the kingdom of God, and the Messiah in Aramaic Isaiah, see Bruce D. Chilton, *The Glory of Israel: The Theology and Provenience of the Isaiah Targum*, JSOTSup 23 (Sheffield: JSOT Press, 1982), 37–46, 77–81, 86–96. Chilton has persuasively argued that the exegetical framework of the Isaiah Targum reflects a period between the two great Jewish rebellions, that is, between 66–70 CE and 132–135 CE. He also rightly observes the presence of early tradition, which in some cases reaches back to the time of Jesus and earlier, and in other cases is quite late.

9. FOR DISCUSSION OF THE FOUR EMPIRES OF DANIEL 2 AND 7: See John E. Goldingay, *Daniel*, WBC 30 (Dallas: Word Books, 1989), 49–52; John J. Collins, *Daniel: A Commentary on the Book of Daniel*, Hermeneia (Minneapolis: Fortress Press, 1993), 165–71. Interest in the concept of the four kingdoms is attested at Qumran, which not only possessed several copies of Daniel and related materials but also had at least two scrolls (i.e., 4Q552 and 4Q553) dedicated to visions about the four kingdoms.

10. ON THE PROBABILITY THAT JESUS SAID SOMETHING ABOUT DESTROYING THE TEMPLE MADE WITH HANDS: See Ed Parish Sanders, *Jesus and Judaism* (London: SCM Press; Philadelphia: Fortress Press, 1985), 71–76; Jacques Schlosser, "La parole de Jésus sur la fin du Temple," *NTS* 36 (1990): 398–414, esp. 412–13; M. Eugene Boring, *Mark: A Commentary*, NTL (Louisville, KY: Westminster John Knox Press, 2006), 412: "There must have been a historical core that goes back to Jesus himself."

11. FOR DISCUSSION OF ALLUSION TO THE SON OF MAN OF DANIEL 7 IN JESUS: See C. F. D. Moule, *The Origin of Christology* (Cambridge and New York: Cambridge University Press, 1977), 11–22; Bruce D. Chilton, "The Son of Man: Human and Heavenly," in *The Four Gospels 1992*, ed. F. Van Segbroeck et al., BETL 100 (Leuven: Leuven University Press, 1992), 203–18, esp. 215–18.

12. ON JESUS' UNDERSTANDING OF THE AUTHORITY OF SON OF MAN: See Craig A. Evans, *Mark 8:27–16:20*, WBC 34B (Nashville: Thomas Nelson, 2001), lxxiii–lxxviii.

13. ON BEING SEATED AT THE RIGHT HAND OF GOD AND COMING WITH THE CLOUDS OF HEAVEN: It is not necessary to think that "two separate scenes" have been awkwardly juxtaposed in Mark 14:62, as is argued in Donald Juel, *Messiah and Temple: The Trial of Jesus in the Gospel of Mark*, SBLDS 31 (Missoula, MT: Scholars Press, 1977), 95.

14. ON THE MEANING AND BACKGROUND OF Ps. 110:1: See Martin Hengel, "'Sit at My Right Hand!': The Enthronement of Christ at the Right Hand of God and Psalm 110," in his *Studies in Early Christology* (Edinburgh: T&T Clark, 1995), 119–225.

15. ON THE AUTHENTICITY OF THE PASSION PREDICTIONS: Scholars are divided on the question of the authenticity of Jesus' predictions of his suffering and death. There is little doubt that these predictions were shaped by the events of the passion, but I think it probable that Jesus did speak of his suffering and death for the following reasons: First, the Words of Institution (1 Cor. 11:23–25; Mark 14:22–25 and parallels) make better sense if Jesus had previously spoken of his death. As for the authenticity of the Words of Institution, it is hard to see how this tradition could have taken hold so early and with such authority if it did not reach back to Jesus himself. Second, the fate of John the Baptist surely impressed itself on Jesus. He must have known that he would likely share it. Third, the story of Jesus' falling on his face and begging God to remove the cup of suffering (Mark 14:33–36) presupposes the anticipation of arrest, suffering, and death. It is hard to see how this story is a pious post-Easter creation, for it shows Jesus apparently unwilling, at least initially, to "take up the cross," as he had instructed his own disciples to do (Mark 8:34). Surely a fictional tradition would depict Jesus in a more courageous or even heroic light. Fourth, Judas Iscariot's decision to betray Jesus is easier to understand if Jesus had made known to his disciples his anticipations of suffering and death. For further discussion, see Craig A. Evans, "Did Jesus Predict His Death and Resurrection?," in *Resurrection*, ed. Stanley E. Porter, Michael A. Hayes, and David Tombs, JSNTSup 186, RILP 5 (Sheffield: Sheffield Academic Press, 1999), 82–97.

16. ON ISRAEL IN "EXILE" IN THE THINKING OF JESUS AND HIS CONTEMPORARIES: See Nicholas Thomas Wright, *Jesus and the Victory of God* (London: SPCK; Minneapolis: Fortress Press, 1996), 126–27, 203–4; Craig A. Evans, "Aspects of Exile and Restoration in the Proclamation of Jesus and the Gospels," in *Exile: Old Testament, Jewish, and Christian Conceptions*, ed. James M. Scott, JSJSup 56 (Leiden: E. J. Brill, 1997), 299–328; John P. Meier, "Jesus, the Twelve and the Restoration of Israel," in *Restoration: Old Testament, Jewish, and Christian Perspectives*, ed. James M. Scott, JSJSup 72 (Leiden: Brill, 2001), 365–404.

17. ON THE ANOINTED ONE OF DAN. 9:26: Many early Christian interpreters assumed that the anointed one of Dan. 9:26 was in reference to Jesus the Messiah (though Eusebius believed the reference was to Hyrcanus II, the last Hasmonean high priest recognized by Rome). Modern critical interpretation is important, to be sure, but we must ask how the text was understood in the time of Jesus and how Jesus himself may have understood and applied it.

18. ON THE DANGER OF CRUCIFIXION: Epictetus commented: "If you want to be crucified, just wait. The cross will come. If it seems reasonable to comply, and the circumstances are right, then it's to be carried through, and your integrity maintained" (*Discourses* 2.2.20). Jesus was fond of proverbial language that did not necessarily derive from Jewish Scripture and tradition. Recall what Jesus said on one occasion: "Doubtless you will quote to me this proverb, 'Physician, heal yourself; what we have heard you did at Capernaum, do here also in your own country'" (Luke 4:23). The proverb "Physician, heal yourself" probably originated in a non-Jewish setting (cf. Euripides, *Fragments* 1086; Plutarch, *Moralia* 32.71F), though eventually it was given expression in Jewish literature (*Gen. Rab.* 23.4 [on Gen. 4:23–25]). Other examples of proverbs include "A prophet is not without honor, except in his own country" (Mark 6:4; Dio Chrysostom 47.6; Philostratus, *Life of Apollonius* 1.354.12); "Wherever the body is, there the vultures will be gathered together" (Matt. 24:28 = Luke 17:37; cf. Cornutus, *On the Nature of the Gods* 21; Seneca, *Epistles* 95.43); and "For if they do this when the wood is green, what

will happen when it is dry?" (Luke 23:31; cf. *Seder Eliyahu Rabbah* §14; *Gen. Rab.* 65.22 [on Gen. 27:27]).

19. ON THE IMPORTANCE OF JUDGMENT IN THE PREACHING AND TEACHING OF JESUS: See the important study by Marius Reiser, *Jesus and Judgment: The Eschatological Proclamation in Its Jewish Context*, trans. Linda M. Maloney (German, 1990; Minneapolis: Fortress Press, 1997). Reiser offers a devastating critique of the noneschatological-Jesus interpretation, which has been fashionable in North America in recent years.

20. ON THE PRIORITY OF THE JEWISH PEOPLE IN THE BOOK OF ACTS: The observation is rightly made in Ben Witherington III, *New Testament History: A Narrative Account* (Grand Rapids: Baker Academic; Carlisle: Paternoster Press, 2001), 234: Acts 13:46 "indicates the missionary principle by which Paul operates: the message must be brought first to the Jews, and if they reject it, Paul will turn to the Gentiles. In Pisidian Antioch, this meant that he would turn to Gentiles once he was no longer welcome in the synagogue. It did not signal a refusal to approach Jews in another city, nor did offering salvation first to the Jews mean that Paul would bypass Gentiles if the first audience [of Jews] largely accepted the good news."

Chapter 3: James as Leader of the Jesus Community

1. ON THE RESURRECTION OF JESUS AS OCCASION FOR THE CONVERSION OF HIS BROTHER JAMES: This is argued in Frederick F. Bruce, "James and the Church of Jerusalem," in his *Men and Movements in the Primitive Church: Studies in Early Non-Pauline Christianity* (Exeter: Paternoster Press, 1977), 86–119, here 87.

2. WHY JAMES BECAME A LEADER IN THE EARLY CHURCH: See Joseph A. Fitzmyer, *The Acts of the Apostles*, AB 31 (New York: Doubleday, 1998), 489. Fitzmyer states that "James acquired such a status in the Jerusalem church because of his kinship to Jesus." This is probably true but only conjecture.

3. FOR TRANSLATION AND CRITICAL STUDY OF THE *GOSPEL OF THE HEBREWS*: See Edgar Hennecke and Wilhelm Schneemelcher, eds., *The New Testament Apocrypha*, vol. 1, *Gospels and Related Writings* (London: SCM Press; Philadelphia: Westminster Press, 1963), 165 (quotation §7); Wilhelm Schneemelcher, ed., *New Testament Apocrypha*, vol. 1, *Gospels and Related Writings*, rev. ed. (Cambridge: James Clarke; Louisville, KY: Westminster/John Knox Press, 1991), 178 (quotation §7); J. Keith Elliott, *The Apocryphal New Testament: A Collection of Apocryphal Christian Literature in an English Translation based on M. R. James* (Oxford: Clarendon Press, 1993), 9–10 (quotation §4). For commentary, see Albertus Frederik Johannes Klijn, *Jewish-Christian Gospel Tradition*, VCSup 17 (Leiden: E. J. Brill, 1992), 79–86.

4. ON THE STATUS OF JAMES IN THE EARLY CHURCH: In 1 Cor. 15:7 Paul simply says, "Then he appeared to James." Nowhere else is there tradition of James's making a vow or fulfilling it in eucharistic fashion in the presence of the risen Jesus.

5. ON THE BACKGROUND OF "PILLARS": See also 11Q19 34.15, which speaks of "twelve pillars ['*amudim*]" in the temple.

6. ON THE MEANING OF "PILLARS": See C. K. Barrett, "Paul and the 'Pillar' Apostles," in *Studia Paulina: In honorem Johannis de Zwaan septuagenarii*, ed. Jan Nicolaas Sevenster and W. C. van Unnik (Haarlem: Erven F. Bohn, 1953), 1–19, here 17. In my view Barrett convincingly argues that Paul grudgingly acknowledges James's pillar status. See also Craig S. Keener, "The Pillars and the Right Hand of Fellowship in Galatians 2.9," *JGRChJ* 7 (2010): 51–58.

7. ON "PILLARS" AS SUPPORT: See Barrett, "Paul and the 'Pillar' Apostles," 4. Reflecting the androcentrism of the time, Iphigeneia declares that "male children are the pillars of homes [*styloi gar oikon*]" (Euripides, *Iphigeneia at Tauris* 57).

8. ON "PILLARS" AS "FOUNDATION": The Hebrew *yesod* normally means "foundation," or the pedestal on which a pillar or altar rests. See the discussion in Richard Bauckham, "James and the Jerusalem Church," in *The Book of Acts in Its Palestinian Setting*, ed. Richard Bauckham (Grand Rapids: Wm. B. Eerdmans Publishing Co., 1995), 415–80, esp. 443–45.

9. ON JAMES AND TEMPLE IMAGERY: See Richard Bauckham, "For What Offence Was James Put to Death?," in *James the Just and Christian Origins*, ed. Bruce D. Chilton and Craig A. Evans, NovTSup 98 (Leiden: E. J. Brill, 1999), 199–232, here 207–8. See also Bauckham, "James and the Jerusalem Church," 441–50.

10. FOR SURVEYS OF TRADITIONS CONCERNED WITH JAMES: See Wilhelm Pratscher, *Der Herrenbruder Jakobus und die Jakobustradition*, FRLANT 139 (Göttingen: Vandenhoeck & Ruprecht, 1987); John Painter, *Just James: The Brother of Jesus in History and Tradition*, Studies on Personalities of the New Testament (Columbia: University of South Carolina Press, 1997; Minneapolis: Fortress Press, 1999; 2nd ed., Columbia, 2004). James appears in other traditions besides those that I have cited.

11. FOR A RECENT STUDY OF THE JEWISH RULER AGRIPPA I: See Daniel R. Schwartz, *Agrippa I: The Last King of Judaea*, TSAJ 23 (Tübingen: Mohr Siebeck, 1990).

12. ON PETER'S SHIFTING FROM JERUSALEM TO ANTIOCH AND THEN TO ROME: See Markus Bockmuehl, "Antioch and James the Just," in Chilton and Evans, *James the Just and Christian Origins*, 155–98, here 183. See also David Wenham, "Did Peter Go to Rome in A.D. 42?," *TynBul* 23 (1972): 94–102; Robert W. Wall, "Successors to the 'the Twelve' according to Acts 12:1–17," *CBQ* 53 (1991): 628–43.

13. ON THE PHARISEES IN ACTS 15: See Fitzmyer, *Acts*, 545.

14. ON PAUL AND THE COUNCIL OF ACTS 15: See ibid., 539–40.

15. ON PAUL AND THE LAW: This does not mean that Paul preached a "law-free" gospel, as is often asserted. The apostle believed that the law is good, revealing God's righteousness and—very importantly—God's oneness. Gentiles not only had to abandon certain vices, in order to join the membership of the church; they also had to abandon their worship of their gods. Only Israel's God, revealed in the books of Moses and in the Prophets, was to be worshiped. This point is rightly driven home by Paula Fredriksen, "Judaizing the Nations: The Ritual Demands of Paul's Gospel," *NTS* 56 (2010): 232–52.

16. ON THE ASSOCIATION OF STRANGLED MEAT WITH PAGAN SACRIFICE: See Philo, *Spec. Laws* 4.122 ("They prepare sacrifices which ought never be offered, strangling their victims, and stifling the essence of life, which they ought to let depart free and unrestrained, burying the blood, as it were, in the body"). "Blood" may refer to the consumption of blood during pagan cultic activity, but it may also refer to murder, i.e., shedding blood. If so, we then have two moral vices to avoid: fornication and murder; and two pagan practices to avoid: idolatry and food related to idolatry. In rabbinic literature (e.g., *b. Pesah.* 25a–b; *b. Sanh.* 74a) three matters are referenced in which compromise was out of the question: (1) idolatry, (2) shedding blood, and (3) incest (the worst form of fornication). The list of vices in the Jerusalem letter (Acts 15:23–29) may approximate an early form of this teaching. For discussion of these possibilities, see C. K. Barrett, *A Critical and Exegetical Commentary on the Acts of the Apostles*, 2 vols., ICC (Edinburgh: T&T Clark, 1994–98), 2:732–35; Fitzmyer, *Acts*, 556–58.

17. On Paul and the Jerusalem Council's decision: The most important discussion of the Jerusalem Council letter and how it relates to Paul is found in Peder Borgen, "Catalogues of Vices, the Apostolic Decree, and the Jerusalem Meeting," in his *Early Christianity and Hellenistic Judaism* (Edinburgh: T&T Clark, 1996), 233–51. See also Bockmuehl, "Antioch and James the Just," 181–82.

18. For a number of primary references in Jewish and non-Jewish literature: See Hans Dieter Betz, *Galatians*, Hermeneia (Philadelphia: Fortress Press, 1979), 100; Richard N. Longenecker, *Galatians*, WBC 41 (Dallas: Word Books, 1990), 58; James D. G. Dunn, *The Epistle to the Galatians*, BNTC (London: A&C Black, 1993), 110–11.

19. For discussion of the Nazirite vow and Acts 21: See Jacob Neusner, "Vow-Taking, the Nazirites, and the Law: Does James' Advice to Paul Accord with Halakhah?," in Chilton and Evans, *James the Just and Christian Origins*, 59–82.

20. On the meaning of the temple warnings: See Joseph M. Baumgarten, "Exclusions from the Temple: Proselytes and Agrippa I," *JJS* 33 (1982): 215–25; Peretz Segal, "The Penalty of the Warning Inscriptions from the Temple of Jerusalem," *IEJ* 39 (1989): 79–84.

21. On James as an "epistle of straw": Luther makes this statement in his Preface to the New Testament, 1522. See Helmut T. Lehmann et al., eds., *Luther's Works*, 55 vols. (Saint Louis: Concordia Publishing House, 1955–), 35:362.

Chapter 4: Phinehan Zeal and Works of the Law

1. For discussion of setting and background of Mount Peor story: See George Buchanan Gray, *A Critical and Exegetical Commentary on the Book of Numbers*, ICC (Edinburgh: T&T Clark, 1903), 381–83; John Sturdy, *Numbers*, The Cambridge Bible Commentary on the New English Bible (Cambridge: Cambridge University Press, 1976), 183–85; Philip Budd, *Numbers*, WBC 5 (Dallas: Word Books, 1984), 281–83; Timothy R. Ashley, *The Book of Numbers*, NICOT (Grand Rapids: Eerdmans, 1993), 516–19.

2. Translation of the Dead Sea Scrolls is based on: Michael O. Wise, Martin G. Abegg Jr., and Edward M. Cook, *The Dead Sea Scrolls: A New Translation* (San Francisco: HarperCollins, 1996), 364. The translation in Elisha Qimron and John Strugnell, *Qumran Cave 4*, part V, *Miqsat Ma'ase Ha-Torah*, DJD 10 (Oxford: Clarendon Press, 1994), 63, fails to sound the scriptural echo.

3. On the grammatical forms of the Hebrew: See Abegg's comment in Wise, Abegg, and Cook, *The Dead Sea Scrolls*, 359.

4. On the importance of the allusion to Phinehas: See Carolyn J. Sharp, "Phinehan Zeal and Rhetorical Strategy in 4QMMT," *RevQ* 18 (1997): 207–22; Dane C. Ortlund, "Phinehan Zeal: A Consideration of James Dunn's Proposal," *JSP* 20 (2011): 299–315.

5. On 4QMMT as offering an important parallel to Paul's language: See Martin G. Abegg Jr., "Paul, 'Works of the Law' and MMT," *BAR* 20, no. 6 (1994): 52–55, 82; idem, "4QMMT C 27,31 and 'Works Righteousness,'" *DSD* 6 (1999): 139–47; idem, "4QMMT, Paul, and 'Works of the Law,'" in *The Bible at Qumran: Text, Shape, and Interpretation*, ed. Peter W. Flint, SDSSRL 5 (Grand Rapids: Wm. B. Eerdmans Publishing Co., 2001), 203–16; Pierre Grelot, "Les oeuvres de la Loi (A propos de 4Q394–398)," *RevQ* 16 (1994): 441–48; John Kampen, "4QMMT and New Testament Studies," in *Reading 4QMMT: New Perspectives on Qumran Law and History*, ed. John Kampen and Moshe J. Bernstein, Symposium 2 (Atlanta: Scholars Press, 1996), 129–44,

esp. 138–43; James D. G. Dunn, "4QMMT and Galatians," *NTS* 43 (1997): 147–53; Martinus C. de Boer, "Paul's Use and Interpretation of a Justification Tradition in Galatians 2.15–21," *JSNT* 28 (2005): 189–216; Jacqueline C. R. de Roo, *"Works of the Law" at Qumran and in Paul*, NTM 13 (Sheffield: Sheffield Phoenix, 2007); Otfried Hofius, "'Werke des Gesetzes"—Zwei Nachträge," in his *Exegetische Studien*, WUNT 223 (Tübingen: Mohr Siebeck, 2008), 89–94.

6. FOR A HELPFUL DISCUSSION OF PAUL'S OBJECTIONS TO WORKS OF THE LAW: See James D. G. Dunn, *The New Perspective on Paul*, rev. ed. (Grand Rapids: Wm. B. Eerdmans Publishing Co., 2008), 23–28. The "new perspective" refers to the major shift in thinking brought on by Ed Parish Sanders, *Paul and Palestinian Judaism: A Comparison of Patterns of Religion* (London: SCM Press; Philadelphia: Fortress Press, 1977). In the years since the publication of this book, ongoing debate and not least the publication of 4QMMT have led to a number of qualifications. A major critique will be found in Donald A. Carson, Peter T. O'Brien, and Mark A. Seifrid, eds., *Justification and Variegated Nomism*, vol. 1, *The Complexities of Second Temple Judaism*, WUNT 2.140 (Tübingen: Mohr Siebeck, 2001); idem, vol. 2, *The Paradoxes of Paul*, WUNT 2.181 (Tübingen: Mohr Siebeck, 2004). The numerous studies in these two volumes have underscored the complexity and diversity of attitudes toward the law in Jewish late antiquity. Several studies in the second volume find that in Galatians and Romans, Paul in all probability was challenging the attempts of some to justify themselves through keeping the law of Moses. On this point, see Gregory K. Beale, "The Overstated 'New' Perspective?," *BBR* 19 (2009): 85–94.

7. THAT TRUE FAITH RESULTS IN RIGHTEOUS DEEDS: See de Roo, *"Works of the Law" at Qumran and in Paul*, 217–22.

8. FOR A SIMILAR COMBINATION OF FAITH AND WORKS: See *4 Ezra* (= 2 Esdras), composed ca. 100 CE: "He who brings the peril at that time will himself protect those who fall into peril, who have works and have faith [Latin: *qui habent operas et fidem*] in the Almighty" (13:23). See also *4 Ezra* 9:7–8 "And it shall be that everyone who will be saved and will be able to escape on account of his works [*per opera sua*], or on account of the faith by which he has believed [*per fidem in qua credidit*], will survive the dangers that have been predicted." For further discussion of texts such as these, see Craig A. Evans, "Paul and 'Works of Law' Language in Late Antiquity," in *Paul and His Opponents*, ed. Stanley E. Porter, PAST 2 (Leiden: E. J. Brill, 2005), 201–26.

9. ON BEING PERFECT: Jesus' "You . . . must be perfect, as your heavenly Father is perfect" (Matt. 5:48) is analogous to the logic expressed in the Holiness Code: "And the LORD said to Moses, 'Say to all the congregation of the people of Israel, You shall be holy; for I the LORD your God am holy'" (Lev. 19:1–2). It is in this context that the command to love one's neighbor as oneself appears (i.e., 19:18).

10. ON THE ROYAL LAW AND LEV. 19:18: See Scot McKnight, *The Letter of James*, NICNT (Grand Rapids: Wm. B. Eerdmans Publishing Co., 2011), 206–7; Wiard Popkes, *Der Brief des Jakobus*, THKNT 14 (Leipzig: Evangelische Verlagsanstalt, 2001), 171–75.

Chapter 5: Jerusalem Communities in Conflict

1. ON THE HISTORY OF CONFLICT BETWEEN THE ARISTOCRATIC PRIESTS AND THE JESUS MOVEMENT: See Eyal Regev, "Temple Concerns and High-Priestly Prosecutions from Peter to James: Between Narrative and History," *NTS* 56 (2010): 64–89.

2. FOR IMPORTANT BACKGROUND ON THE ARISTOCRATIC PRIESTS AND POLITICS: See also Richard A. Horsley, "High Priests and the Politics of Roman Palestine," *JSJ* 17 (1986):

23–55. Horsley broadens the scope of discussion in important ways, showing how the ruling priests, in their attempts to maintain law and order (as Rome expected), frequently came into conflict with various reform and peasant movements, which often were led by charismatics inspired by Israel's stories of deliverance.

3. ON DAVID IN THE ARAMAIC VERSION OF PS. 118: David appears in vv. 26 and 28: "'We bless you from the house of the sanctuary of the Lord,' said David" (v. 26); "'You are my God, and I will give thanks before you; O my God, I will praise you,' said David" (v. 28). Translation by David M. Stec, *The Targum of Psalms: Translated, with a Critical Introduction, Apparatus, and Notes*, ArBib 16 (Collegeville, MN: Liturgical Press, 2004), 210.

4. ON RABBINIC INTERPRETATION OF PS. 118: Part of the midrash reads: "'Open to me the gates of righteousness.' . . . And David said: 'I have done all these things. Therefore let all the gates be opened for me.'" Translation by William G. Braude, *The Midrash on Psalms*, 2 vols., YJS 13 (London and New Haven: Yale University Press, 1959), 2:243.

5. ON TRIUMPHAL ENTRIES: David Catchpole cites twelve examples of celebrated entries (most entries into Jerusalem), six from 1 and 2 Maccabees, and six from Josephus, of a "more or less fixed pattern of entry." See David R. Catchpole, "The 'Triumphal' Entry," in *Jesus and the Politics of His Day*, ed. Ernst Bammel and C. F. D. Moule (Cambridge: Cambridge University Press, 1984), 319–35, esp. 319–21.

6. ON THE MEANING OF JESUS' DEMONSTRATION IN THE TEMPLE PRECINCTS: See Ed Parish Sanders, *Jesus and Judaism* (London: SCM Press; Philadelphia: Fortress, 1985), 61–76. Sanders rightly challenges the notion that Jesus protested the practice of sacrifice.

7. ON THE CURRENCY OF ISA. 56: See 1 Macc. 7:34–38; Nicholas Perrin, *Jesus the Temple* (London: SPCK; Grand Rapids: Baker Academic, 2010), 84–88.

8. FOR A SURVEY OF EVIDENCE FOR PERCEIVING CORRUPTION IN THE FIRST-CENTURY TEMPLE: See Craig A. Evans, "Jesus' Action in the Temple and Evidence of Corruption in the First-Century Temple," in *Society of Biblical Literature 1989 Seminar Papers*, ed. David J. Lull, SBLSP 28 (Atlanta: Scholars Press, 1989), 522–39.

9. ON JESUS' RESPECT FOR THE LAW OF MOSES: Recall that when Jesus healed the leper, he ordered him to go and show himself to the (local, village) priest and do as Moses commanded (Mark 1:40–44).

10. ON THE INTERPRETATION OF ISA. 5:1–7: The anti-temple-establishment orientation of Isa. 5:1–7 is attested in the Aramaic paraphrase and in rabbinic interpretation (cf. *t. Me'il.* 1.16; *t. Sukkah* 3.15). The antiquity of this interpretation is attested by 4Q500. On this point, see Joseph M. Baumgarten, "4Q500 and the Ancient Conception of the Lord's Vineyard," *JJS* 40 (1989): 1–6; George J. Brooke, "4Q500 1 and the Use of Scripture in the Parable of the Vineyard," *DSD* 2 (1995): 268–94.

11. ON THE TESTIMONY OF JOSEPHUS REGARDING JESUS: For an able defense of this position, see John P. Meier, "Jesus in Josephus: A Modest Proposal," *CBQ* 52 (1990): 76–103; Victor Ulrich, "Das Testimonium Flavianum: Ein authentischer Text des Josephus," *NovT* 52 (2010): 72–82. Ulrich rightly observes that much of the skepticism with respect to the authenticity of this testimonium grows out of misunderstanding what it really says. See also Shlomo Pines, *An Arabic Version of the Testimonium Flavianum and Its Implications* (Jerusalem: Israel Academy of Sciences and Humanities, 1971). Pines thinks the Arabic version of the passage, which lacks some of the glossed material, may be close to the original form of the text. The Arabic version of the passage is found in Agapius, Melkite bishop of Manbij in Syria (tenth century CE), *Kitab al-'Unwan*

[*Book of Headings/Titles* = *Universal History*]. For more recent support of this suggestion, see David Flusser, "Bericht des Josephus über Jesus," in his *Entdeckungen im Neuen Testament*, vol. 1 (Neukirchen-Vluyn: Neukirchener Verlag, 1992), 216–25; and, with some important qualifications, Alice Whealey, "The Testimonium Flavianum in Syriac and Arabic," *NTS* 54 (2008): 573–90.

12. ON JOSEPHUS AND HIS REFERENCES TO THE JEWISH LEADERS: See *Ant.* 11.140–41; 18.121; Luke 19:47 ("the principal men of the people").

13. ON PETER AND THE TEMPLE: See Regev, "Temple Concerns and High-Priestly Prosecutions," 66–67.

14. ON THE LINGUISTIC ELEMENTS THAT LIE BEHIND THE STORY OF STEPHEN'S MARTYRDOM: See Martin Hengel, *Between Jesus and Paul: Studies in the Earliest History of Christianity* (Philadelphia: Fortress Press, 1983), 1–18.

15. ON THE QUARREL WITH STEPHEN: The accusations against Stephen originate among persons who are part of the "Synagogue of the Freedman," whose membership includes persons from the Diaspora (Acts 6:9). The famous Theodotos Synagogue Inscription mentions rooms available for those from abroad (*CII* 2.332–35 §1404; http://members .bib-arch.org/publication.asp?PubID=BSBA&Volume=29&Issue=4&ArticleID=14). For this reason some scholars wonder if this is the very synagogue mentioned in Acts 6:9.

16. ON STEPHEN'S DEATH UNDER THE AUTHORITY OF CAIAPHAS: That Stephen, an early martyr of the Jesus movement, was killed by the same high-priestly leadership that had opposed Jesus is not lost on Eusebius, the fourth-century church historian, who remarks: "Stephen . . . was stoned to death . . . by the slayers of the Lord" (*Hist. eccl.* 2.1.1; cf. 3.5.2).

17. ON THE STONING OF STEPHEN: See Regev, "Temple Concerns and High-Priestly Prosecutions," 67: "a kind of public lynching." For more on the question of Stephen's blasphemy and death, see Hengel, *Between Jesus and Paul*, 19–25.

18. ON THE MEANING OF "LAID VIOLENT HANDS" (ACTS 12:1): The text literally reads, "laid hands to do evil" (*epebalen . . . tas cheiras kakōsai*).

19. ON THE MOTIVE FOR KILLING JAMES SON OF ZEBEDEE: See Regev, "Temple Concerns and High-Priestly Prosecutions," 67. The account in Eusebius is hagiographic and in any case offers no motive (*Hist. eccl.* 2.9.1–4).

20. ON KILLING JAMES TO AVOID POLITICAL DISTURBANCE: See Daniel R. Schwartz, *Agrippa I: The Last King of Judaea*, TSAJ 23 (Tübingen: Mohr Siebeck, 1990), 119–24.

21. Joseph A. Fitzmyer, *The Acts of the Apostles*, AB 31 (New York: Doubleday, 1998), 487: "We are not told why Herod takes such action against Christians in Judea."

22. ON AGRIPPA'S MOTIVES: Ibid., 487: "Herod's actions are marked by caprice." On the contrary, Agrippa's motives were probably far more intentional.

23. ON THE APPOINTMENT OF ANANIAS SON OF NEDEBAEUS: Ananias was appointed by the Roman procurator Ventidius Cumanus in 47 CE and served until 59 CE (cf. Josephus, *Ant.* 20.103).

24. ON PAUL'S CONFLICT WITH TEMPLE AUTHORITIES: See Regev, "Temple Concerns and High-Priestly Prosecutions," 68–69.

25. ON PAUL IN CUSTODY: See ibid., 69.

26. A VERSION OF THE STORY OF JAMES'S DEATH IS RECOUNTED in Eusebius, *Hist. eccl.* 2.23.21–24.

27. ON THE MOTIVES FOR KILLING JAMES: See Richard Bauckham, "For What Offence was James Put to Death?," in *James the Just and Christian Origins*, ed. Bruce D. Chilton and Craig A. Evans, NovTSup 98 (Leiden: E. J. Brill, 1999), 199–232. Bauckham believes James was put to death for leading the people astray in the sense of the false prophet, who entices Israel to go after other gods (cf. Deut. 13).

28. ON COMPETING FOR THE HEARTS OF THE JEWISH PEOPLE: See James S. McLaren, "Ananus, James, and the Earliest Christianity: Josephus's Account of the Death of James," *JTS* 52 (2001): 1–25.

29. ON ATTITUDES TOWARD THE TEMPLE: See Regev, "Temple Concerns and High-Priestly Prosecutions," 88.

30. ON THE STORY OF JESUS BEN ANANIAS: Eusebius recounts a version of this story in *Hist. eccl.* 3.8.7–9.

31. ON THE PARALLELS BETWEEN THE EXPERIENCES OF JESUS OF NAZARETH AND JESUS BEN ANANIAS: These parallels are delineated in Craig A. Evans, "Jesus and the 'Cave of Robbers': Toward a Jewish Context for the Temple Action," *BBR* 3 (1993): 93–110, esp. 105–7. Impressed by these parallels, Theodore Weeden has argued that Mark's story of Jesus depends on Josephus's story of Jesus ben Ananias. See Theodore J. Weeden, "Two Jesuses, Jesus of Jerusalem and Jesus of Nazareth: Provocative Parallels and Imaginative Imitation," *Forum* 6 (2003): 137–341. This is most unlikely, not least in light of the fact that Mark's Gospel was written before 70 CE, and *Jewish Wars* was written no earlier than 74 CE. The parallels between Mark and Josephus bear witness to Roman juridical process in pre-70-CE Jerusalem, in which the Jewish priestly aristocracy and Roman authority collaborated in maintaining law and order. There is no hint anywhere in the Gospel of Mark of the influence of the writings of Josephus. See also Dale C. Allison Jr., *Constructing Jesus: Memory, Imagination, and History* (Grand Rapids: Baker Academic, 2010), 237 n. 67. Allison finds Weeden's interpretation implausible and unnecessary.

32. FOR A CRITICAL STUDY OF THE ORACLE UTTERED BY JESUS BEN ANANIAS: See Anna Maria Schwemer, "Irdischer und himmlischer König: Beobachtungen zur sogenannten David-Apokalypse in Hekhalot Rabbati §§122–126," in *Königsherrschaft Gottes und himmlischer Kult im Judentum, Urchristentum und in der hellenistischen Welt*, ed. Martin Hengel and Anna Maria Schwemer (Tübingen: Mohr Siebeck, 1991), 309–59, here 352–58.

Chapter 6: The Church between Paul, James, and Ignatius

1. ON THE PARTING OF THE CHRISTIAN CHURCH FROM THE JEWISH PEOPLE AND JUDAISM: In recent years scholarly literature concerned with this topic has mushroomed. For a sample, see James D. G. Dunn, *The Partings of the Ways: Between Christianity and Judaism and Their Significance for the Character of Christianity* (London: SCM Press, 1991; 2nd ed., 2006); idem, ed., *Jews and Christians: The Parting of the Ways, A.D. 70 to 135*, WUNT 66 (Tübingen: Mohr Siebeck, 1992; repr., Grand Rapids: Wm. B. Eerdmans Publishing Co., 2001). Of course, important lines of continuity remained. See Adam H. Becker and Annette Yoshiko Reed, eds., *The Ways That Never Parted: Jews and Christians in Late Antiquity and the Middle Ages*, TSAJ 95 (Tübingen: Mohr Siebeck, 2003; repr., Minneapolis: Fortress Press, 2007); Oskar Skarsaune and Reidar Hvalvik, eds., *Jewish Believers in Jesus: The Early Centuries* (Peabody, MA: Hendrickson Publishers, 2007).

2. FOR CAUTIONS ABOUT DEFINING ETHNIC AND RELIGIOUS CATEGORIES TOO SHARPLY: See David Frankfurter, "Beyond 'Jewish Christianity': Continuing Religious Sub-Cultures

of the Second and Third Centuries and Their Documents," in Becker and Reed, *The Ways That Never Parted*, 131–43. Other essays in this volume make similar points.

3. ON ANTI-SEMITISM AND THE EARLY CHRISTIAN MOVEMENT: See Craig A. Evans and Donald A. Hagner, eds., *Anti-Semitism and Early Christianity: Issues of Polemic and Faith* (Minneapolis: Fortress Press, 1993). Among other things, the contributors to this volume found no anti-Semitism in the New Testament, but did find some in its later interpretation and use. This important topic has recently been explored further in Terence L. Donaldson, *Jews and Anti-Judaism in the New Testament* (London: SPCK; Waco: Baylor University Press, 2010).

4. ON THE MATTHEAN COMMUNITY AS A JEWISH SECT: See J. Andrew Overman, *Matthew's Gospel and Formative Judaism: A Study of the Social World of the Matthean Community* (Minneapolis: Fortress Press, 1990).

5. ON MATTHEW AS A JEWISH TEACHER: See Anthony J. Saldarini, *Matthew's Christian-Jewish Community*, CSHJ (Chicago: University of Chicago Press, 1994).

6. ON THE MATTHEAN COMMUNITY AS JEWS WHO BELIEVE IN JESUS: See David C. Sim, *The Gospel of Matthew and Christian Judaism: The History and Social Setting of the Matthean Community* (Edinburgh: T&T Clark, 1998). To an important degree, the studies of Overman, Saldarini, and Sim (see previous notes) confirm essential elements of the groundbreaking redaction-critical studies of Günther Bornkamm, Gerhard Barth, and Heinz Joachim Held, *Tradition and Interpretation in Matthew* (Philadelphia: Westminster, 1963); *Überlieferung und Auslegung im Matthäusevangelium*, 5th ed. (Neukirchen-Vluyn: Neukirchener Verlag, 1968).

7. ON MATTHEW'S PORTRAIT OF JESUS AS FULFILLER OF THE LAW: See Scot McKnight, "A Loyal Critic: Matthew's Polemic with Judaism in Theological Perspective," in Evans and Hagner, eds., *Anti-Semitism and Early Christianity*, 55–79; Donaldson, *Jews and Anti-Judaism*, 30–54.

8. FOR FURTHER DISCUSSION OF THE MESSIAH PASSAGE IN THE MISHNAH: See Craig A. Evans, "Mishna and Messiah 'in Context': Some Comments on Jacob Neusner's Proposals," *JBL* 112 (1993): 267–89.

9. IF ZECHARIAH IS THE SON OF JEHOIADA: We may have examples of murder from the beginning of Hebrew Scripture (i.e., Abel in Gen. 4) to its end (i.e., Zechariah in 2 Chr. 24).

10. FOR A DISCUSSION OF THE VARIOUS INTERPRETATIONS THAT HAVE BEEN PUT FORWARD CONCERNING THE IDENTITY OF ZECHARIAH: See Dale C. Allison Jr. and W. D. Davies, *A Critical and Exegetical Commentary on the Gospel according to Saint Matthew*, vol. 3, *Commentary on Matthew XIX–XXVIII*, ICC (Edinburgh: T&T Clark, 1997), 318–19.

11. ON JOHN AND THE SYNAGOGUGE: See Donaldson, *Jews and Anti-Judaism*, 81–108.

12. THAT JOHN'S *IOUDAIOI* SHOULD BE TRANSLATED "JUDEANS": See Steve Mason, "Jews, Judeans, Judaizing, Judaism: Problems of Categorization in Ancient History," in his *Josephus, Judea, and Christian Origins: Methods and Categories* (Peabody, MA: Hendrickson Publishers, 2009), 141–84.

13. ON THE GOSPEL OF JOHN AND EXPULSION FROM THE SYNAGOGUE: See J. Louis Martyn, *History and Theology in the Fourth Gospel* (New York: Harper & Row, 1968); 3rd ed., with an introduction by D. Moody Smith (Louisville, KY: Westminster John Knox Press, 2003). Part of Martyn's thesis was anticipated by Kenneth L. Carroll, "The Fourth Gospel and the Exclusion of Christians from the Synagogue," *BJRL* 40 (1957–58): 19–32.

14. ON THE TWELFTH BENEDICTION OF THE AMIDAH: For critical discussion and notes, see Ismar Elbogen, *Jewish Liturgy: A Comprehensive History* (Philadelphia: The Jewish Publication Society; New York and Jerusalem: The Jewish Theological Seminary of America, 1993), 45–46 and 397–98 (notes). See also the text and critical apparatus in Gustaf H. Dalman, *Die Worte Jesu: Mit Berücksichtigung des nachkanonischen jüdischen Schrifttums und der aramäischen Sprache* (Leipzig: Hinrichs, 1898), 303.

15. FOR SCHOLARLY DISCUSSION OF MARTYN'S HYPOTHESIS: See Wayne A. Meeks, "Breaking Away: Three New Testament Pictures of Christianity's Separation from the Jewish Communities," in *"To See Ourselves as Others See Us": Christians, Jews, "Others" in Late Antiquity*, ed. Jacob Neusner and Ernest S. Frerichs (Chico, CA: Scholars Press, 1985), 93–115. His criticisms notwithstanding, Meeks does accept the essence of Martyn's thesis.

16. FOR FURTHER SCHOLARLY DISCUSSION OF MARTYN'S HYPOTHESIS: See D. Moody Smith's introductory essay in Martyn, *History and Theology in the Fourth Gospel*, 3rd ed. (2003), 1–23.

17. ON THE APOLOGETIC FUNCTION OF SCRIPTURE IN THE GOSPEL OF JOHN: See Craig A. Evans, "On the Quotation Formulas in the Fourth Gospel," *BZ* 26 (1982): 79–83; idem, *Word and Glory: On the Exegetical and Theological Background of John's Prologue*, JSNTSup 89 (Sheffield: JSOT Press, 1993), 173–81.

18. ON THE COMPOSITION OF THE *DIALOGUE WITH TRYPHO*: Justin Martyr's *Dialogue with Trypho* is artificial. In all probability Justin has edited a Jewish tract, perhaps actually authored by a man named Trypho, and inserted his answers. The important point is that the objections and arguments attributed to Trypho are authentically Jewish and circulated in the early decades of the second century. See Timothy J. Horner, *Listening to Trypho: Justin Martyr's Dialogue Reconsidered*, CBET 28 (Leuven: Peeters, 2001).

19. FOR STUDY OF THE LETTERS TO THE SEVEN CHURCHES IN ASIA MINOR: In addition to the major commentaries, see Colin J. Hemer, *The Letters to the Seven Churches of Asia in Their Local Setting*, JSNTSup 11 (Sheffield: JSOT Press, 1986).

20. ON THE DATE AND TEXTUAL COMPLEXITY OF THE LETTERS OF IGNATIUS: See the succinct summary in Michael W. Holmes, *The Apostolic Fathers: Greek Texts and English Translations*, 3rd ed. (Grand Rapids: Baker Academic, 2007), 166–73.

21. ON THE MEANING OF THE "ARCHIVES" IN THE LETTER *TO THE PHILADELPHIANS*: See Joseph B. Lightfoot, *The Apostolic Fathers: Clement, Ignatius, and Polycarp*, 5 vols. (London: Macmillan, 1889–90), 2:270–71. Lightfoot believes *archeia*, the old books, stand in contrast to the new, the *euangelion*. He cites *2 Clement* 14.2 (*ta biblia kai hoi apostoloi*, "the books and the apostles") as a parallel.

22. ON THE MEANING OF "I DO NOT BELIEVE IT" IN THE LETTER *TO THE PHILADELPHIANS*: See Lightfoot, *The Apostolic Fathers*, 2:271–72.

23. ON THE PLACE OF THE OLD TESTAMENT IN THE LETTERS OF IGNATIUS: See Hemer, *Letters to the Seven Churches*, 169.

24. ON THE EFFORTS TO LURE JEWS BACK TO THE SYNAGOGUE: This is plausibly suggested by Hemer, *Letters to the Seven Churches*, 169–70. I disagree with Lightfoot (*The Apostolic Fathers*, 2:242) when he says Ignatius is attacking "Docetic Judaism." There is nothing docetic here.

25. FOR DISCUSSION OF THE CONTINUITY BETWEEN REV. 3:9 AND THE LETTER *TO THE PHILADELPHIANS* 8.2: See Hemer, *Letters to the Seven Churches*, 168–70.

26. On docetism in the letter *To the Magnesians*: I do not agree with Lightfoot, *The Apostolic Fathers*, 2:103, 124. There is no clear evidence of docetism in *To the Magnesians*.

27. On Sunday as the Lord's day: See Rev. 1:10; *Did.* 14.1; cf. 1 Cor. 16:2.

28. For additional commentary on *To the Magnesians* 10: See Lightfoot, *The Apostolic Fathers*, 2:124–34; Robert M. Grant, *The Apostolic Fathers: A Translation and Commentary*, vol. 4, *Ignatius of Antioch* (New York: Thomas Nelson, 1966), 62–64.

29. Tradition attributed to Rabbi Simeon ben Yohai: "Rabbi Simeon ben Yohai taught: 'Aqiba, my master, used to interpret "a star [*kokav*] goes forth from Jacob" [Num. 24:17]—Kozeba [*kozeva'*] goes forth from Jacob.'" Rabbi Aqiba, when he saw Bar Kozeba, said: 'This is the King Messiah.'" Thanks to the discovery of some of his letters in the Cave of Letters of Nahal Hever, we know Simon's name in Greek was spelled *Simon Chosiba* (cf. P.Yadin 59 line 2). The various Aramaic and Hebrew spellings encountered in rabbinic literature—*koseba'*, *kosebah*, *kosbah*, *kozebah*, *kozeba'*, and others (the last from *kazav*, "to lie," "to disappoint")—represent exegesis and puns, whether positive or negative.

30. On Aqiba's recognition of Simon ben Kosiba as the Messiah: See Peter Schäfer, "R. Aqiva und Bar Kokhba," in his *Studien zur Geschichte und Theologie des rabbinischen Judentums*, AGJU 15 (Leiden: E. J. Brill, 1978), 65–121; idem, "Rabbi Aqiva and Bar Kokhba," in *Approaches to Ancient Judaism*, ed. William S. Green, vol. 2, BJS 9 (Chico, CA: Scholars Press, 1980), 113–30. Less cautious is Adele Reinhartz ("Rabbinic Perceptions of Simeon bar Kosiba," *JSJ* 20 [1989]: 171–94) who speaks of "irrefutable evidence for the messianic identification of Bar Kosiba" (192). I believe that the evidence is compelling, but hardly irrefutable.

31. For a review of the primary literature relating to Simon: See Craig A. Evans, "Was Simon ben Kosiba Recognized as Messiah?," in his *Jesus and His Contemporaries: Comparative Studies*, AGJU 25 (Leiden: E. J. Brill, 1995), 183–211.

32. One of Simon ben Kosiba's letters: "Simeon bar Kosiba to Yehonathan: . . . You are to deliver to me Eleazar, . . . and whoever raises a clamor against you on this sort of matter, dispatch him to my side, and I will exact punishment" (P.Yadin 50); "[col. 1] Simeon bar Kosiba, the Prince over Israel, to Yehonathan and to Masabala: Peace! You are to examine and to seize the wheat that he brought up. . . . And place them under guard, because they were found to be stolen. . . . [col. 2] And any Teko'an man who is found with you—let the house in which they reside be burned down, and from you I shall exact punishment. And seize Yeshua, son of the Palmyrene, and send him to me under guard. Do not fail to seize the sword that is on him" (P.Yadin 54). For Aramaic and Hebrew texts, with English translation, see Yigael Yadin et al., eds., *The Documents from the Bar-Kokhba Period in the Cave of Letters*, vol. 3, part 1, *Hebrew, Aramaic and Nabataean-Aramaic Papyri*; part 2, *Plates* (Jerusalem: Israel Exploration Society, 2002), 290 and 308. For additional examples that speak of punishment, see 314 (P.Yadin 55), 319 (P.Yadin 56), and 364 (P.Yadin 59).

33. On the question of the society founded by Jesus: See Géza Vermès, *The Religion of Jesus the Jew* (London: SCM Press; Minneapolis: Fortress Press, 1993), 215. Although I disagree with Professor Vermès at this point, I do agree with many other points he makes in this insightful book.

Appendix: Root Causes of the Jewish-Christian Rift

1. On the parting of the ways: See esp. James D. G. Dunn, ed., *Jews and Christians: The Partings of the Ways A.D. 70 to 135*, WUNT 66 (Tübingen: Mohr Siebeck, 1992);

idem, *The Partings of the Ways* (London: SCM Press; Philadelphia: Trinity Press International, 1991).

2. ON THE USEFULNESS OF "PARTING OF THE WAYS" LANGUAGE: See Judith Lieu, "'The Parting of the Ways': Theological Construct or Historical Reality?," *JSNT* 56 (1994): 101–19.

3. FOR A MAJOR TREATMENT OF THE ORIGINS OF THE DIVINITY OF JESUS: See Larry W. Hurtado, *Lord Jesus Christ: Devotion to Jesus in Earliest Christianity* (Grand Rapids: Wm. B. Eerdmans Publishing Co., 2003).

4. FOR DISCUSSION OF THE CHURCH'S USE OF THE SEPTUAGINT: See Martin Hengel, with the assistance of Roland Deines, *The Septuagint as Christian Scripture: Its Prehistory and the Problem of Its Canon*, with an introduction by Robert Hanhart, Old Testament Studies (Edinburgh: T&T Clark, 2002).

5. ON ALLUSION IN *BARNABAS* TO JEWISH HOPES TO REBUILD THE TEMPLE: See William Horbury, "Jewish-Christian Relations in Barnabas and Justin Martyr," in Dunn, *Jews and Christians*, 315–45. See additional commentary in Robert A. Kraft, *The Apostolic Fathers: A Translation and Commentary*, vol. 3, *Barnabas and the Didache* (New York: Thomas Nelson, 1965), 130–31.

6. ON JEWISH MEN WHO MAY HAVE BEEN REGARDED AS MESSIANIC CLAIMANTS: See Richard A. Horsley, "Popular Messianic Movements around the Time of Jesus," *CBQ* 46 (1984): 471–95; Richard A. Horsley and John S. Hanson, *Bandits, Prophets, and Messiahs: Popular Movements at the Time of Jesus* (San Francisco: Harper & Row, 1985), 88–134; Craig A. Evans, *Ancient Texts for New Testament Studies: A Guide to the Background Literature* (Peabody, MA: Hendrickson Publishers, 2005), 431–43. However, Marinus de Jonge (*Christology in Context: The Earliest Christian Response to Jesus* [Philadelphia: Westminster Press, 1988]) has his doubts and comments: "This is an attractive theory, but unfortunately difficult to substantiate from literary sources: we have only Josephus' very one-sided presentation of the facts" (164). This is true, but Josephus's bias tends to downplay the messianic elements and accompanying scriptural foundations.

7. MORE ON MESSIANIC CLAIMANTS: It is probable that both Menahem and Simon bar Giora (in the first war with Rome: 66–70 CE) made messianic claims of one sort or another, while it is virtually certain that Simon ben Kosiba (in the second war with Rome: 132–35) claimed to be Israel's Messiah. See Craig A. Evans, *Jesus and His Contemporaries: Comparative Studies*, AGJU 25 (Leiden: E. J. Brill, 1995), 183–211.

8. FOR A SURVEY OF PRIMARY LITERATURE RELATING TO CRUCIFIXION IN LATE ANTIQUITY: See Martin Hengel, *Crucifixion in the Ancient World and the Folly of the Message of the Cross* (Philadelphia: Fortress Press, 1977), 1–10; idem, "Christological Titles in Early Christianity," in *The Messiah: Developments in Earliest Judaism and Christianity*, ed. James H. Charlesworth (Minneapolis: Fortress Press, 1992), 425–48, esp. 425–30.

9. ON JEWISH CHRISTIANITY AND ITS RELATIONSHIP TO THE LARGER, PREDOMINANTLY GENTILE CHURCH: see Ray A. Pritz, *Nazarene Jewish Christianity: From the End of the New Testament Period until Its Disappearance in the Fourth Century* (Jerusalem: Magnes; Leiden: E. J. Brill, 1988); and the essays by Oskar Skarsaune (on the Ebionites) and Wolfram Kinzig (on the Nazoreans) in *Jewish Believers in Jesus: The Early Centuries*, ed. Oskar Skarsaune and Reidar Hvalvik (Peabody, MA: Hendrickson Publishers, 2007), 419–62 and 463–87, respectively.

10. ON THE AFTERMATH OF THE BAR KOKHBA WAR: Following the defeat of Simon in 135 CE, it would be three centuries before the reappearance of messianic fervor. Based on various calculations, it was believed that the Messiah would come either in 440

CE (cf. *b. Sanh.* 97b) or in 471 CE (cf. *b. 'Abod. Zar.* 9b). Other dates were suggested. Answering this expectation, one "Moses of Crete" (ca. 448 CE) promised to lead the Jewish people through the sea, dry-shod, from Crete to Palestine. At his command many of his followers threw themselves into the Mediterranean. Some drowned; others were rescued. Moses himself disappeared (cf. Socrates Scholasticus, *Historia ecclesiastica* 7.38; 12.33). Evidently Moses typology had continued to play an important role in shaping restoration hopes. A variety of other pseudo-messiahs appeared in the Islamic period (esp. in the eighth century), during the later Crusades (esp. in the twelfth and thirteenth centuries), and even as late as the sixteenth, seventeenth, and eighteenth centuries (cf. *Jewish Encyclopedia* [1906], 10:252–55, http://www.jewishencyclopedia .com/articles/12416-pseudo-messiahs).

Suggestions for Further Reading

The Time between the Testaments

Barclay, J. M. G. *Jews in the Mediterranean Diaspora: From Alexander to Trajan (323 BCE–117 CE)*. Edinburgh: T&T Clark, 1996.

Grabbe, Lester L. *Judaism from Cyrus to Hadrian*. Vol. 1, *The Persian and Greek Periods*. Vol. 2, *The Roman Period*. Minneapolis: Fortress Press, 1992.

Hayes, John H., and Sara R. Mandell. *The Jewish People in Classical Antiquity: From Alexander to Bar Kochba*. Louisville, KY: Westminster John Knox Press, 1998.

Horbury, William, et al., eds. *The Cambridge History of Judaism*. Vol. 3, *The Early Roman Period*. Cambridge: Cambridge University Press, 1999.

Reicke, Bo. *The New Testament Era*. Philadelphia: Fortress Press, 1974.

Russell, David S. *The Jews from Alexander to Herod*. Oxford: Oxford University Press, 1967.

Stern, Menahem. *Greek and Latin Authors on Jews and Judaism*. 3 vols. Jerusalem: The Israel Academy of Sciences and Humanities, 1974, 1980, 1984.

The Time of Jesus and the Early Church

Barnett, Paul. *Jesus and the Rise of Early Christianity: A History of New Testament Times*. Downers Grove, IL: InterVarsity Press, 1999.

Bond, Helen K. *Caiaphas: Friend of Rome and Judge of Jesus?* Louisville, KY: Westminster John Knox Press, 2004.

———. *Pontius Pilate in History and Interpretation*. SNTSMS 100. Cambridge: Cambridge University Press, 1998.

Bruce, Frederick F. *New Testament History*. New York: Doubleday, 1972.

Chilton, Bruce D., and Craig A. Evans, eds. *James the Just and Christian Origins*. NovTSup 98. Leiden: E. J. Brill, 1999.

———, eds. *The Missions of James, Peter, and Paul: Tensions in Early Christianity*. NovTSup 115. Leiden: E. J. Brill, 2004.

Chilton, Bruce D., and Jacob Neusner, eds. *The Brother of Jesus: James the Just and His Mission*. Louisville, KY: Westminster John Knox Press, 2001.

Duriez, Colin. *AD 33: The Year That Changed the World*. Downers Grove, IL: InterVarsity Press, 2007.

Goodman, Martin. *The Ruling Class of Judaea: The Origins of the Jewish Revolt against Rome, A.D. 66–70*. Cambridge: Cambridge University Press, 1987.

Hengel, Martin. *The "Hellenization" of Judaea in the First Century after Christ*. London: SCM Press; Philadelphia: Trinity Press International, 1989.

———. *Jews, Greeks and Barbarians: Aspects of the Hellenization of Judaism in the Pre-Christian Period*. London: SCM Press, 1980.

———. *Judaism and Hellenism: Studies in Their Encounter in Palestine during the Early Hellenistic Period*. 2 vols. Philadelphia: Fortress Press, 1974. Repr. as one vol., 1981.

———. *Was Jesus a Revolutionist?* FBBS 28. Philadelphia: Fortress Press, 1971.

———. *The Zealots: Investigations into the Jewish Freedom Movement in the Period from Herod I until 70 A.D.* Edinburgh: T&T Clark, 1989.

Horsley, Richard A. *Galilee: History, Politics, People*. Valley Forge, PA: Trinity Press International, 1995.

———. *Jesus and the Spiral of Violence: Popular Jewish Resistance in Roman Palestine*. San Francisco: Harper & Row, 1987.

Horsley, Richard A., and John S. Hanson. *Bandits, Prophets, and Messiahs: Popular Movements at the Time of Jesus*. New Voices in Biblical Studies. Minneapolis: Winston, 1985. Repr., San Francisco: Harper & Row, 1988.

Jeffers, James S. *The Greco-Roman World of the New Testament Era: Exploring the Background of Early Christianity*. Downers Grove, IL: InterVarsity Press, 1999.

Jensen, Morten H. *Herod Antipas in Galilee*. 2nd ed. WUNT 2/215. Tübingen: Mohr Siebeck, 2010.

Mendels, Doron. *The Rise and Fall of Jewish Nationalism: Jewish and Christian Ethnicity in Ancient Palestine*. Grand Rapids: Wm. B. Eerdmans Publishing Co., 1992.

Painter, John. *Just James: The Brother of Jesus in History and Tradition*. Studies on Personalities of the New Testament. Columbia: University of South Carolina Press, 1997. Minneapolis: Fortress Press, 1999. 2nd ed., Columbia, 2004.

Rhoads, David M. *Israel in Revolution 6–74 C.E.* Philadelphia: Fortress Press, 1976.

Richardson, Peter. *Herod: King of the Jews and Friend of the Romans*. Columbia: University of South Carolina Press, 1996.

Schnabel, Eckhard J. *Early Christian Mission*. Vol. 1, *Jesus and the Twelve*. Vol. 2, *Paul and the Early Church*. Downers Grove, IL: InterVarsity Press, 2004.

Schürer, Emil. *The History of the Jewish People in the Age of Jesus Christ*. 3 vols. Revised by Géza Vermès, Fergus Millar, and Matthew Black. Edinburgh: T&T Clark, 1973–87.

Smallwood, E. Mary *The Jews under Roman Rule: From Pompey to Diocletian: A Study in Political Relations*. SJLA 20. Leiden: E. J. Brill, 1976. Repr. with corrections, 1981.

Witherington, Ben, III. *New Testament History: A Narrative Account*. Grand Rapids: Baker Academic; Carlisle: Paternoster Press, 2001.

Commentaries and Studies on the Book of Acts

Barrett, Charles Kingsley. *A Critical and Exegetical Commentary on the Acts of the Apostles*. 2 vols. ICC. Edinburgh: T&T Clark, 1994–98.

Bauckham, Richard, ed. *The Book of Acts in Its Palestinian Setting*. Grand Rapids: Wm. B. Eerdmans Publishing Co., 1995.

Bruce, Frederick F. *Commentary on the Book of Acts*. Rev. ed. NICNT. Grand Rapids: Wm. B. Eerdmans Publishing Co., 1988.

Fitzmyer, Joseph A. *The Acts of the Apostles*. AB 31. New York: Doubleday, 1998.

Foakes-Jackson, Frederick J., and Kirsopp Lake. *The Beginnings of Christianity*. 5 vols. London: Macmillan, 1920–33.

Pervo, Richard I., and Harold W Attridge. *Acts: A Commentary*. Hermeneia. Minneapolis: Fortress Press, 2008.

Peterson, David G. *The Acts of the Apostles*. PNTC. Grand Rapids: Wm. B. Eerdmans Publishing Co., 2009.

Porter, Stanley E. *The Paul of Acts: Essays in Literary Criticism, Rhetoric and Theology*. WUNT 115. Tübingen: Mohr Siebeck, 1999.

Talbert Charles. H. *Reading Acts: A Literary and Theological Commentary on the Acts of the Apostles*. Reading the New Testament. New York: Crossroad, 1997.

Witherington, Ben, III. *Acts of the Apostles: A Socio-Rhetorical Commentary*. Grand Rapids: Wm. B. Eerdmans Publishing Co., 1998).

Index of Ancient Sources

Index of Modern Names

Index of Subjects